1001 Cocktails

&other decadent drinks

1001 Cocktails
& other decadent drinks

This edition published in 2011
LOVE FOOD is an imprint of Parragon Books Ltd

Parragon
Queen Street House
4 Queen Street
Bath BA1 1HE, UK

ISBN: 978-1-4454-4414-7

Printed in Indonesia

Internal design by Andrew Easton @ Ummagumma
Additional photography by Charlie Richards, Clive Streeter, Günter Beer and Mike Cooper
Edited by Fiona Biggs
Introduction and chapter opener text by Fran Eamas

Notes for the Reader
This book uses both metric and imperial measurements. Follow the same units of
measurement throughout; do not mix metric and imperial. All spoon measurements are
level: teaspoons are assumed to be 5 ml, and tablespoons are assumed to be 15 ml. Unless
otherwise stated, milk is assumed to be full fat, eggs and individual vegetables are medium,
and pepper is freshly ground black pepper.

Recipes using raw or very lightly cooked eggs should be avoided by infants, the elderly,
pregnant women, convalescents and anyone suffering from an illness. Pregnant and
breastfeeding women are advised to avoid eating peanuts and peanut products. Sufferers
from nut allergies should be aware that some of the ready-made ingredients used in the
recipes in this book may contain nuts. Always check the packaging before use.

Please drink alcohol responsibly.

CONTENTS

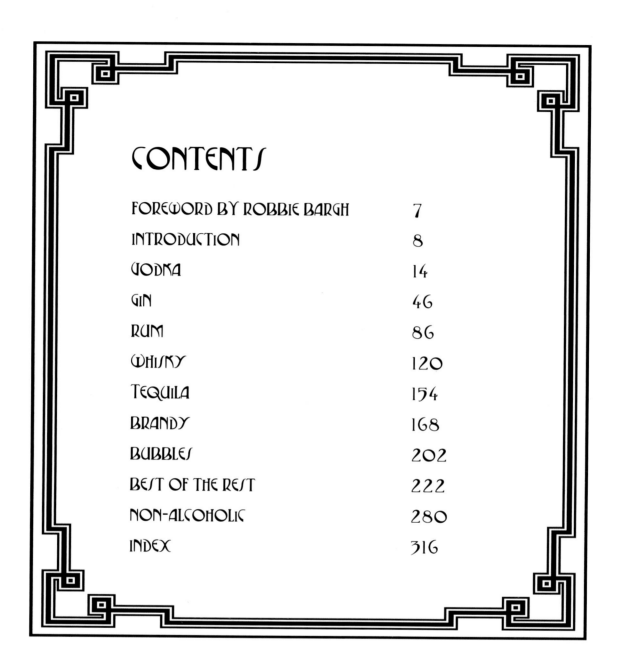

FOREWORD

Having been involved in the opening of some of the best cocktail establishments around the world and having sipped some of the finest cocktails ever made, I can categorically say there is a cocktail for every mood and every occasion. From weddings to divorce parties, from premieres to tea parties, from birthday parties to coming-out parties, every occasion has the perfect cocktail tipple. Long drinks, short drinks, built drinks, blended drinks, shaken drinks, daiquiris, slings, punches – the list is endless, as, of course, are the occasions.

For me the cocktail is a statement, an opportunity to show off and a singular way of expressing the personality and inner mood of the person doing the ordering. Even before taking a sip, the confidence from within is immediately let loose and we see a story unfold before us. Reading people from the cocktails they order is a pastime well worth taking up. Forget about the colours they wear or the perfume they use – the preference of a cocktail at any given occasion or, indeed, at any particular part of the day can tell plenty about a person.

Another reason why cocktails are such wonderful things is the fabulous sense of occasion you can get from sipping that particular cocktail. Bellinis remind me of summer weekends in Venice, Margaritas of Tulum in Mexico, Gin Martinis of dating in New York, and the Martinez of my mid-afternoon cocktails at the Dorchester Hotel in London. For all these reasons, the cocktail should be nothing short of celebrated.

What makes a good cocktail is the finest of ingredients, the best tools you can buy, the perfect occasion and a little bit of patience with a dash of love, care and attention. Bartending is an art, and making drinks at home is the perfect way to awaken those creative energies – and for that reason we all have the potential to be great artists. Mixology is a labour of love; choosing that perfect cocktail can determine how successful a party will be, and making the damn thing requires the time, the ingredients, the recipe and that little bit of magic that every great artist must possess. So go on, get the party started, and 'go create'.

Robbie Bargh
Founder and Managing Director
Gorgeous Group
www.gorgeousgroup.com

INTRODUCTION

EXQUISITE COCKTAILS!

Cocktails are as much about style and glamour as they are about taste and texture, and you can be sure that everyone will immediately be able to tell you what their favourite one is.

Our long-running romance with the cocktail is testament to the fact that everyone deserves to enjoy a little bit of decadence. Whether you're throwing a lavish black-tie affair, having a few drinks with friends or curling up on the sofa with a glass of something comforting, you are sure to find just the right cocktail in this book.

FROM DISREPUTABLE BEGINNINGS

Although the word 'cocktail' first appeared in the early 1800s, the trend for a tipple with a twist really took off during the Prohibition Era in the US in the 1920s. During this time the art of mixing drinks became more and more important to mask the raw taste of bootlegged alcohol. After the repeal of Prohibition, the skills that had been developed in the proliferation of illegal bars became widespread and heralded the golden era of the cocktail, the 1930s. However, one of the oldest known cocktails, the Cognac-based Sazerac, dates from

1850s New Orleans, as many as 70 years prior to Prohibition. And, like most things, cocktails change with the times. Until the 1970s, cocktails were made predominantly with gin, whisky or rum, and less commonly with vodka. From the 1970s onwards, the popularity of vodka increased dramatically, and by the 1980s it was the predominant base for mixed drinks. Many cocktails traditionally made with gin, such as the Gimlet or the Martini, are now frequently made with vodka as the main ingredient instead.

Today, all kinds of delicious tastes await us, including different types of spirits and flavourings and a variety of liqueurs, fruit juices, sauces, honey, milk, cream and spices.

BECOME A CONNOISSEUR

In order to really know your cocktails and become a bit of an expert, you need to put together a tool kit of ingredients and equipment. Once you have built up a store of the essentials, you won't have to keep investing for every party or gathering.

- Spirits: The basis of every cocktail is a principal spirit, or occasionally a mixture of two. If you are going for some of the

most popular spirits, you will definitely need vodka, gin, white and dark rum, whisky, brandy and tequila. For a walk on the wild side try champagne, Japanese sake or cherry brandy, or how about some chilli vodka to spice up your list! And remember, it is always good to think about taste rather than cost. While some spirits can be picked up fairly cheaply, try not to opt for the really budget buys, as they will probably taste awful! Think of colour, as well – half the fun of cocktails is the rainbow of wonderful colours that can be mixed into a drink. Try curaçao, which comes in a range of rich colours, from orange to blue, grenadine, which imparts a rich red hue to the most mundane alcoholic and non-alcoholic combinations, and green crème de menthe and Midori for a cool, elegant effect.

- Mixers: These provide the cocktail with its soul and add depth to the taste of your chosen spirit. Mixers are also very important when making non-alcoholic cocktails, so you'll need plenty of fruit juices. Make sure to have a stock of orange, pineapple, tomato, apple, carrot and cranberry juices. For that essential fizz, buy soda water, tonic water and cola.

- Liqueurs: Most liqueurs range between 15 and 70 per cent alcohol by volume and are made from herbs, fruit or nuts. Try coffee liqueurs, cream liqueurs, raspberry, strawberry, or banana-flavoured liqueurs, or perhaps mint- or nut-flavoured tipples. Tropical-tasting liqueurs are always popular – perhaps because they bring back happy holiday memories – especially those with a hint of coconut, among others.

- Flavourings and decoration: These may seem insignificant, but can make or break a cocktail! Stock up on Worcestershire sauce, lemons and limes, cream and hot pepper sauce. You may also need some household items, such as salt and eggs. Syrups are also useful – for example, grenadine, maple, chocolate and raspberry syrups – and are ideal for giving an exotic flavour to a non-alcoholic cocktail. For decoration, think colour and flair. You will definitely need olives, lemon rind, cocktail cherries, sugar for frosting glasses, and fruit pieces, such as strawberries or peach slices.

But of course it's not all about the ingredients. You also need to think about the methods of stirring, mixing and, don't forget, the all-important serving of the drink. Read on for a comprehensive list of all the equipment you will need.

ESSENTIAL EQUIPMENT

- Blender: This should be top of your list as it mixes together fruits, liquids and ice.

- Glasses: Martini glasses, long glasses, tumblers and shot glasses are essential. You'll need to use the right glass for the right cocktail – the shape of the glass can make a difference to the impression created by a cocktail!

- Measures: You can buy stainless steel measures in 25 ml/³/4 fl oz, 35 ml/1 1/4 fl oz, 50 ml/1³/4 fl oz, and 125 ml/4 fl oz varieties. You can also buy glass measures with the same volumes.

- Shaker: This is very important, and is also impressive when you are performing your new-found cocktail-shaking skills. A chrome 1930s-inspired design will look particularly effective.

- Strainer: Very useful to strain out seeds and fruit pieces.

- Bar spoon and pourer: These add a touch of professionalism and make things a little less messy.

- Straws: You can get a variety these days – black straws for a chic look or colourful ones for a summer's day barbecue party.

- Ice: You'll need plenty of it! You can buy in large bags from your local shop, which is often better than trying to make your own. However, if you are having a small gathering, you could use novelty ice cubes, which you can buy. Some involve adding water, but others may not.

Once you have built up your store of ingredients and equipment, you can get on with experimenting with all kinds of tastes and textures. You will soon build up a repertoire of cocktails, making the business of creating and serving cocktails as easy as

can be. When you are comfortable with the general principles of cocktail making you can begin to play around. You could design your own cocktails or perhaps have themed parties, which match the food with particular cocktails. You can learn how to layer different ingredients so that you produce a sophisticated, subtly striped masterpiece rather than an unattractive murky mess.

Until you become really proficient, try to limit the number of cocktails available to three or four – otherwise you'll spend the entire party mixing and pouring and miss out on all the fun!

Cocktails tend to be reserved for special events, but they don't have to be kept for special occasions or parties. Once you find your way around the best *1001 Cocktails*, you will soon realize that cocktails are also the perfect drink for more everyday use – a refreshing drink on a summer's evening, a winter warmer when the nights draw in, or simply a treat after a hard week's work. The following chapters take each spirit at a time and provide you with the most popular recipes, together with a few new twists on classic cocktails. So get practising and discover the delights of the tastiest *1001 Cocktails* – you can be sure you'll come back for more.

VODKA

Vodka is an essential in any cocktail cabinet and is perfect for giving those cocktails a real kick. How about a Vodkatini for a variation on the traditional martini recipe, or a couple of glasses of Harvey Wallbanger? From cold Russian winters to hot New York parties, vodka cocktails will always be on the menu.

1 COSMOPOLITAN (see right-hand page for picture)

This rosy-pink cocktail has a bittersweet flavour that will quench any thirst.

SERVES 1

2 measures vodka
1 measure triple sec
1 measure fresh lime juice
1 measure cranberry juice
ice
orange peel twist, to decorate

Shake all the liquid ingredients over ice until well frosted. Strain into a chilled cocktail glass. Dress with a twist of orange peel.

2 THE LEGEND MARTINI

This version of the ubiquitous martini really is the stuff of which legends – at least in the world of cocktails – are made.

SERVES 1

2 measures iced vodka
1 measure blackberry liqueur
1 measure fresh lime juice
dash sugar syrup

Shake all the ingredients together until really well frosted. Strain into an iced martini glass.

3 SCREWDRIVER

This cocktail has universal appeal, and is great to serve to guests at a party if you are not sure of individual tastes. Freshly squeezed orange juice is a must.

SERVES 1

cracked ice
2 measures vodka
orange juice
orange slice, to decorate

Fill a chilled glass with cracked ice. Pour the vodka over the ice and top up with orange juice. Stir well to mix and dress with a slice of orange.

4 BARBED WIRE

There's nothing too barbed about this one – although it may sharpen the party experience!

SERVES 1

3 measures vodka
1 tsp sweet vermouth
1/2 tsp Pernod
1/2 measure dry sherry
ice
lemon peel twist, to decorate

Shake all the liquid ingredients over ice until well frosted. Strain into a chilled cocktail glass and dress with a twist of lemon peel.

5 SELF-DESTRUCT

Nobody's sure if it's the drink or the drinker who is supposed to self-destruct. There's only one way to find out…

SERVES 1

3 measures vodka
1/2 tsp lime juice
1/2 tsp triple sec
ice

Shake the liquid ingredients over ice until well frosted and strain into a chilled cocktail glass.

6 A SLOE KISS

Sloe gin has a rich fruity flavour that mixes well and is a great base for long drinks.

SERVES 1

1/2 measure sloe gin
1/2 measure Southern Comfort
1 measure vodka
1 tsp amaretto
ice
splash Galliano
orange juice
orange peel twist, to decorate

Shake the first four ingredients over ice until well frosted. Strain into a chilled long glass filled with ice. Splash on the Galliano and top up with a little orange juice. Dress with a twist of orange peel and a stirrer.

7 LONG ISLAND ICED TEA

This dates back to Prohibition when it was drunk out of cups to fool the FBI.

SERVES 1

2 measures vodka
1 measure gin
1 measure white tequila
1 measure white rum
1/2 measure white crème de menthe
2 measures lemon juice
1 tsp sugar syrup
cracked ice
cola
lime wedge, to decorate

Shake the vodka, gin, tequila, rum, crème de menthe, lemon juice and sugar syrup vigorously over ice until well frosted. Strain into an ice-filled tall glass and top up with the cola. Dress with a lime wedge.

8 ANGELIC

It may look angelic, but, unless you are very liberal with the fruit juice, this is certainly not a mild cocktail.

SERVES 1

$^1/_2$ measure Galliano
$^1/_2$ measure Southern Comfort
1 measure vodka
dash egg white
ice
orange or pineapple juice, to taste
pineapple slice, to decorate

Shake the first four ingredients over ice until well frosted. Strain into an ice-filled tall glass and top up with orange or pineapple juice to taste. Dress with a slice of pineapple.

10 DRY SMILE

If you like really dry mixes, go easy on the pineapple juice.

SERVES 1

1 measure Cinzano extra dry
1 measure mandarin vodka
$^1/_2$ measure orange curaçao
juice of $^1/_2$ lemon
1 tbsp strawberry syrup
ice
pineapple juice
strawberry slice, to decorate

Shake the first five ingredients well over ice. Pour into a long glass and top up with pineapple juice to taste. Dress with a slice of strawberry.

9 BAY BREEZE

White cranberry juice is perfect for mixing a refreshing cocktail combination. It's not as sharp as red cranberry juice, but is very fruity.

SERVES 1

2 measures white cranberry and apple juice
2 measures pineapple juice
2 measures vodka
ice
tonic water
lime and pineapple slices, to decorate

Shake the first three ingredients well over ice until frosted. Strain into a tall glass and top up with tonic to taste. Dress with slices of lime and pineapple.

11 SEX ON THE BEACH

Holiday drinks are often long and fruity and this refreshing cocktail is reminiscent of happy days in the sun.

SERVES 1

1 measure peach schnapps
1 measure vodka
2 measures fresh orange juice
3 measures cranberry and peach juice
cubed and crushed ice
dash lemon juice
piece of orange peel, to decorate

Shake the peach schnapps, vodka, orange juice and cranberry and peach juice over ice until well frosted. Strain into a glass filled with crushed ice and squeeze on the lemon juice. Dress with orange peel.

12 TWISTER

Fresh lime juice and lime slices swirled through help to make this a seriously sharp, but long and refreshing mix.

SERVES 1

2 measures vodka
juice of 1/2 fresh lime
ice
1/2 fresh lime, sliced
lemonade

Stir the vodka and lime juice over ice in a large tumbler with slices of fresh lime. Top up with lemonade to taste.

14 CORDLESS SCREWDRIVER

Cordless, perhaps, but certainly not running on empty!

SERVES 1

2 measures chilled vodka
orange wedge
icing sugar

Pour the vodka into a shot glass. Dip a wedge of orange into the sugar. Down the vodka in one go and suck the orange.

13 SALTY DOG

When this cocktail first appeared, gin-based mixes were by far the most popular, but nowadays, a Salty Dog is more frequently made with vodka.

SERVES 1

1 tbsp granulated sugar
1 tbsp coarse salt
lime wedge
cracked ice
2 measures vodka
grapefruit juice

Mix the sugar and salt in a saucer. Rub the rim of a chilled cocktail glass with the lime wedge, then dip it in the sugar and salt mixture. Fill the glass with ice and pour over the vodka. Top up with grapefruit juice and stir.

15 CREAMY SCREWDRIVER

Not cream, but egg yolk, gives this its smooth and creamy texture.

SERVES 1

2 measures vodka
6 measures orange juice
1/2 tsp sugar syrup
1 egg yolk
crushed and cracked ice

Blend the liquid ingredients with the egg yolk and some crushed ice until smooth. Half fill a tall chilled tumbler with cracked ice and pour the cocktail over without straining.

16 COOL YULE MARTINI

Just the right martini to help you celebrate the festive season.

SERVES 1

3 measures vodka
1/2 measure dry vermouth
1 tsp peppermint schnapps
ice
fresh mint sprig, to decorate

Shake the liquid ingredients over ice until well frosted. Strain into a chilled cocktail glass and dress with a sprig of mint.

17 MARS EXPLOSION

We may never know what happens on Mars but we can let the imagination wander.

SERVES 1

2 measures orange juice, chilled
1 measure vodka, frozen
ice
1/4 measure white rum, frozen
1 dash grenadine, chilled
cocktail cherry and orange peel twist, to decorate

Stir the orange juice and vodka over ice until well frosted. Strain into a chilled goblet or wine glass. Stir the rum and grenadine together and pour slowly into the middle of the juice so the red colour spreads gently outwards. Dress with a cocktail cherry and a twist of orange peel.

18 MOSCOW MULE

This cocktail came into existence through a happy coincidence in the 1930s. An American bar owner had overstocked ginger beer and a representative of a soft drink company invented the Moscow Mule to help him out.

SERVES 1

2 measures vodka
1 measure lime juice
cracked ice
ginger beer
lime slice, to decorate

Shake the vodka and lime juice vigorously over ice until well frosted. Half fill a chilled tall glass with cracked ice and strain the cocktail over. Top up with ginger beer and dress with a slice of lime.

19 KAMIKAZE

No turning back on this one. It's so delicious you won't be able to put it down.

SERVES 1

1 measure vodka
1 measure triple sec
1/2 measure fresh lime juice
1/2 measure fresh lemon juice
ice
dry white wine, chilled
cucumber and lime slices, to decorate

Shake the vodka, triple sec, lime juice and lemon juice together over ice until well frosted. Strain into a chilled glass and top up with wine. Dress with slices of cucumber and lime.

20
BLUE LAGOON (see right-hand page for picture)

Let your imagination carry you away while you sink into this luxuriously blue cocktail. It has a refreshing lemon zing and sparkle too.

SERVES 1

1 measure blue curaçao
1 measure vodka
dash fresh lemon juice
lemonade

Pour the curaçao into a highball or cocktail glass, followed by the vodka. Add the lemon juice and top up with lemonade to taste.

21
LUMBERJACK

When you put in a day's hard work, you deserve something with a bit of a kick in it to refresh you at the end.

SERVES 1

2 measures vodka
2 measures apple brandy
1 measure lemon juice
1/2 measure sugar syrup
6 cherries, stoned
crushed ice
soda water
fresh cherry, to decorate

Mix the first six ingredients together in a small blender until slushy. Pour into a tall chilled glass. Top up with soda water and dress with a fresh cherry.

22
DELFT DONKEY

Well, it would be a truly Dutch donkey if made with gin – perhaps the vodka will help you pin the tail to the right spot?

SERVES 1

2 measures vodka
1 measure lime juice
cubed and cracked ice
ginger beer
lime slice, to decorate

Shake the vodka and lime juice vigorously over ice until well frosted. Half fill a chilled tall glass with cracked ice and strain the cocktail over. Top up with ginger beer and dress with a slice of lime.

⍺23

ILLUSIONS

Start adding the orange juice to this blue-green combination and you will be having illusions as it changes its colour once again.

SERVES 1

1 measure vodka
1 measure Malibu
1/2 measure Midori
1/2 measure blue curaçao
ice
fresh orange juice
melon slices, to decorate

Stir the first four ingredients over ice until frosted. Strain into a chilled highball glass or large cocktail or wine glass, and top up with more ice and orange juice to taste. Dress with slices of melon.

⍺25

PEARTINI

Pear brandy has a delicate fragrance and lovely flavour, but don't confuse it with pear liqueur.

SERVES 1

1 tsp caster sugar
pinch ground cinnamon
1 lemon wedge
cracked ice
1 measure vodka
1 measure pear brandy,
   such as Poire William or
   Pera Segnana

Mix the sugar and cinnamon in a saucer. Rub the outside rim of a cocktail glass with the lemon wedge, then dip it into the sugar and cinnamon mixture. Set aside. Put the ice into a jug and pour in the vodka and pear brandy. Stir well and strain into a glass.

⍺24

BLUE MONDAY

The lovely colour and fruity flavour of this cocktail is guaranteed to make Monday your favourite day of the week.

SERVES 1

cracked ice
1 measure vodka
1/2 measure Cointreau
1 tbsp blue curaçao

Put the cracked ice into a mixing glass or jug and pour in the vodka, Cointreau and curaçao. Stir well and strain into a cocktail glass.

⍺26

WOO-WOO

Be sure to woo your friends with this refreshing and simple drink. It's also great for parties.

SERVES 1

cracked ice
2 measures vodka
2 measures peach schnapps
4 measures cranberry juice
Cape gooseberry,
   to decorate

Half fill a chilled cocktail glass with cracked ice. Pour the vodka, peach schnapps and cranberry juice over the ice. Stir well to mix and dress with a Cape gooseberry.

27 LINE LIGHTNING

This unusual liqueur made from caraway seeds makes a great long drink with most mixers and other flavours.

SERVES 1

1 measure vodka
1 measure kümmel
ice
tonic water
red berries, to decorate

Stir the vodka and kümmel together with ice in a tall glass. Top up with tonic water to taste and dress with berries.

28 VODKA ESPRESSO

This makes for a fabulous after-dinner treat. It's usually made with Stolichnaya vodka and Amarula, a South African cream liqueur with a caramel flavour.

SERVES 1

cracked ice
2 measures espresso or other strong brewed coffee, cooled
1 measure vodka
2 tsp caster sugar
1 measure Amarula

Put the cracked ice into a cocktail shaker, pour in the coffee and vodka, and add the sugar. Cover and shake vigorously for 10–20 seconds, until the outside of the shaker is misted. Strain into a cocktail glass, then float the Amarula on top.

29 FLYING GRASSHOPPER

There are two versions of this cocktail – one made with green crème de menthe and chocolate liqueur and this one made with equal quantities of white and green crème de menthe.

SERVES 1

cracked ice
1 measure vodka
1 measure green crème de menthe
1 measure white crème de menthe

Put the cracked ice into a mixing glass or jug and pour in the vodka and crème de menthe. Stir well and strain into a cocktail glass.

30 METROPOLITAN

This sophisticated cocktail for city slickers shares its name, but not its ingredients, with an equally urbane classic from the past.

SERVES 1

1 lemon wedge
1 tbsp caster sugar
cracked ice
1/2 measure vodka
1/2 measure framboise
1/2 measure cranberry juice
1/2 measure orange juice

Rub the rim of a cocktail glass with the lemon wedge and dip into the sugar. Put the ice into a shaker and pour in the liquid ingredients. Cover and shake for 10–20 seconds, until the outside of the shaker is misted. Strain into the glass.

31 BELLINITINI

Bellini, martini – it's the sweet peachy ingredients that make all the difference.

SERVES 1

2 measures vodka
1 measure peach schnapps
1 measure peach juice
ice
chilled champagne

Shake the vodka, schnapps, and peach juice vigorously over ice until well frosted. Strain into a chilled goblet and top up with chilled champagne.

33 CHOCOLATE MARTINI

For those with a sweet tooth, this variation of the classic martini will go down wonderfully.

SERVES 1

2 measures vodka
1/4 measure crème de cacao
2 dashes orange flower water
ice
cocoa powder
orange peel twist,
  to decorate

Shake the vodka, crème de cacao and orange flower water over ice until really well frosted. Strain into a martini glass rimmed with cocoa and dress with an orange peel twist.

32 ROAD RUNNER 2

A cool and sophisticated tropical delight with more than a hint of bitter almonds.

SERVES 1

1 measure vodka
1/2 measure Malibu
1/2 measure amaretto
ice

Shake the liquid ingredients vigorously over ice until well frosted. Strain into a chilled cocktail glass.

34 PEAR & CINNAMON SLING

If you can't find cinnamon syrup, you may have to make your own!

SERVES 1

2 measures vodka
2 measures pear purée
3/5 measure cinnamon syrup
4/5 measure cranberry and
  blackcurrant juice
ice
champagne, chilled

Shake the first four ingredients together over ice until frosted. Strain into a chilled glass and top up with champagne.

35 THE MODERN MARTINI

Now more popularly based on vodka and often flavoured with fresh fruits – this one uses pomegranate. Other good fruits to try are kiwi fruit, cranberry, pear and watermelon.

SERVES 1

1 very ripe pomegranate
2 measures vodka
ice

Spoon the flesh of the pomegranate into a shaker and lightly crush or muddle. Add the vodka and ice and shake well. Strain into an iced martini glass.

36 GENOA VODKA

Or it could just be called Italian vodka – Genoa has no special claim to the bittersweet liqueur.

SERVES 1

2 measures vodka
1 measure Campari
3 measures orange juice
ice
orange slice, to decorate

Shake the vodka, Campari and orange juice vigorously over ice until well frosted. Strain into a small chilled tumbler. Dress with a slice of orange.

37 IS THIS ALL?

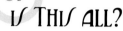

And if it were, it should be enough for any cocktail connoisseur.

SERVES 1

2 measures lemon vodka
1 measure triple sec
1 measure lemon juice
1 egg white
cracked ice

Shake the liquid ingredients with the egg white over ice until well frosted. Strain into a chilled cocktail glass.

38 VODKATINI

The celebrated 007 popularized the use of vodka, rather than gin, as the base of the Martini, and the Vodkatini is now widely accepted as an incredibly stylish and tasty alternative.

SERVES 1

1 measure vodka
ice
dash dry vermouth
lime peel twist,
    to decorate

Pour the vodka over a handful of ice in a mixing glass. Add the vermouth, stir well, and strain into a cocktail glass. Dress with a twist of lime peel.

39 BALALAIKA

A very lemony cocktail but it works well and you could always add the lemon gradually, to your taste.

SERVES 1

1/2 measure vodka, chilled
1/4 measure Cointreau, chilled
1/4 measure fresh lemon juice
lemon slice
ice

Pour the three liquids into a small cocktail glass. Stir gently, then add a slice of lemon and one ice cube.

40 CAIPIROSKA

This is a very fresh version of vodka and lime. If you find it too sharp, add a little more sugar to taste.

SERVES 1

1 lime, cut into 6 wedges
3 tsp confectioners' sugar
a really good slug of vodka
crushed ice

Put the lime wedges and sugar in a tumbler and mash the wedges to release the juice and combine well with the sugar. Pour on the vodka and add crushed ice to fill the glass. For maximum kick, drink through a straw!

41 PEACH FLOYD

Shots look stunning in the right type of glass, but as they are for drinking down in one, keep them small and have everything really well chilled.

SERVES 1

1 measure peach schnapps, chilled
1 measure vodka, chilled
1 measure white cranberry and peach juice, chilled
1 measure cranberry juice, chilled
ice

Stir all the liquid ingredients together over ice and pour into an iced shot glass.

42 VODKA ZIP

This mix relies on being really cold, so you should serve it over ice.

SERVES 1

2 measures vodka
1 measure freshly squeezed lemon juice
crushed ice
lemon peel strip, to decorate

Shake the vodka and lemon juice with half the crushed ice until well frosted. Strain into an iced wine glass or large cocktail glass filled with more crushed ice. Dress with a strip of lemon peel.

43
BLACK RUSSIAN

History records only White and Red Russians. The omission of the Black Russian is a sad oversight. For a coffee liqueur, you can use either Tia Maria or Kahlúa, depending on your personal taste – the latter is sweeter.

SERVES 1

2 measures vodka
1 measure coffee liqueur
cracked ice

Pour the vodka and coffee liqueur over cracked ice cubes in a small chilled glass. Stir to mix.

45
SILVER BERRY

This drink is perfect for one of those very special occasions – except that you really can't drink very many!

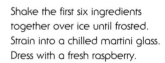

SERVES 1

1 measure raspberry vodka, iced
1 measure cassis, iced
1 measure Cointreau, iced
frozen berry, to decorate

Carefully and slowly layer the three liqueurs in the order listed, in a well-iced shot glass or tall thin cocktail glass. They must be well iced first and may need time to settle into their layers. Dress with a frozen berry.

44
BLOODY MARY

This classic was invented in 1921 at the legendary Harry's Bar in Paris.

SERVES 1

dash Worcestershire sauce
dash Tabasco sauce
cracked ice
2 measures vodka
splash dry sherry
6 measures tomato juice
juice 1/2 lemon
pinch celery salt
pinch cayenne pepper
celery stick with leaves and lemon slice, to decorate

Dash the Worcestershire sauce and Tabasco sauce over ice in a shaker and add the vodka, splash of dry sherry, tomato juice and lemon juice. Shake vigorously until frosted. Strain into a tall chilled glass, add a pinch of celery salt and a pinch of cayenne pepper and decorate with the celery stick and a slice of lemon.

46
THE SPRAY

If you can't find raspberry vodka, you can make your own simply by marinating about 10 berries in a bottle of vodka for about 12 hours. Then remove the berries and the vodka is good enough on its own!

SERVES 1

1 measure raspberry vodka
1/2 measure framboise
1/2 measure Cointreau
3/4 measure cranberry juice
2 dashes orange bitters
1 dash lime cordial
ice
1 raspberry

Shake the first six ingredients together over ice until frosted. Strain into a chilled martini glass. Dress with a fresh raspberry.

47 THE AWOL

As its name suggests, you won't last long drinking many of these in an evening!

SERVES 1

1 measure melon liqueur, iced
1/2 measure lime juice, chilled
1/2 measure vodka, iced
1/2 measure white rum, iced
ice

Stir all the liquid ingredients together over ice and strain into a chilled cocktail glass.

48 LAST MANGO IN PARIS

Things might have turned out differently if Brando had gone for the mango instead of the tango.

SERVES 1

2 measures vodka
1 measure framboise
1 measure lime juice
1/2 mango, peeled, pitted, and chopped
2 halved strawberries
lime slice, to decorate

Mix the ingredients in a blender until slushy. Pour into a chilled goblet and dress with a slice of lime.

49 THUNDERBIRD

Enjoy the heady perfume of all these ingredients as you sip this iced delight.

SERVES 1

2 measures iced vodka
dash Parfait Amour
dash cassis
small piece of orange zest
one rose or violet petal

Pour the vodka into a frosted martini glass. Add the other ingredients slowly and stir only once. Dress with the rose petal.

50 FULL MONTY

The expression 'full monty', meaning not holding anything back, has been around for a long time, but was given a new lease of life by the highly successful film of the same title. However, you can keep your clothes on when drinking this.

SERVES 1

1 measure vodka
1 measure Galliano
cracked ice
grated ginseng root (use fresh ginger if you can't find ginseng)

Shake the vodka and Galliano vigorously over ice until well frosted. Strain into a chilled cocktail glass and sprinkle with grated ginseng.

51
BLACK BEAUTY

For a very different version, try it with one of the black vodkas that have recently appeared on the market. The dramatic colour and subtle flavour are worth experiencing.

SERVES 1

2 measures vodka
1 measure black Sambuca
ice
black olive, to decorate

Stir the vodka and Sambuca with ice in a mixing glass until frosted. Strain into an iced martini glass and add the olive.

53
PERFECT LOVE

This is the literal translation for an unusual purple liqueur flavoured with rose petals, almonds and vanilla.

SERVES 1

1 measure vodka
1/2 measure Parfait Amour
1/2 measure maraschino
crushed ice

Shake all the liquid ingredients together over ice until frosted. Strain into a chilled tall thin glass with more ice.

52
RASPBERRINI

Wonderfully fresh tasting with a smell of summer that will take away all your cares...

SERVES 1

30 g/1 oz fresh or frozen raspberries
1 tbsp icing sugar
1–2 drops fresh lemon juice
splash framboise
ice
2 measures vodka, well iced

Retain 2–3 raspberries to add later. Crush the rest in a bowl with the sugar, lemon and framboise. Strain well. Pour the vodka into an iced martini glass and add the purée and reserved raspberries.

54
SPOTTED BIKINI

A playful name for an amusing cocktail. It also tastes great, although you may like to add a little sugar to taste.

SERVES 1

1 ripe passion fruit
2 measures vodka
1 measure white rum
1 measure cold milk
juice of 1/2 lemon
ice
slice of lemon peel,
   to decorate

Scoop the passion fruit flesh into a jug. Shake the liquid ingredients over ice until well frosted. Strain into a chilled cocktail glass and add the passion fruit at the last minute. Dress with a slice of lemon peel.

55
ANOUCHKA (see right-hand page for picture)

Sambuca is liquorice-flavoured and therefore not to everyone's taste. However, used here with a dash of blackberry liqueur and the iced vodka, it's a great combination.

SERVES 1

1 measure vodka, iced
dash black Sambuca
dash blackberry liqueur
a few blackberries, fresh or
frozen, to decorate

Pour the vodka into a chilled shot glass. Add the Sambuca and the blackberry liqueur. Dress with the blackberries.

56
NINETY-NINE PARK LANE

London's Park Lane was once a prestigious road of smart apartments, with only the very occasional bright neon light!

SERVES 1

1 measure vodka
1 measure Cointreau
2 measures orange juice
1 small egg white
crushed ice
1/2 measure green crème de menthe

Shake the first four ingredients together over crushed ice. Pour into a medium-sized cocktail glass or goblet over more crushed ice. Shake or sprinkle on the crème de menthe.

57
ALLIGATOR

This delicious variety competes fiercely with its cousin, the Crocodile!

SERVES 1

2 measures vodka
1 measure Midori
1/2 measure dry vermouth
1/4 tsp lemon juice
ice
melon balls, to decorate

Pour the liquid ingredients over ice and shake vigorously until well frosted. Strain into a chilled cocktail glass and decorate with melon balls.

58 MELON BALL

This vibrantly lovely melon-flavoured cocktail is also full of refreshing pineapple.

SERVES 1

2 measures vodka
2 measures Midori
4 measures pineapple juice
cubed and cracked ice
melon wedge, to decorate

Pour the liquid ingredients over ice and stir well to mix. Half fill a chilled tumbler with cracked ice and strain the cocktail over. Decorate with a melon wedge.

60 GOLDEN TANG

Summery colours combine with the autumn flavours of fruit and herbs to produce a delicious and refreshing mix.

SERVES 1

2 measures vodka
1 measure Strega
1/2 measure crème de banane
1/2 measure orange-flavoured
    drink
ice
cherry and orange slice,
    to decorate

Shake the first four ingredients together over ice until well frosted. Strain into a chilled glass and dress with a cherry and a slice of orange.

59 CROCODILE

This is certainly a snappy cocktail with a bit of bite. However, it probably gets the name from its spectacular colour. Midori, a Japanese melon-flavoured liqueur, is a startling shade of green.

SERVES 1

2 measures vodka
1 measure triple sec
1 measure Midori
2 measures lemon juice
cracked ice

Shake the vodka, triple sec, Midori and lemon juice vigorously over ice until well frosted. Strain into a chilled cocktail glass.

61 HARVEY WALLBANGER

This well-known contemporary classic cocktail is a great party drink – mix it strong at first, then weaker as the evening goes by – or without alcohol for drivers and no one would know!

SERVES 1

ice
3 measures vodka
8 measures orange juice
2 tsp Galliano
cherry and orange slice,
    to decorate

Half fill a tall glass with ice, pour the vodka and orange juice over the ice cubes and float Galliano on top. Dress with a cherry and a slice of orange.

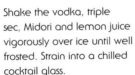

62
PEPPER PUNCH

There is a long and honourable culinary tradition of seasoning pineapple with pepper and spices.

SERVES 1

2 measures vodka
1 measure golden rum
4 measures pineapple juice
1/2 measure orgeat
1 tsp lemon juice
cracked ice
1/4 tsp cayenne pepper
dash Tabasco sauce

Pour the vodka, rum, pineapple juice, orgeat and lemon juice over ice in a shaker and add the cayenne pepper and Tabasco sauce. Shake vigorously until well frosted. Strain into a chilled glass.

63
GODMOTHER

Amaretto is an Italian liqueur, so the inspiration for this cocktail may come from the wife of Don Corleone, the protagonist in Mario Puzo's best-selling novel.

SERVES 1

cracked ice
2 measures vodka
1 measure amaretto

Put some cracked ice into a small chilled tumbler. Pour the vodka and amaretto over the ice. Stir to mix.

64
MOON LANDING

Try a few of these and decide if they really have any gravity-defying properties.

SERVES 1

1 measure vodka
1 measure Tia Maria
1 measure amaretto
1 measure Bailey's Irish Cream
ice

Shake the liquid ingredients over ice until well frosted. Strain into a chilled shot glass.

65
GRAND DUCHESS

Definitely a cocktail fit for a duchess… or a princess… or even a queen.

SERVES 1

cracked ice
2 measures vodka
1 measure triple sec
3 measures cranberry juice
2 measures orange juice

Put some cracked ice into a mixing glass and pour the ingredients over the ice. Stir well to mix. Half fill a small chilled tumbler with cracked ice and strain the cocktail over.

66 YELLOW QUIVER

Three fruits mixed with three different alcoholic drinks, topped with a swirl of blue curaçao for a glamorous touch.

SERVES 1

1/2 measure Mandarine
  Napoleon
1/2 measure vodka
1/4 measure Galliano
1/2 measure pineapple juice
1/4 measure lemon juice
1/2 egg white
crushed ice
dash blue curaçao

Shake all but the curaçao over crushed iced until well frosted. Pour into an iced cocktail glass and spoon the curaçao on top at the last moment.

67 SEABREEZE

Pink grapefruit juice is much sweeter and subtler than its paler cousin, so it is ideal for mixing in cocktails where you want just a slight sharpness.

SERVES 1

1 1/2 measures vodka
1/2 measure cranberry juice
ice
pink grapefruit juice, to taste

Shake the vodka and cranberry juice over ice until frosted. Pour into a chilled tumbler or long glass and top up with pink grapefruit juice to taste.

68 EARLY EVENING

A variation on the classic Pimm's that is a little stronger and more appley, yet still a great summer cocktail for special occasions.

SERVES 1

1 measure vodka
1 measure Pimm's No. 1
1 measure apple juice
ice
lemonade
cucumber strips and apple
  slices, to decorate

Shake the first three ingredients over ice until frosted. Strain into a chilled highball glass and top up with lemonade. Dress with cucumber strips and apple slices.

69 SEEING RED

There is a real kick to this cocktail and the vivid colour comes from the cranberry juice.

SERVES 1

1 measure red vodka
1 measure peach schnapps
3 measures cranberry juice
crushed ice
soda water
frozen cranberries, to
  decorate

Shake the first three ingredients over ice until well frosted. Strain into a tall chilled cocktail glass, top up with soda water and float a few frozen cranberries on the top.

70 CHICA CHICA

You can buy most flavoured vodkas, but you can also make your own. Add a small quantity of the flavouring you require to a bottle of vodka and set aside for 12 hours.

SERVES 1

2 measures raspberry vodka
1 measure Chambord
2 measures cranberry and
   raspberry juice
crushed ice
1 measure apple juice
lemonade
apple slices, to decorate

Mix the first three ingredients well with crushed ice in a chilled highball glass. Stir in the apple juice and top up with lemonade to taste. Dress with slices of apple.

71 CRANBERRY COLLINS

The classic Collins drink is made with gin, but its many variations are made with other spirits, so try this one for size.

SERVES 1

2 measures vodka
3/4 measure elderflower cordial
3 measures white cranberry
   and apple juice, or to taste
ice
soda water
cranberries and slice of lime,
   to decorate

Shake the vodka, elderflower cordial and white cranberry and apple juice over ice until well frosted. Strain into a Collins glass with more ice and add soda water to taste. Dress with cranberries and a slice of lime.

72 ON THE BEACH

This refreshing cocktail is reminiscent of happy days in the sun.

SERVES 1

1 measure peach schnapps
1 measure vodka
2 measures fresh orange juice
3 measures cranberry juice
crushed ice
dash lemon juice
lime peel, to decorate

Shake the first four ingredients over ice until well frosted. Strain into a highball glass filled with crushed iced and squeeze on the lemon juice. Dress with lime peel.

73 CINNAMON PARK

Hints of cinnamon or other spices can make all the difference to fruit-based cocktails. Add to taste or sprinkle more on the top before drinking.

SERVES 1

1 measure vodka
2 measures pink grapefruit
   juice
1/2 measure Campari
1 dash sugar syrup
pinch or two cinnamon
1 egg white
ice

Shake the first six ingredients well over ice and strain into a chilled cocktail glass.

74 MIMI

This is a delicious mix without the kick of the vodka, so make a batch for non-alcohol drinkers and add the vodka for yourself!

SERVES 1

2 measures vodka
1/2 measure coconut cream
2 measures pineapple juice
crushed ice
fresh pineapple slice or fan, to decorate

Mix the vodka, coconut cream, pineapple juice and crushed ice in a blender for a few seconds until frothy. Pour into a chilled cocktail glass and dress with a slice of pineapple.

75 THE BLOOD ORANGE COCKTAIL

Although available only briefly, early in the Spanish orange season, blood oranges are ideal for enhancing the fruity bitter sweetness of Campari. Mind you, it might be too bitter for some, so sugar-crust the rim to sweeten the first taste.

SERVES 1

juice of 1 blood orange
icing sugar
1 measure red vodka
1 measure Campari
cracked ice

Rub the rim of an old-fashioned glass with a little orange juice and dip into the sugar. Set aside to dry. Shake the liquid ingredients over ice until well frosted. Fill the glass with ice and pour in the mixture.

76 MELON STATE BALL

Even though this is full of healthy orange juice, the vibrant green Midori gives it a decadent appearance.

SERVES 1

2 measures vodka
1 measure Midori
2 measures orange juice
ice

Pour the liquid ingredients over ice and shake vigorously until well frosted. Strain into a chilled cocktail glass.

77 FUZZY NAVEL

This is another one of those cocktails with a name that plays on the ingredients – fuzzy to remind you that it contains peach schnapps and navel because it is mixed with orange juice.

SERVES 1

2 measures vodka
1 measure peach schnapps
1 cup orange juice
cracked ice
physalis, to decorate

Shake the vodka, peach schnapps and orange juice vigorously over cracked ice until well frosted. Strain into a chilled cocktail glass and dress with a physalis.

78 BULLSHOT

This is not unlike drinking chilled consommé – but with a noticeable kick. It is best really cold.

SERVES 1
1 measure vodka
2 measures beef consommé or good stock
dash fresh lemon juice
2 dashes Worcestershire sauce
ice
celery salt
strip of lemon peel, to decorate

Shake all the liquid ingredients well with ice and strain into a glass with extra ice. Sprinkle with celery salt and dress with the strip of lemon peel.

79 GRIMACE & GRIN

Cocktails flavoured with sweets are in fashion at the moment.

SERVES 6
100 g/3¹/₂ oz sharp-flavoured jelly beans, such as sour cherry, lemon and apple
³/₄ bottle vodka

Set aside 30 g/1 oz of the jelly beans and place the remainder in a microwave-proof bowl. Add about 4 tablespoons of the vodka. Microwave until the jelly beans have melted. Pour the mixture through a funnel into the bottle with the remaining vodka, and add the reserved jelly beans. Replace the lid and chill in the refrigerator for at least 2 hours.

80 SPUTNIK

If you are making several of these, they can be prepared in advance with different coloured cherries in orbit on top.

SERVES 1
1 measure vodka
1 measure light cream
1 tsp maraschino
ice
maraschino cherry, to decorate

Shake all the liquid ingredients well over ice and strain into a glass. Dress with a cherry, supported on crossed cocktail sticks.

81 BERRY BLUSH

If you can't find any framboise, use fraise instead, or try it with cassis for a complete change.

SERVES 1
2 measures vodka
1 measure framboise
1 scoop vanilla ice cream
¹/₂ measure strawberry syrup
fresh strawberry, to decorate

Mix all the ingredients in a blender for about 10 seconds, until smooth and frothy. Pour into a cocktail glass, and dress with a strawberry.

82
ICED LEMON CREAM

This really is like drinking a very adult and alcoholic slush – perfect for a hot day.

SERVES 1

1½ measures lemon vodka or Citroen
¾ measure Galliano
¾ measure light cream
small scoop lemon sorbet
mint leaf, to decorate

Blend all the ingredients together to a smooth slush. Pour into a chilled shallow cocktail glass and dress with a mint leaf. Drink with a straw.

83
RUSSIAN DOUBLE

Vodka and schnapps are both very strong drinks, so handle with care!

SERVES 1

1 measure vodka, iced
strips of lemon peel or orange peel
1 measure lemon vodka or schnapps, iced

Layer the ingredients carefully in a chilled shot glass, putting the strips of peel in the first layer. Drink immediately.

84
ROMPOPE

This is Mexico's version of the better-known Dutch advocaat, a thick, yellow, custardy treat for the sweet-toothed.

SERVES 1

350 ml/12 fl oz sweetened condensed milk
300 ml/10 fl oz chilled milk
4 egg yolks
¼ tsp vanilla extract
150 ml/5 fl oz vodka
¼ tsp cinnamon, for dusting
cinnamon stick, to decorate

Reserve the cinnamon and mix all the other ingredients in a blender at top speed for 45 seconds. Strain and chill. Pour into glasses and dust with cinnamon. For a finishing touch, use a cinnamon stick as a stirrer.

85
TAILGATE

Tailgating – best avoided, if you want to keep body and soul together. Have one of these instead.

SERVES 1

cracked ice
dash orange bitters
2 measures vodka
1 measure green Chartreuse
1 measure sweet vermouth

Put some cracked ice into a mixing glass. Dash the orange bitters over the ice and pour in the remaining ingredients. Stir well to mix, then strain into a chilled cocktail glass.

86
WHITE SPIDER

As subtle as the finest spider's web, the white crème de menthe hides in the corners of this clear cocktail.

SERVES 1
cracked ice
1 measure vodka
1 measure white crème de menthe

Put some cracked ice into a mixing glass. Pour the vodka and crème de menthe over the ice. Stir well and strain into a chilled cocktail glass.

87
GENOESE

A misleadingly pure-looking Italian offering with fiery Sambuca and more than a touch of the unforgiving grappa.

SERVES 1
1 measure vodka
1 measure grappa
1/2 measure Sambuca
1/2 measure dry vermouth
ice

Shake the liquid ingredients vigorously over ice until well frosted. Strain into a chilled cocktail glass.

88
GOLDEN FROG

As a rule, classic vodka cocktails were intended to provide an alcoholic drink with no telltale signs on the breath and were usually fairly simple mixes of non-alcoholic flavours. Contemporary vodka cocktails often include other spirits.

SERVES 1
ice
1 measure vodka
1 measure Strega
1 measure Galliano
1 measure lemon juice

Mix 4–6 ice cubes in a blender with the vodka, Strega, Galliano and lemon juice. Blend until slushy. Pour into a chilled cocktail glass.

89
VODGA

This may look fresh and innocuous, but one too many could push you over the edge.

SERVES 1
2 measures vodka
1 measure Strega
1/2 measure orange juice
cracked ice

Shake the vodka, Strega and orange juice vigorously over ice until well frosted. Strain into a chilled cocktail glass.

90

HOT & DIRTY MARTINI

(see right-hand page for picture)

The chilli vodka provides the heat, the olive brine gives the dirt.

SERVES 1

3 measures chilli vodka
1/2 measure dry vermouth
1 tsp olive brine
ice
stuffed green olive,
   to decorate

Shake the vodka, vermouth and olive brine over ice until well frosted. Strain into a chilled cocktail glass and dress with a stuffed olive.

91

GOLDEN FLIP

Sherry and almond liqueur are the bases for this flip, with an added kick of vodka.

SERVES 1

1 measure vodka
1 measure sweet sherry
1 measure amaretto
1 egg yolk
1 tbsp icing sugar
ice
grated nutmeg, for sprinkling

Shake all the ingredients except the nutmeg well over ice until frosted. Strain into a chilled small wine glass and sprinkle with freshly grated nutmeg.

92

SERENADE

Nuts and fruit mixed with vodka need little but thorough icing to produce a great-tasting cocktail.

SERVES 1

1 measure vodka
1 measure amaretto
1/4 measure coconut cream
1 measure pineapple juice
crushed ice

Mix all the ingredients together in a blender on slow speed for 5–10 seconds, until frozen and slushy. Pour into a chilled cocktail glass and serve with a straw.

93 FUZZY MARTINI

Flavoured vodkas are very popular in Russia and Poland and add great variety to the range of vodka cocktails.

SERVES 1

2 measures vanilla vodka
1/2 measure coffee vodka
1 tsp peach schnapps
ice
peach slice, to decorate

Shake the vodkas and schnapps over ice until well frosted. Strain into a chilled cocktail glass and dress with a peach slice.

95 YORSH

A marriage of two great traditions in a fairly ordinary looking cocktail – it's stronger than it looks!

SERVES 1

225 ml/8 fl oz pale ale
2 measures vodka

Pour the ale into a chilled beer glass or tankard, then pour in the vodka.

94 CHILLY WILLY

Truly a cocktail for the brave-hearted – the heat depends on the type of chilli (some are much more fiery than others) as well as the quantity you add and whether the chilli was deseeded first. For even more spice, use chilli vodka as well!

SERVES 1

2 measures vodka
1 tsp chopped fresh chilli
cracked ice

Shake the vodka over ice with the chilli until a frost forms. Strain into a small chilled tumbler.

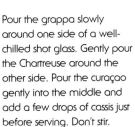

96 AURORA BOREALIS

Like a pousse-café, this spectacular coloured drink should not be mixed or stirred. Let it swirl around the glass, creating a multi-coloured effect, and try to guess the various flavours.

SERVES 1

1 measure grappa or vodka, iced
1 measure green Chartreuse, iced
1/2 measure orange curaçao, iced
few drops cassis, iced

Pour the grappa slowly around one side of a well-chilled shot glass. Gently pour the Chartreuse around the other side. Pour the curaçao gently into the middle and add a few drops of cassis just before serving. Don't stir.

97
THE
CHOCOLATE DIVA

Chocoholics will not be able to resist this wicked alcohol and chocolate combination, but it really needs to be very cold.

SERVES 1

4 squares good-quality milk
   chocolate, melted
1 measure Grand Marnier
1 measure vodka
1 measure crème de cacao
1 tbsp fresh orange juice
fresh edible petals, to decorate

Mix the melted chocolate gently with the liqueurs and orange juice until well blended. Pour into a chilled cocktail glass and float petals on the top to dress.

98
SILVER
SLIPPER

The caraway flavour of the kümmel comes through strongest in this creamy combination, but do choose a good pure vanilla ice cream.

SERVES 1

1 measure kümmel
1 measure vodka
1 scoop vanilla ice cream

Mix all the ingredients together in a blender on slow speed until thick. Pour into a chilled cocktail glass.

99
CUCUMBER CRUSH

Perfect to enjoy after your sauna, swim, or work-out, but this cocktail does have some added inner strength!

SERVES 1

1/4 cucumber, peeled
juice of 1 lime
1 measure vodka
crushed and cubed ice
soda water
cucumber slice and mint sprig,
   to decorate

Put the cucumber, lime juice, vodka and ice in a blender and mix almost to a purée. Serve poured over ice, topped up with soda water to taste, and dress with a slice of cucumber and a mint sprig.

100
STOCKHOLM

A citrussy cocktail that's as cool and sparkling as a winter's day in the Swedish capital.

SERVES 1

1 sugar cube
2 measures lemon vodka
1 measure lemon juice
chilled sparkling wine

Put the sugar cube in a goblet with the vodka and lemon juice. Stir to dissolve the sugar. Top up with sparkling wine.

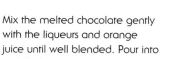

GIN

Gin's unique blend of juniper botanicals and berries adds a deliciously delicate flavour to any cocktail cabinet. You can add fruit juices and mixers, or vermouth. There is, of course, the Ultimate Classic Martini, but why not try other variations, such as the Sapphire Martini or the Bellini Martini?

101
SINGAPORE SLING

In the days of the British Empire, the privileged would gather at their clubs in the relative cool of the evening to gossip about the day's events. A Singapore Sling is still the ideal thirst-quencher.

SERVES 1

2 measures gin
1 measure cherry brandy
1 measure lemon juice
1 tsp grenadine
cracked ice
soda water
lime peel and cocktail cherries,
    to decorate

Shake the gin, cherry brandy, lemon juice and grenadine vigorously over ice until well frosted. Half fill a chilled glass with cracked ice and strain in the cocktail. Top up with soda water and dress with lime peel and cocktail cherries.

102
MARTINI

For many, this is the ultimate cocktail. It is named after its inventor, Martini di Arma di Taggia, not the famous brand of vermouth! It can vary hugely, from the Original (see below) to the Ultra Dry, when the glass is merely rinsed out with vermouth.

SERVES 1

3 measures gin
1 tsp dry vermouth, or to taste
cracked ice
green cocktail olive,
    to decorate

Pour the gin and vermouth over the ice in a mixing glass and stir well to mix. Strain into a chilled cocktail glass and dress with a cocktail olive.

103
GIN FIZZ

This could be the forerunner to gin and tonic, as it makes a great drink – long, economical and refreshing.

SERVES 1

1 1/2 measures gin
1 tsp sugar
few long shreds lemon peel
crushed ice
soda water

Mix the gin, sugar and lemon peel together until the sugar has dissolved. Pour into a long glass full of crushed ice and top up with chilled soda water.

104
FIREFLY

A light and frothy mixture that looks delicate and innocent – but watch out, there are three spirits in this brew!

SERVES 1

1 measure gin
1/2 measure tequila
1/2 measure dry orange
    curaçao
1/2 measure lemon juice
dash egg white
ice
orange peel, to decorate

Shake the first five ingredients well over ice until frosted. Strain into a chilled cocktail glass and dress with a twist of orange peel.

105
ALICE SPRINGS

This fruity cocktail, with a generous kick of gin, can be diluted to taste.

SERVES 1

3 measures gin
1/2 tsp grenadine
1 measure orange juice
1 measure lemon juice
ice
soda water
3 drops Angostura bitters

Shake the first four ingredients together over ice until frosted. Strain into a chilled tall glass and top up with soda water. Sprinkle in the Angostura bitters.

107
ORANGE GIN SLING

The dazzling marriage of the two ingredients make this look more complex than it is – one to impress with!

SERVES 1

2 measures gin
4 dashes orange bitters

Pour the gin into a cocktail glass, then carefully splash on the orange bitters.

106
GIN SLING COCKTAIL

This is a great variation on the classic Singapore Sling for those who don't like cherry brandy.

SERVES 1

ice
juice of 3/4 lemon
1/2 tbsp icing sugar
1 measure gin
lemon slice, to decorate
dash Angostura bitters,
    to serve

Put a large chunk of ice into a tumbler with the lemon juice, sugar and gin. Top up with water and float a slice of lemon on top with a dash of Angostura bitters.

108
RUBY FIZZ

This low-alcohol fizz is very refreshing and can be made with almost any rich sweet fruit syrup. It's especially good with home-made syrups, such as redcurrant shrub.

SERVES 1

juice of 1/2 lemon
2 tsp icing sugar
1 small egg white
2 dashes raspberry syrup or
    grenadine
2 measures sloe gin
ice
soda water

Shake all the ingredients except the soda water well over ice until frosted. Strain into a chilled long glass and top up with soda water.

109
GIN SLING

Many say the original gin sling was hot, but there are numerous cool variations to enjoy too!

SERVES 1

1 sugar cube
1 measure dry gin
freshly grated nutmeg
lemon slice, to serve

Dissolve the sugar in 125 ml/4 fl oz hot water in an old-fashioned glass. Stir in the gin, sprinkle with nutmeg and serve with a slice of lemon.

110
LEAPFROG

Gin and tonic fans will enjoy this variation with its gutsy flavour of lemon and gin.

SERVES 1

1 ice cube
juice of 1/2 lemon
2 measures gin
ginger ale
orange slice, to decorate

Chill a long tumbler and then add the ice, lemon juice and gin. Stir just once. Top up with ginger ale to taste and dress with a slice of orange.

111
MOTHER-IN-LAW'S GIN

Made up in advance so no one need know how much gin you put in!

SERVES 4

5 measures gin
7 measures orange juice
7 measures lemon juice
2 measures sugar syrup
1 small egg white
ice
tonic water
lemon peel, to decorate

Blend the first four ingredients together and chill until required. Mix with the egg white and ice in a blender until frothy. Pour into long chilled glasses and top up with tonic water. Dress with lemon peel.

112
BEE'S KNEES

Use a well-flavoured honey for this drink – acacia, orange blossom or heather, for instance. It makes all the difference to the final cocktail.

SERVES 1

1 measure gin
1/3 measure fresh lemon juice
2/3 measure clear honey
ice
bitter lemon, to taste
lemon zest, to decorate

Shake the first three ingredients over ice until well frosted. Strain into a tall ice-filled glass and top up with bitter lemon. Dress with a few shreds of lemon zest.

113 BULLDOG

A refreshing variation on the classic gin and orange.

SERVES 1

2 measures gin
1 measure fresh orange juice
ice
ginger ale
orange slice

Stir the gin and orange over ice in a medium tumbler. Top up with ginger ale and add a slice of orange.

114 BELLE COLLINS

A Collins is a tall, iced cocktail, perfect for drinking on a long summer's afternoon. This southern-inspired version is even cooler, with old world minty charm.

SERVES 1

2 fresh mint sprigs
crushed ice
2 measures gin
1 measure lemon juice
1 tsp sugar syrup
sparkling water, to fill
fresh mint sprig, to decorate

Crush the mint sprigs and place in a tall chilled tumbler. Add 4–6 crushed ice cubes and pour in the gin, lemon juice and sugar syrup. Top up with sparkling water, stir gently and dress with a fresh mint sprig.

115 TEARDROP

The gin, fruit and cream make a nice long cocktail, and the pink syrup gently sinking through gives it that final touch of the exotic.

SERVES 1

1 measure gin
2 measures apricot or peach nectar
1 measure single cream
crushed ice
1/2 measure strawberry syrup

Blend the first three ingredients in a blender for 5–10 seconds, until thick and frothy. Pour into a long glass filled with crushed ice. Splash the strawberry syrup on the top.

116 MAIDEN'S PRAYER

Gin and orange with a dry twist.

SERVES 1

1 measure gin
1 measure triple sec
1 tsp orange juice
1 tsp lemon juice
ice
lemon peel twist, to decorate

Shake the first four ingredients vigorously over ice until well frosted. Strain into a chilled cocktail glass and dress with a twist of lemon peel.

117
SLOE GIN RICKEY (see right-hand page for picture)

Just like a Gin Rickey but with sloe gin instead of dry gin.

SERVES 1

cracked ice
2 measures sloe gin
1 measure lime juice
soda water
lime slice

Fill a chilled highball glass or goblet with ice. Pour the gin and lime juice over the ice. Top up with soda water. Stir gently to mix and dress with a lime slice.

118
BLEU BLEU BLEU

It may well be blur blur blur after this heady combination, so don't rush for the second one.

SERVES 1

1 measure gin
1 measure vodka
1 measure tequila
1 measure blue curaçao
1 measure fresh lemon juice
2 dashes egg white
crushed ice
soda water

Shake all the ingredients except the soda water together over ice until frosted. Pour into a tall glass filled with ice and top up with soda water to taste.

119
OASIS

This bright blue shining pool is as refreshing as it looks, thanks to lots of ice and refreshing soda water.

SERVES 1

1 measure blue curaçao
2 measures gin
soda water
ice
lemon wedge,
   to decorate

Shake all the liquid ingredients over ice until well frosted. Strain into a chilled cocktail glass. Dress with a wedge of lemon.

120
GIN RICKEY

The classic version of this cocktail is based on gin, but other spirits are also used, mixed with lime or lemon juice and soda water, with no sweetening.

SERVES 1

cracked ice
2 measures gin
1 measure lime juice
soda water
lemon slice, to decorate

Fill a chilled highball glass or goblet with ice. Pour the gin and lime juice over the ice. Top up with soda water. Stir gently to mix and dress with a lemon slice.

122
GIMLET

The fresh aromatic scent of lime is so much nicer with gin than the traditional lemon – this cocktail is seriously tangy.

SERVES 1

1 measure gin
1/2 measure fresh lime juice
ice
tonic water
lime slices, to decorate

Pour the gin and lime juice over ice in a chilled old-fashioned glass. Top up with tonic water and dress with slices of lime.

121
BLUE BLOODED

A sinister looking drink until it has settled down – but don't let that put you off because it tastes great and is very light and fruity.

SERVES 1

1 measure gin
1 measure passion fruit nectar
4 cubes melon or mango
crushed ice
1–2 tsp blue curaçao

Mix all the ingredients except the curaçao in a blender until smooth and frosted. Pour into a chilled tall glass filled with more ice and, finally, top with the curaçao so it trickles through like blue blood!

123
STAR DAISY

Although it looks more like a hangover cure than a cocktail, don't be fooled – this is a strong one that could have you seeing stars.

SERVES 1

2 measures gin
1 1/2 measures apple brandy
1 1/2 measures lemon juice
1 tsp sugar syrup
1/2 tsp triple sec
crushed ice
soda water

Pour the first five ingredients over ice and shake vigorously until well frosted. Strain into a tumbler half filled with ice, then top up with soda water.

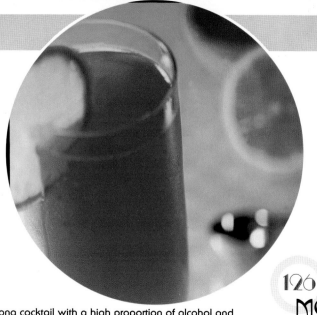

124
DAISY

A Daisy is a long cocktail with a high proportion of alcohol and sweetened with fruit syrup. Perhaps it gets its name from the now old-fashioned slang when the word 'daisy' referred to something exceptional and special.

SERVES 1
3 measures gin
1 measure lemon juice
1 tbsp grenadine
1 tsp sugar syrup
cracked ice
soda water
orange slice, to decorate

Pour the gin, lemon juice, grenadine and sugar syrup over cracked ice and shake vigorously until well frosted. Strain into a chilled highball glass and top up with soda water. Stir gently, then dress with an orange slice.

125
LEAVE IT TO ME

Pretty, but with a sting to its tail, this is a good party cocktail, because you can easily make several at once.

SERVES 1
1/2 measure gin
1/4 measure dry vermouth
1/4 measure apricot brandy
dash lemon juice
crushed ice
dash grenadine
lemon peel, to decorate

Shake the first four ingredients well over ice and strain into a cocktail glass. At the last minute swirl in the grenadine and decorate with a piece of lemon peel.

126
MOONLIGHT

This light wine-based cocktail is ideal to make for several people at once.

SERVES 4
3 measures grapefruit juice
4 measures gin
1 measure kirsch
4 measures white wine
1/2 tsp lemon zest
ice

Shake all the ingredients together well and strain into chilled glasses.

127
ST. CLEMENT'S GIN

This can be seriously strong or very refreshing, so add soda water to your taste.

SERVES 1
juice of 1/2 orange
juice of 1/2 lemon
1 tsp icing sugar
2 measures gin
ice
soda water
orange and lemon slices, to decorate

Mix the orange juice, lemon juice, sugar and gin together and pour over ice in a highball glass. Top up with soda water and dress with slices of orange and lemon.

128
CHERRY FIZZ

A fizz used to be a morning drink, perhaps as a refresher. Add plenty of soda water to make this one as long as you like.

SERVES 1

³/4 measure gin
¹/4 measure cherry brandy
3 dashes kirsch
juice of ¹/2 lime
1 tsp sugar syrup
ice
soda water

Shake all the ingredients except the soda water over ice until frosted. Strain into an ice-filled highball glass and top up with soda water to taste.

129
GIN SLINGER

Unlike a Singapore Sling, this doesn't dilute its strength with fizz.

SERVES 1

1 tsp icing sugar
1 measure lemon juice
1 tsp water
2 measures gin
ice
orange twist, to decorate

Stir the sugar, lemon juice and water together. Pour in the gin and stir. Half fill a small, chilled tumbler with ice and strain the cocktail over. Dress with an orange twist.

130
DIAMOND HEAD

Guaranteed to leave you with something a bit different from a clear head!

SERVES 2

4 measures gin
2 measures lemon juice
1 measure apricot brandy
1 tsp sugar syrup
1 egg white
ice
lemon peel, to decorate

Shake the first five ingredients vigorously over ice until well frosted. Strain into two chilled cocktail glasses and dress with lemon peel.

131
THIRD DEGREE

A serious drink, this could persuade you that you'd been given the third degree.

SERVES 1

cracked ice
1 measure dry vermouth
2 measures gin

Put some cracked ice into a mixing glass. Pour the vermouth over the ice and pour in the gin. Stir well to mix, then strain into a chilled cocktail glass.

132
SUFFERING FOOL

You will have to make up your own mind whether this cocktail is a cure or whether it is the cause of suffering still to come!

SERVES 1

1 tbsp Angostura bitters
cracked ice
2 measures gin
1 1/2 measures brandy
1/2 measure lime juice
1 tsp sugar syrup
ginger beer
cucumber and lime slices
   and a fresh mint sprig,
   to decorate

Pour the bitters into a chilled Collins glass and swirl around to coat the inside of the glass. Discard the excess. Half fill the glass with cracked ice. Pour the gin, brandy, lime juice and sugar syrup over the ice. Stir well. Top up with ginger beer. Dress with cucumber, lime and mint.

133
LONDONER

The soft fruitiness of berries and the herbal aroma of vermouth make this gin mix a lovely long cocktail.

SERVES 1

2 measures London dry gin
1/2 measure fraise, rosehip or
   any fruit syrup
2 measures lemon juice
1/2 measure dry vermouth
ice
soda water
lemon peel twist, to decorate

Mix the first four ingredients over ice in a highball glass or large tumbler. Top up with soda water and dress with a twist of lemon peel.

134
MEDITERRANEAN

Whatever the weather, this eye-catching drink should transport your imagination to the blue skies and seas of the Mediterranean. The exotic colour needs no decoration to set it off.

SERVES 1

ice
2 measures gin
1 measure blue curaçao
lemonade

Put the ice in a glass and pour the gin and curaçao over them. Add lemonade to taste.

135
NEW ORLEANS GIN FIZZ

The cocktail is part of New Orleans' society and it is always flamboyantly presented, so go to town on this one!

SERVES 1

juice of 1/2 lemon
2 tsp icing sugar
1 small egg white
2 measures gin
2 dashes orange flower water
1 tbsp single cream
ice
soda water
orange peel and a flower,
   to decorate

Shake the first six ingredients over ice until well frosted. Strain into a chilled tall tumbler and top up with soda water to taste. Dress with a shred of orange peel and a flower.

136 GORDON BENNETT

Don't be too surprised that this is no simple gin – it has more than a little kick and lots of limey zing.

SERVES 1

1 measure gin, iced
1 measure Cointreau, iced
cracked ice
lime slices
soda water

Place the gin, Cointreau and ice in a chilled highball glass and stir until well frosted. Squeeze the lime slices and add to the glass. Add soda water to taste.

138 MISSISSIPPI MULE

You may find a mule that doesn't have a kick – this certainly isn't one!

SERVES 1

2 measures gin
1/2 measure cassis
1/2 measure lemon juice
cubed and crushed ice

Shake the liquid ingredients vigorously over ice until well frosted. Strain over crushed ice into a small chilled tumbler.

137 BRIDE'S MOTHER

Lots of vitamin C to build up her strength for the big day – lots of gin to drown her sorrows with.

SERVES 1

1 1/2 measures sloe gin
1 measure gin
2 1/2 measures grapefruit juice
1/2 measure sugar syrup
cubed and crushed ice
grapefruit slices, to decorate

Shake the liquid ingredients vigorously over ice until well frosted. Strain over crushed ice and dress with grapefruit slices.

139 SLOW COMFORTABLE SCREW

Always use freshly squeezed orange juice to make this refreshing cocktail – it is just not the same with bottled juice. This simple, classic cocktail has given rise to numerous and increasingly elaborate variations.

SERVES 1

2 measures sloe gin
orange juice
cracked ice
orange slice, to decorate

Shake the sloe gin and orange juice over ice until well frosted and pour into a chilled glass. Dress with a slice of orange.

140 COSTA DEL SOL

Pure and golden, just like the endless Spanish sun.

SERVES 1

2 measures gin
1 measure apricot brandy
1 measure triple sec
ice

Shake the liquid ingredients vigorously over ice until well frosted and strain into a chilled glass.

142 SEVENTH HEAVEN

Which is where you'll be after a few of these!

SERVES 1

2 measures gin
1/2 measure maraschino
1/2 measure grapefruit juice
ice
fresh mint sprigs, to decorate

Shake the liquid ingredients vigorously over ice until well frosted. Strain into a chilled cocktail glass. Dress with fresh mint.

141 PALM BEACH SOUR

Low on alcohol, high on taste, this is the perfect midday drink for all those beach babes.

SERVES 1

1/3 measure gin
1/3 measure grapefruit juice
1/6 measure dry vermouth
2–3 drops Angostura bitters
1 tsp icing sugar
1 egg white
ice

Shake all the ingredients together and pour into a chilled cocktail glass.

143 BIRD OF PARADISE COOLER

This might well take you to Paradise...

SERVES 1

2 measures gin
1 measure lemon juice
1 tsp grenadine
1 tsp sugar syrup
1 egg white
cracked ice
sparkling water
star fruit slice, to decorate

Shake the gin, lemon juice, grenadine, sugar syrup and egg white vigorously over cracked ice until well frosted. Half fill a chilled tumbler with cracked ice and pour the cocktail over it. Top up with sparkling water and dress with a slice of star fruit.

144
BLUE BIRD

So simple, so jewel-like. Perhaps this is the original blue bird of happiness.

SERVES 1

3 measures gin
1 measure blue curaçao
dash Angostura bitters
cracked ice

Shake the liquid ingredients vigorously over cracked ice until well frosted. Strain into a chilled cocktail glass.

146
PINK GIN

Originally devised as a remedy for stomach complaints, the Pink Gin was subsequently adopted by the British Navy as part of its medicine chest.

SERVES 1

1 measure Plymouth gin
few drops Angostura bitters
1 measure water, iced
maraschino cherry, to decorate

Pour the first three ingredients into a mixing glass and stir. Strain into a cocktail glass and dress with a maraschino cherry.

145
APPLE CLASSIC

Apple lovers and cider makers will put this at the top of their list, but it is definitely better made with sweet rather than dry cider.

SERVES 1

1/2 measure gin
1/2 measure brandy
1/2 measure Calvados
ice
sweet cider
apple slice, to decorate

Shake the gin, brandy and Calvados over ice until frosted. Strain into a glass and top up with cider to taste. Dress with a slice of apple.

147
GIN FIX

A fix should contain spirit, sugar, fruit and often a lot of fizz. It works very well with gin but other spirits are great too, so try some variations.

SERVES 1

2 1/2 measures gin
1 measure lemon juice
1 tsp sugar syrup
crushed ice
lemon slice, to decorate

Pour the gin, lemon juice and syrup into a tumbler filled with crushed ice and stir once. Dress with the slice of lemon.

148
END OF THE ROAD

Best to keep this till the end of the party – that pastis could really see you all the way to the end of the road!

SERVES 1

3 measures gin
1 measure crème de menthe
1 measure pastis
ice
soda water (optional)
fresh mint sprig, to decorate

Stir the first three ingredients over ice. Strain into a tall glass filled with ice and dress with a sprig of mint. Top up with soda water for a longer drink.

150
ROAD RUNNER

Whether it is named after the real bird or after Wile E Coyote's nemesis, this is a cocktail for slowing down after a fast-moving day, not for speeding things up.

SERVES 1

2 measures gin
1/2 measure dry vermouth
1/2 measure Pernod
1 tsp grenadine
cracked ice

Shake the gin, vermouth, Pernod and grenadine vigorously over ice until well frosted. Strain into a chilled wine glass.

149
BREAKFAST

It is difficult to believe that anyone would actually have the stomach to cope with cocktails first thing in the morning – but then, for those who party all night and sleep all day, cocktail time coincides with breakfast.

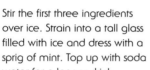

SERVES 1

2 measures gin
1 measure grenadine
cracked ice
1 egg yolk

Pour the gin and grenadine over ice in a shaker and add the egg yolk. Shake vigorously until frosted. Strain into a chilled glass.

151
ALASKA

Yellow Chartreuse is slightly sweeter than green Chartreuse, so it does benefit from being really well chilled.

SERVES 1

1/2 measure gin
1/2 measure yellow Chartreuse
ice

Shake the gin and Chartreuse over ice until well frosted. Strain into a chilled glass.

152
FALLEN ANGEL

Mint and lemon make an unusual addition to gin, but do make sure it is a green mint liqueur or it will not have the same visual impact.

SERVES 1

1 dash Angostura bitters
juice of 1 lemon or lime
2 measures gin
ice
2 dashes green crème de menthe

Shake the first three ingredients over ice and strain into a cocktail glass. Top with two dashes of crème de menthe at the last minute.

153
WEDDING BELLE

Probably best to have this after the ceremony – it's usually recommended to remain standing while exchanging vows.

SERVES 1

2 measures gin
2 measures Dubonnet
1 measure cherry brandy
1 measure orange juice
ice

Shake the liquid ingredients over ice until well frosted. Strain into a cocktail glass.

154
MAIDENLY BLUSH

This is a very maidenly blush, so pale as to be unnoticeable. Perhaps drinking it will bring a bit of colour to the cheeks?

SERVES 1

2 measures gin
1 measure Pernod
ice

Stir the gin and Pernod over ice to mix, then strain into a chilled cocktail glass.

155
CAT'S EYE

A cat's eye is many things (apart from what a cat sees with!) including a semi-precious stone and a striped marble. Now, it's a highly potent cocktail, as pretty as any gemstone.

SERVES 1

2 measures gin
1 1/2 measures dry vermouth
1/2 measure kirsch
1/2 measure triple sec
1/2 measure lemon juice
cracked ice
1/2 measure iced water, to serve

Shake the gin, vermouth, kirsch, triple sec and lemon juice over ice until well frosted. Strain into a chilled goblet, adding a touch of iced water to serve.

156 LEAP YEAR

Definitely deserving of a little attention more than once every four years.

SERVES 1

2 measures gin
1/2 measure Grand Marnier
1/2 measure sweet vermouth
1/2 tsp lemon juice
ice

Shake the liquid ingredients vigorously over ice until well frosted. Strain into a chilled cocktail glass.

158 SAPPHIRE MARTINI

Only a blue diamond could compete with this.

SERVES 1

cracked ice
2 measures gin
1/2 measure blue curaçao
cocktail cherry, to decorate

Put some cracked ice into a mixing glass. Pour the gin and blue curaçao over. Stir well to mix, then strain into a chilled cocktail glass. Dress with the cocktail cherry.

157 PARTY SPECIAL

It's clear why this was designed for parties – but whatever the reason, go ahead, celebrate.

SERVES 1

2 measures gin
1 1/2 measures apricot brandy
1 measure dry vermouth
1/2 measure lemon juice
cocktail cherry, to decorate

Shake the liquid ingredients vigorously over ice until well frosted. Strain into a chilled cocktail glass. Dress with a cocktail cherry.

159 KARINA

The mandarin liqueur comes through nicely to give this cocktail a good citrus tang.

SERVES 1

1 measure gin
1/2 measure Dubonnet
1/2 measure mandarin liqueur
juice of 1/2 lemon
ice

Mix the liquid ingredients together in a large tumbler filled with ice and stir until the glass is frosted.

160 MAIDEN'S BLUSH

The name of this cocktail aptly describes its pretty colour. It could also be a warning, however, that too much of this concoction could be the cause of the maiden's blush.

SERVES 1

cracked ice
2 measures gin
1/2 tsp triple sec
1/2 tsp grenadine
1/2 tsp lemon juice

Put the ice into a cocktail shaker. Shake the gin, triple sec, grenadine and lemon juice vigorously over the ice until well frosted. Strain into a chilled cocktail glass or small highball glass.

161 ABSINTHE FRIEND

The original absinthe was a popular cocktail ingredient and digestif. It was banned by law for many years from 1915 because it was then flavoured with wormwood and was said to react with alcohol and cause brain damage. Any pastis, such as Pernod and Ricard, will do instead.

SERVES 1

1 measure gin
1 measure Pernod
dash Angostura bitters
dash sugar syrup
cracked ice

Shake the liquid ingredients vigorously over ice until well frosted. Strain into a chilled medium-sized glass or tumbler.

162 BLUE STAR SHAKER

A stunningly pretty cocktail for blues fans who love the rich flavours of Lillet, a French aperitif made from red or white wine fortified with Armagnac, herbs and fruit.

SERVES 2

2/3 measure blue curaçao
2/3 measure gin
1 measure Lillet
crushed ice
lime slices, to decorate

Place the three liquids into a cocktail shaker with ice. Shake until frosted, then pour into shallow cocktail glasses and dress with a slice of lime.

163 ORANGE BLOOM

Some orange juices are made from the whole fruit and have a very bitter back taste. Avoid these in cocktails as they will overpower the spirits.

SERVES 1

1 measure gin
1/2 measure fresh orange juice
1/2 measure Cointreau
1/4 measure dry vermouth
cracked ice

Shake the liquid ingredients together over ice until really well frosted. Strain into a chilled cocktail glass.

164
BRONX

Like Manhattan, the New York borough of the Bronx – and also the river of the same name – has been immortalized in cocktail bars throughout the world.

SERVES 1

2 measures gin
1 measure orange juice
1/2 measure dry vermouth
1/2 measure sweet vermouth
cracked ice

Pour the gin, orange juice, dry vermouth and sweet vermouth over ice in a mixing glass. Stir to mix and strain into a chilled cocktail glass.

166
MAGNOLIA BLOSSOM

Creamy, light and smooth – and not a magnolia in sight!

SERVES 1

2 measures gin
1 measure lemon juice
1 measure single cream
ice

Shake the liquid ingredients vigorously over ice until well frosted. Strain into a chilled cocktail glass.

165
HAWAIIAN ORANGE BLOSSOM

There's definitely an aroma of exotic tropical days and balmy nights in this fruity confection.

SERVES 1

2 measures gin
1 measure triple sec
2 measures orange juice
1 measure pineapple juice
ice

Shake the liquid ingredients vigorously over ice until well frosted. Strain into a chilled wine glass.

167
ORANGE BLOSSOM

During the Prohibition era in the US, gin was often quite literally made in the bath and flavoured with fresh orange juice to conceal its filthy flavour. Made with good quality gin, which needs no such concealment, this drink is delightfully refreshing.

SERVES 1

2 measures gin
2 measures orange juice
cracked ice
orange slices, to decorate

Shake the gin and orange juice vigorously over ice until well frosted. Strain into a chilled cocktail glass and dress with orange slices.

168
GOOD NIGHT LADIES

Sweetly scented with apricot and pomegranate, this is a great nightcap for all cocktail lovers.

SERVES 1

1/2 measure gin
1/6 measure apricot brandy
1/6 measure grenadine
1/6 measure lemon juice
ice
peach slice, to decorate

Shake the liquid ingredients over ice and strain into a cocktail glass. Dress with a slice of peach.

169
GOLDEN DAWN

Like the golden sun rising, the bright red of the grenadine peeps through the brandy and orange.

SERVES 1

1/2 measure gin
1/2 measure Calvados
1/2 measure apricot brandy
1/2 measure mango juice
ice
dash grenadine

Mix the first four ingredients together over ice. Strain into a cocktail glass and gradually add a dash grenadine so the colour ripples through.

170
JUPITER ONE

Beautifully perfumed by the Parfait Amour – yet without the distinguishing purple colour.

SERVES 1

2 tsp Parfait Amour
2 tsp orange juice
1 measure dry vermouth
1 measure gin
ice
lemon zest, to decorate

Shake the liquid ingredients well over ice and strain into a cocktail glass. Dress with lemon zest.

171
CLOVER CLUB

The grenadine really does give this cocktail the lovely colour of a clover flower.

SERVES 1

2 measures gin
1 measure lime juice
1 measure grenadine
1 egg white
ice

Pour the first four ingredients over ice. Shake vigorously until well frosted. Strain into a chilled cocktail glass.

172
GRAND ROYAL CLOVER CLUB

In this subtle variation on the Clover Club, lemon juice is substituted for the lime juice of the original.

SERVES 1

2 measures gin
1 measure lemon juice
1 measure grenadine
1 egg white
ice
lime peel, to decorate

Pour the first four ingredients over ice. Shake vigorously until well frosted. Strain into a chilled cocktail glass and dress with lime peel.

174
CLUB

Groucho Marx is well known for claiming that he wouldn't want to belong to any club that was prepared to accept him as a member. This Club and its many associates are unlikely ever to have any shortage of willing members.

SERVES 1

dash yellow Chartreuse
cracked ice
2 measures gin
1 measure sweet vermouth

Dash the Chartreuse over ice in a mixing glass and pour in the gin and vermouth. Stir well to mix and strain into a chilled cocktail glass.

173
RACKET CLUB

The clear sophistication of the Racket Club reflects the suave superiority of the club members.

SERVES 1

dash orange bitters
ice
1 measure gin
1 measure dry vermouth
orange peel twist, to decorate

Dash the orange bitters over ice in a mixing glass and pour in the gin and vermouth. Stir well to mix, then strain into a chilled cocktail glass. Dress with a twist of orange peel.

175
BELLINI MARTINI

This will go down like silk, especially with the velvety addition of the peach purée instead of the more usual peach schnapps.

SERVES 1

1 measure gin
1/2 measure brandy
1/2 measure peach purée
splash of sweet vermouth
ice
peach slice, to decorate

Shake the first four ingredients over ice until well frosted. Strain into an iced martini glass and dress with a slice of peach.

176
DIRTY MARTINI

Infinitely better than it sounds, the 'dirt' is simply the brine from the cocktail olives.

SERVES 1

3 measures gin
1 measure dry vermouth
1/2 measure brine from jar of
   cocktail olives
ice
cocktail olive, to decorate

Shake the first three ingredients vigorously over ice until well frosted. Strain into a chilled cocktail glass and dress with an olive.

177
MONTGOMERY

Named after the World War II general, or just a good one for the wartime nightclubs? Conquer a few today.

SERVES 1

3 measures gin or vodka
1 tsp vermouth
ice
lemon zest, to decorate

Stir the gin and vermouth with ice, strain into a chilled cocktail glass and dress with lemon zest.

178
SAKETINI

East meets West in this delicious Japanese variation on the Martini theme.

SERVES 1

3 measures gin
1/2 measure sake
ice
lemon peel twist, to decorate

Shake the gin and sake vigorously over ice until well frosted. Strain into a chilled cocktail glass and dress with a twist of lemon peel.

179
FIFTY FIFTY

This version of the Martini uses equal measures of gin and dry vermouth.

SERVES 1

2 measures gin
2 measures dry vermouth
ice
cocktail olive, to decorate

Shake the gin and vermouth vigorously over ice until well frosted. Strain into a chilled cocktail glass and dress with an olive.

180
GIBSON

Said to have been created for magazine illustrator Charles Dana Gibson in the 1930s, enough of these will make you see pretty pictures!

SERVES 1

cracked ice
3 measures gin
1 measure dry vermouth
cocktail onions, to decorate

Fill a cocktail glass with ice and pour over the gin and vermouth. Dress with 2–3 cocktail onions.

181
TOPAZ MARTINI

Named for its jewelled appearance, this one really stands out from the rest.

SERVES 1

cracked ice
2 measures gin
1/2 measure orange curaçao
orange peel twist, to decorate

Put some cracked ice into a mixing glass. Pour the gin and orange curaçao over the ice. Stir well to mix then strain into a chilled cocktail glass. Dress with a twist of orange peel.

182
THE ULTIMATE CLASSIC MARTINI

Drier than a Dry Martini, the vermouth is simply an aftertaste.

SERVES 1

dash vermouth, iced
2 measures gin
cocktail olive, to decorate

Put a dash of vermouth in an iced martini glass, swirl it around and discard. Pour in the gin and dress with a cocktail olive.

183
DRY MARTINI

Unlike the Martini, this drink has almost no vermouth in it. Traditionalists will tell you simply to wave the bottle over the glass!

SERVES 1

1 measure London Dry Gin
dash dry vermouth
ice
cocktail olive, to decorate

Shake the gin and vermouth over ice until well frosted and combined. Strain into a chilled glass. Dress with an olive.

184 MARTINEZ

The original recipe may go back to 1849 and was made with a gin called Old Tom that was slightly sweetened.

SERVES 1

2 measures gin, iced
1 measure Italian vermouth
dash Angostura bitters
dash maraschino
ice
twisted lemon slice,
   to decorate

Shake the gin, vermouth, bitters and maraschino over ice until frosted. Strain into a chilled cocktail glass and dress with a twisted lemon slice.

186 DUBARRY

The Comtesse du Barry, the mistress of King Louis XV of France, was renowned for her extraordinary beauty. This delicious concoction is just as dazzling as its famous namesake.

SERVES 1

dash Pernod
dash Angostura bitters
2 measures gin
1 measure dry vermouth
ice
lemon peel twist, to decorate

Stir the Pernod, Angostura bitters, gin and vermouth in a mixing glass with ice. Strain into a chilled cocktail glass or wine glass and dress with a lemon peel twist.

185 THE JOURNALIST

Practice makes perfect with this one, as the balance of sweet to dry is important to the final drink.

SERVES 1

1½ measures gin
dash sweet vermouth
dash dry vermouth
1–2 dashes fresh lemon juice
2 dashes triple sec
2 dashes Angostura bitters
ice
cocktail cherry, to decorate

Shake the liquid ingredients over ice until really well frosted. Strain into an iced martini glass and dress with a cocktail cherry.

187 TOM COLLINS

This cooling long drink is a celebrated cocktail and was the inspiration for several generations of Collins drinks across the globe.

SERVES 1

3 measures gin
2 measures lemon juice
½ measure sugar syrup
cracked ice
soda water
lemon slice, to decorate

Shake the gin, lemon juice and sugar syrup vigorously over ice until well frosted. Strain into a tall, chilled tumbler and top up with soda water. Dress with a slice of lemon.

188
PINK PHANTOM

The classic combination of gin and Noilly Prat is sweetened with grenadine and a serious kick of absinthe.

SERVES 1

1/2 measure dry gin
1/2 measure Noilly Prat
2 dashes grenadine
2 dashes absinthe
ice
lemon juice

Stir the first four ingredients over ice, strain into a cocktail glass and squeeze lemon juice over the top.

189
INCA

The legendary lost gold of the Incas – the 'sweat of the sun' to those sun-worshippers – inspired the name of this golden cocktail.

SERVES 1

1 measure gin
1 measure sweet vermouth
1 measure dry sherry
dash orgeat
dash orange bitters

Pour all the ingredients into a glass and stir. This is one that does not need to be chilled.

190
NEGRONI

This aristocratic cocktail was created for Count Negroni in Florence, although, since then, the proportions of gin to Campari have altered.

SERVES 1

cracked ice
1 measure gin
1 measure Campari
1/2 measure sweet vermouth
orange peel twist, to decorate

Put some ice into a mixing glass. Pour the gin, Campari and vermouth over the ice and stir well to mix. Strain into a chilled glass and dress with an orange peel twist.

191
MAH-JONG

No Chinese games here, but you may not be walking in perfectly straight lines if you drink too many!

SERVES 1

1 measure gin
1/4 measure Cointreau
1/4 measure white rum
ice
orange peel twist, to decorate

Stir the liquid ingredients over ice in a mixing glass and strain into a chilled small cocktail glass. Dress with a twist of orange peel.

192
DOG'S NOSE (see right-hand page for picture)

A traditional English cocktail made with traditional English ingredients.

SERVES 1

1 cup pale ale
1 measure gin

Pour the ale into a chilled beer glass or tankard, then pour in the gin.

193
THE BLUE BIRD

Orange and bittersweet, but not too strong.

SERVES 1

1 measure gin
3–4 dashes Angostura bitters
1–2 tsp orange curaçao
ice
maraschino cherry

Shake the liquid ingredients together over ice and strain into a small cocktail glass. Serve with a cherry on its stalk.

194
JOCKEY CLUB SPECIAL

A short cocktail with a good kick in its tail, but you can mellow it by serving on the rocks if you prefer!

SERVES 1

1 measure gin
1/2 measure crème de noyaux
good splash lemon juice
2 dashes orange bitters
2 dashes Angostura bitters
ice
lemon wedge, to decorate

Stir the liquid ingredients well over ice and strain into a cocktail glass. Dress with a lemon wedge.

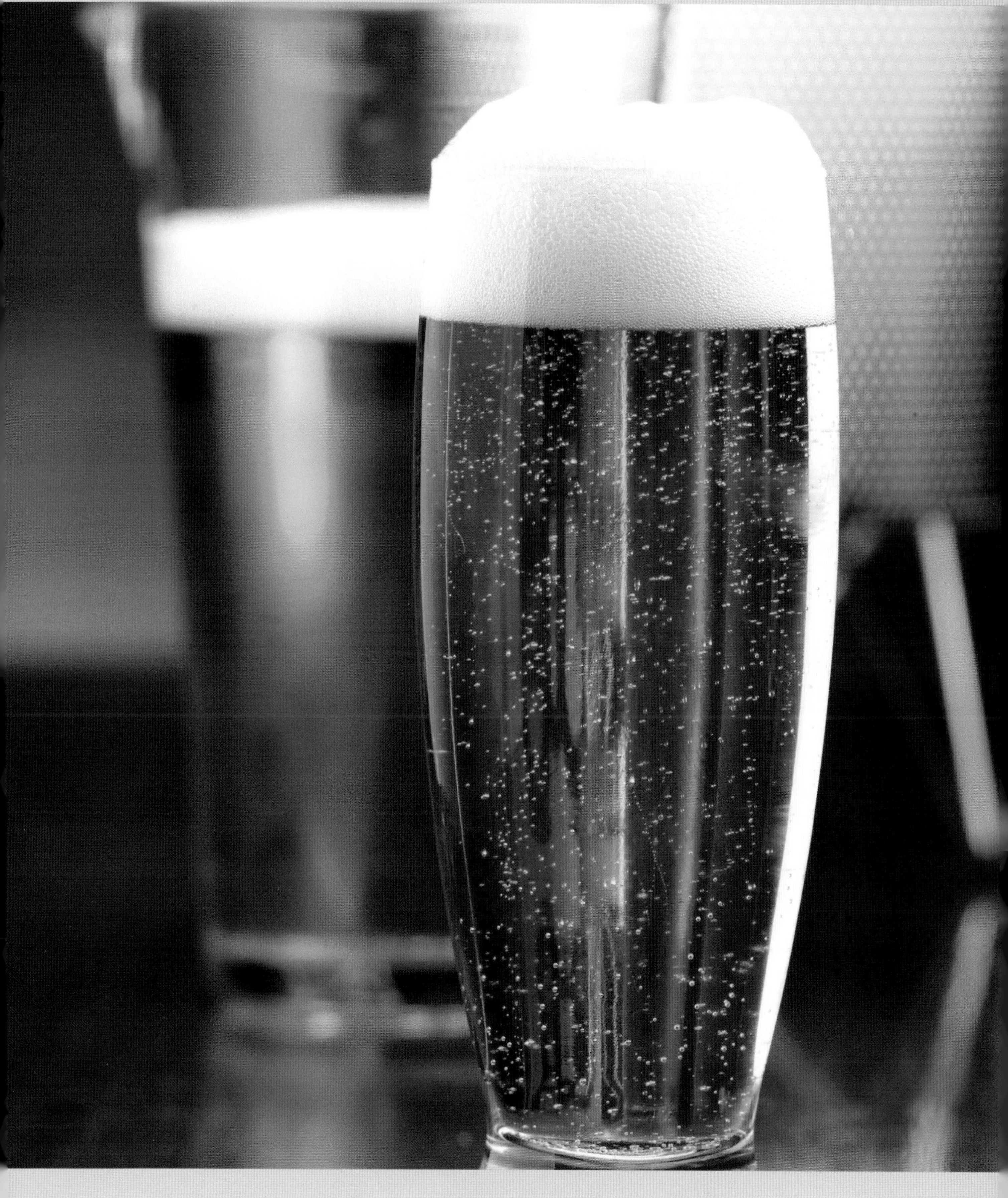

195 SPRING IN THE AIR

This fresh and zingy cocktail will make you feel as if spring is definitely on the way.

SERVES 1

1 measure gin
1 measure lime cordial
1/2 measure green Chartreuse
ice
lime peel twist, to decorate

Stir the liquid ingredients over ice in a mixing glass and strain into a chilled cocktail glass. Add one lump of fresh ice and dress with a twist of lime peel.

196 STRESSED OUT

This well-iced cocktail will soon relax you and take away all the stresses of the day.

SERVES 1

1 measure gin, iced
1/2 measure green Chartreuse, iced
1/2 measure lime juice, chilled
dash pastis, iced
sugar syrup, to taste
cubed and crushed ice
lime wedge, to decorate

Stir all the liquid ingredients together over ice until well frosted. Strain into a small cocktail glass filled with crushed ice and add a lime wedge.

197 CREOLE LADY

It may look ladylike, but this will soon have your inhibitions sashaying down the street!

SERVES 1

2 measures gin
1 1/2 measures Madeira
1 tsp grenadine
cracked ice
cocktail cherries, to decorate

Pour the liquid ingredients over ice in a mixing glass. Stir well to mix, then strain into a chilled cocktail glass. Dress with cocktail cherries.

198 FAIR LADY

As fair as an English rose, this is the perfect cocktail for those long, hazy days of summer.

SERVES 1

2 measures gin
1 measure orange juice
1 measure lime juice
ice
1 egg white
dash strawberry liqueur
strawberry slice, to decorate

Shake the gin, orange juice and lime juice vigorously over ice until well frosted. Add the egg white and strawberry liqueur. Strain into a chilled cocktail glass and dress with a strawberry slice.

199
GREEN LADY

Lightly tinted rather than bilious, this will pick you up, not knock you down.

SERVES 1

2 measures gin
1 measure green Chartreuse
dash lime juice
ice

Shake the liquid ingredients vigorously over ice until well frosted. Strain into a chilled cocktail glass.

201
WHITE LADY

Simple, elegant, subtle and much more powerful than appearance suggests, this is the perfect cocktail to serve before an al fresco summer dinner.

SERVES 1

2 measures gin
1 measure triple sec
1 measure lemon juice
cracked ice

Shake the gin, triple sec and lemon juice vigorously over ice until well frosted. Strain into a chilled cocktail glass.

200
LADY

Deceptively frothy, this delicious concoction packs a powerful punch.

SERVES 1

2 measures gin
1 measure peach brandy
1 measure lemon juice
1 tsp egg white
ice
lemon slice, to decorate

Shake the first four ingredients over ice until well frosted. Strain into a chilled cocktail glass and dress with a lemon slice.

202
THIS IS IT

Is this it? With its tangy lightness, it's certainly the one that will have you coming back for more.

SERVES 1

2 measures gin
1 measure triple sec
1 measure lemon juice
1 egg white
cracked ice
lemon peel twist, to decorate

Shake the first four ingredients vigorously over ice until well frosted. Strain the mixture into a chilled cocktail glass. Dress with a twist of lemon peel.

203
WHAT THE DICKENS?

A simple combination that would have kept you warm even in the chilly fog of Dickens' London.

SERVES 1

2 measures gin
1¹/2 tsp icing sugar
hot water
lemon peel twist, to decorate

Pour the gin into a heatproof tumbler and stir in the sugar. Top up with hot water and dress with a twist of lemon peel.

205
ALEXANDER

A creamy, chocolate-flavoured, gin-based cocktail, decorated with grated nutmeg.

SERVES 1

1 measure gin
1 measure crème de cacao
1 measure single cream
cracked ice
freshly grated nutmeg,
    to decorate

Shake the first three ingredients vigorously over ice until well frosted. Strain into a chilled cocktail glass and dress with grated nutmeg.

204
WHY NOT?

And, indeed, why not? This is one that will warm the cockles of your heart.

SERVES 1

cracked ice
dash lemon juice
2 measures gin
1 measure peach brandy
1 measure Noilly Prat
lemon peel twist, to decorate

Put some ice into a mixing glass. Dash lemon juice over the ice. Pour in the gin, peach brandy and Noilly Prat. Stir to mix. Strain into a chilled cocktail glass and dress with a twist of lemon peel.

206
GIVE ME HOPE

Cheer yourself up when you are at a loose end, or when everything seems to have gone wrong, with this simple but delicious concoction.

SERVES 1

cracked ice
dash lime juice
1 measure gin
1 measure apricot brandy
1 measure dry vermouth
lemon peel twist,
    to decorate

Put some ice into a mixing glass. Dash lime juice over the ice and pour in the gin, apricot brandy and vermouth. Stir well to mix. Strain into a chilled cocktail glass and dress with a twist of lemon peel.

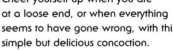

207
VESPERS

A calming drink to enjoy in quiet solitude and repose and certainly not a drink to be rushed.

SERVES 1

1 1/2 measures gin, iced
1 measure vodka, iced
1/2 measure dry vermouth or Lillet
ice
lemon peel, to decorate

Shake the liquid ingredients over ice until frosted. Strain into a frosted martini glass. Dress with lemon peel.

208
SILVER STREAK

This short drink can be made with either gin or vodka. Be sure both spirits are really cold and don't stir, just leave the kümmel to sink through the gin and enjoy as a nightcap.

SERVES 1

ice
1 measure gin, iced
1 measure kümmel, iced

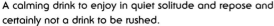

Fill a small old-fashioned glass or tumbler with ice and pour in the gin. Slowly pour on the kümmel and then drink before they become too mingled.

209
BACK TO THE FUTURE

You may not be sure exactly where you are after you've downed a few of these.

SERVES 1

2 measures gin
1 measure slivovitz
1 measure lemon juice
ice
lemon peel twist, to decorate

Shake the liquid ingredients vigorously over ice until well frosted. Strain into a chilled cocktail glass and dress with a twist of lemon peel.

210
STAR WARS

This almond-flavoured cocktail with a hint of bitterness will soon have you in orbit.

SERVES 1

2 measures gin
2 measures lemon juice
1 measure Galliano
1 measure crème de noyaux
ice
lemon peel twist, to decorate

Shake the first four ingredients vigorously over ice until well frosted. Strain into a chilled cocktail glass and dress with a twist of lemon peel.

211 HARLEM

Spanish, Dutch or New York, New York? The origins may be clouded, but the cocktail is clearly delicious.

SERVES 1

2 measures gin
1 1/2 measures pineapple juice
1 tsp maraschino
1 tbsp chopped fresh
   pineapple
ice
lime leaf, to decorate

Shake the first four ingredients vigorously over ice until well frosted. Strain into a small chilled tumbler and dress with a lime leaf.

213 OLD ETONIAN

With its clever sophistication, this is definitely one to oil the wheels of the old boy network!

SERVES 1

cracked ice
dash crème de noyaux
dash orange bitters
1 measure gin
1 measure Lillet

Put some ice into a mixing glass and add the liquid ingredients. Stir to mix well, then strain into a chilled cocktail glass.

212 ROLLS-ROYCE 2

This really is in a class all of its own.

SERVES 1

ice
3 measures gin
1 measure dry vermouth
1 measure sweet vermouth
1/4 tsp Benedictine

Put 4–6 ice cubes into a mixing glass. Pour the liquid ingredients over the ice. Stir well to mix, then strain into a chilled cocktail glass.

214 STREGA SOUR

Made from almost 100 aromatic herbs, Strega is the Italian word for 'witch'. You'll be under a spell!

SERVES 1

2 measures gin
1 measure Strega
1 measure lemon juice
ice
lemon slice, to decorate

Shake the gin, Strega and lemon juice vigorously over ice until well frosted. Strain into a cocktail glass and dress with a slice of lemon.

215
GLASS SLIPPER

Is this why Cinderella was so anxious to get to the ball – and why she missed her midnight curfew?

SERVES 1

3 measures gin
1 measure blue curaçao
ice

Shake the gin and curaçao over ice until well frosted. Strain into a chilled cocktail glass.

217
GIN SANGAREE

Sangria and sangaree are usually red, but there is a precedent for a white drink in sangria blanco, made with white wine.

SERVES 1

cracked ice
2 measures gin
1/2 tsp sugar syrup
sparkling water
1 tbsp port
freshly grated nutmeg,
   for sprinkling

Put some ice into a chilled tumbler. Pour the gin and sugar syrup over the ice, then top up with sparkling water. Stir gently to mix, then float the port on top. Sprinkle with freshly grated nutmeg.

216
MOONSHOT

This apparently strange combination of gin and clam juice will really hit the spot.

SERVES 1

cracked ice
dash Tabasco sauce
2 measures gin
3 measures clam juice
celery stick, to decorate

Put some ice into a mixing glass. Dash Tabasco sauce over the ice and pour in the gin and clam juice. Stir well to mix, then strain into a chilled tumbler. Dress with a celery stick.

218
KGB

Komityet Gosudarstvyennoi Byezopasnosti may no longer be with us, but the memory lives on.

SERVES 1

11/2 measures gin
1/2 measure kümmel
ice
dash apricot brandy

Shake the gin and kümmel vigorously over ice with a dash of apricot brandy until well frosted. Strain into a chilled cocktail glass.

219
CHELSEA SIDECAR

Like a Sidecar, but with gin replacing the traditional brandy.

SERVES 1

2 measures gin
1 measure triple sec
1 measure lemon juice
ice
lemon peel twist,
   to decorate

Pour the gin, triple sec and lemon juice over ice and shake vigorously until well frosted. Strain into a chilled cocktail glass. Dress with a twist of lemon peel.

220
POLISH SIDECAR

This not only replaces brandy with gin, it replaces triple sec with blackberry brandy – hardly deserving of a sidecar licence, but who's arguing?

SERVES 1

2 measures gin
1 measure blackberry brandy
1 measure lemon juice
ice

Pour the gin, blackberry brandy and lemon juice over ice and shake vigorously until well frosted, then strain into a chilled cocktail glass.

221
BLOODHOUND

Far more sweet and delicate than its name suggests, this will send you on a hunt for more.

SERVES 1

2 measures gin
1 measure sweet vermouth
1 measure dry vermouth
3 strawberries
crushed ice

Mix the first four ingredients in a blender with a little crushed ice until smooth. Strain into a chilled cocktail glass.

222
BULLDOG
BREED

A drink that's every bit as straightforward and British as its canine namesake.

SERVES 1

cracked ice
1 measure gin
2 measures orange juice
ginger ale, chilled

Half fill a chilled tumbler with ice. Pour the gin and orange juice over and top up with chilled ginger ale. Stir.

223
GREAT DANE

There's nothing very straitlaced and Danish about this – perhaps that's what makes it so great?

SERVES 1

2 measures gin
1 measure cherry brandy
1/2 measure dry vermouth
1 tsp kirsch
ice
lemon peel, to decorate

Shake the gin, cherry brandy, vermouth and kirsch vigorously over ice until well frosted. Strain into a chilled cocktail glass. Dress with lemon peel.

225
CRUSTED GREEN MONSTER

Crusted cocktails suit sharp-flavoured mixes, such as this.

SERVES 1

1/3 measure lemon juice
1 tsp icing sugar
1/3 measure kümmel
1/3 measure green crème de menthe
1/2 measure gin
4 dashes peach bitters
ice

Rub a little lemon around the rim of a chilled cocktail glass and then dip it in sugar. Shake all the liquid ingredients over ice until well frosted and strain into the chilled crusted glass.

224
BACHELOR'S BAIT

Is this pink froth supposed to be bait for the unwary bachelor, or is the bachelor doing the baiting? You decide.

SERVES 1

2 measures gin
1 tsp grenadine
1 egg white
ice
dash orange bitters

Shake the gin, grenadine and egg white over ice with a dash orange bitters until well frosted. Strain into a chilled cocktail glass.

226
THE CHARLESTON

A real mix of flavours with a lively kick!

SERVES 1

1/6 measure dry gin
1/6 measure kirsch
1/6 measure orange curaçao
1/6 measure dry vermouth
1/6 measure sweet vermouth
lemon peel, to decorate

Shake all the liquid ingredients together and strain into a cocktail glass. Dress with lemon peel.

227

PINK PUSSYCAT (see right-hand page for picture)

Deadlier than a leopard, this feline could knock your spots off!

SERVES 1

cracked ice
dash grenadine
2 measures gin
pineapple juice
pineapple, to decorate

Half fill a chilled tumbler with cracked ice. Dash grenadine over the ice and pour in the gin. Top up with pineapple juice and dress with pineapple.

228

SAND MARTIN

This looks dangerous and slips down very easily.

SERVES 1

¹/₂ measure green Chartreuse
¹/₂ measure sweet vermouth
¹/₂ measure gin
ice

Shake the liquid ingredients well over ice and strain into a cocktail glass.

229

SOUTHERN FIZZ

This fizz is packed with fruity flavour and a subtle taste of frozen gin.

SERVES 1

2 measures gin
1 measure fresh lime juice
1 measure passion fruit juice
¹/₄ measure sugar syrup
3 dashes orange flower
  water
1 measure soda water
crushed ice

Mix all the ingredients together in a blender on fast for a few seconds or until really frothy. Pour into a large iced cocktail glass or highball glass.

230
FRUIT CRAZY

Melon and mango both have powerful flavours and perfumes, making this an exotic and delicious concoction.

SERVES 1

1 measure gin
1/2 measure melon liqueur
1 measure mango nectar
1 measure grapefruit juice
1 small egg white
ice cubes
mango slice, to decorate

Shake the first five ingredients together over ice until frosted. Strain into a chilled long glass with more ice to fill, and dress with a slice of mango.

231
BIRD OF PARADISE

This is sometimes made with blue curaçao, but orange curaçao gives a much more appetizing finishing colour. However, it's up to you, so try them both!

SERVES 1

1 thick watermelon slice
   (reserve a piece to decorate)
1 measure chilled gin
1 measure chilled passion fruit
   nectar
1/2 measure chilled orange
   curaçao
crushed ice

Deseed the watermelon. Blend the liquid ingredients together with the ice until partly frozen. Pour into a tumbler or large cocktail glass and dress with a wedge of melon. You may need a spoon!

232
JAPANESE JEWEL

Sugared fruits always look spectacular as a finishing touch. Prepare them in advance if you are making several drinks.

SERVES 1

4–5 green grapes
1–2 tsp egg white, lightly
   beaten
icing sugar
1 measure melon liqueur
1 measure gin
2 measures kiwi juice
crushed ice

Pick out the best two grapes to dip in egg white and then sugar. Set aside to dry. Blend all the remaining ingredients in a blender with a little crushed ice for about 10 seconds until slushy. Pour into a medium-sized cocktail glass with more ice and dress with the sugared grapes.

233
MY FAIR LADY

A very light and airy cocktail, perfect to enjoy during a long evening of light entertainment.

SERVES 1

1 measure gin
1/2 measure lemon juice
1/2 measure orange juice
1/2 measure fraise
1 egg white
ice

Shake the first five ingredients over ice and strain into a cocktail glass.

234 SNOWBALL COCKTAIL

Almost as white as snow but certainly not as pure!

SERVES 1

2/3 measure gin
1/3 measure anisette
1/3 measure crème de violette
1/3 measure white crème de menthe
1/3 measure single cream, slightly sweetened
ice
cocktail cherry, to decorate

Mix the first five ingredients well in a glass over ice and strain into a cocktail glass. Dres with a cocktail cherry.

235 FREEDOM FIGHTER

Crème Yvette is a liqueur flavoured with Parma violets. It has a distinctive taste, so you'll either love it or hate it – but it certainly makes pretty coloured cocktails.

SERVES 1

3 measures sloe gin
1 measure Crème Yvette
1 measure lemon juice
1 egg white
cracked ice

Shake the gin, Crème Yvette, lemon juice and egg white vigorously over ice until well frosted. Strain into a chilled glass.

236 LEMON SHERBET

This turns into a delicious fluffy thick drink that you may well need a spoon for.

SERVES 1

2 measures gin
1 measure lemon juice
1 measure cream
1/2 measure orange curaçao
1 tsp icing sugar
dash orange flower water
crushed ice

Mix all the ingredients together in a blender for 10–15 seconds. Pour into a chilled small tumbler.

237 TONY BENNETT

The old crooner enjoyed his favourite drink before any show but especially when there was cold and damp in the air.

SERVES 1

1 measure gin
1 measure crème de cassis
1 measure triple sec
1/2 measure lemon juice
cracked ice
soda water

Stir all the liquid ingredients except the soda water over ice until well chilled. Strain into a long glass filled with ice and add a touch of soda water, or to taste.

RUM

Born in the tropics, rum cocktails capture the Caribbean spirit of sun, sea and sweet spirits. Live on the sunny side of life as you delve into a Daiquiri, a favourite with beachside aficionados. Or ignite the Latino spirit with an historic toast to Cuban independence and the emblematic Cuba Libre.

238
CLUB MOJITO

Dark rum is rich in flavour and redolent of sunshine holidays.

SERVES 1

1 tsp sugar syrup
few mint leaves, plus extra
    to decorate
juice of 1/2 lime
ice
2 measures Jamaican rum
soda water
dash Angostura bitters

Put the syrup, mint leaves and lime juice in a cocktail glass and crush or muddle the mint leaves. Add ice and the rum, then top up with soda water to taste. Finish with a dash of Angostura bitters and dress with the mint leaves.

239
MAI TAI

Created in 1944 by restaurateur 'Trader Vic', it was described as 'Mai Tai – Roe Ae, meaning 'out of this world'.

SERVES 1

2 measures white rum
2 measures dark rum
1 measure orange curaçao
1 measure lime juice
1 tbsp orgeat
1 tbsp grenadine
cracked ice
fruit slices, to decorate

Shake the white and dark rums, curaçao, lime juice, orgeat and grenadine vigorously over ice until well frosted. Strain into a chilled cocktail glass and dress with fruit slices.

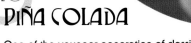

240
PIÑA COLADA

One of the younger generation of classics, this became popular during the cocktail revival of the 1980s and has remained so ever since.

SERVES 1

crushed ice
2 measures white rum
1 measure dark rum
3 measures pineapple juice
2 measures coconut cream
pineapple wedges,
    to decorate

Mix some crushed ice in a blender with the white rum, dark rum, pineapple juice and coconut cream until smooth. Pour, without straining, into a tall, chilled glass and dress with pineapple wedges.

241
LOUNGE LIZARD

A cocktail for the dedicated lounge lizard – lots of cola to quench the thirst, and plenty of rum to give it a kick.

SERVES 1

cracked ice
2 measures dark rum
1 measure amaretto
cola

Half fill a tall chilled tumbler with cracked ice. Pour the rum and amaretto over the ice. Top up with cola and stir gently.

242
ANKLE BREAKER

A warning to all cocktail drinkers – watch your step!

SERVES 1

2 measures dark rum
1 measure cherry brandy
1 measure lime juice
1 tsp sugar syrup
ice

Shake the rum, cherry brandy, lime juice and sugar syrup over ice until well frosted. Strain into a chilled tumbler.

243
MELLOW MULE

Perhaps this mule is the most easygoing of the breed – at any rate, this will make you as mellow as a Caribbean sunset.

SERVES 1

2 measures white rum
1 measure dark rum
1 measure golden rum
1 measure Falernum
   (wine-based ginger syrup)
1 measure lime juice
ice
ginger beer
pineapple wedges and stem
   ginger, to decorate

Shake the first five ingredients vigorously over ice until well frosted. Strain the mixture into a tall chilled tumbler. Top up with ginger beer and dress with pineapple wedges and stem ginger.

244
BARBADOS SUNSET

There is certainly a warm evening glow to this cocktail and you can make it even pinker with some more strawberry syrup.

SERVES 1

1 1/2 measures golden rum
1 measure coconut rum
2 measures orange juice
2 measures pineapple juice
dash strawberry syrup
ice
cocktail cherry and fruit slices,
   to decorate

Shake the first five ingredients well over ice and pour into a chilled glass. Add more ice to taste and dress with a cherry and slices of fruit.

245
JAMAICAN COOLER

A long, refreshing and very simple cocktail – perfect for inveterate rum lovers.

SERVES 1

1 1/2 measures Jamaican rum
ice cubes
soda water
lemon or lime slices, to
   decorate

Pour the rum into an ice-filled highball glass. Top up with soda water to taste and dress with lemon slices.

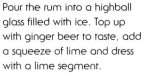

246 JAMAICAN MULE

Jamaican rum is dark and strong, perfect to dilute and makes a great long drink with numerous mixers.

SERVES 1

2 measures Jamaican rum
ice
ginger beer
squeeze of lime juice
lime segments, to decorate

Pour the rum into a highball glass filled with ice. Top up with ginger beer to taste, add a squeeze of lime and dress with a lime segment.

247 FAT MAN RUNNING

Blue curaçao can make beautiful cocktails of strange colours – you may find you prefer to use a clear curaçao in this cocktail!

SERVES 1

2 measures dark rum
1/2 measure blue curaçao
1/2 measure lime juice
crushed ice
ginger ale

Blend all the ingredients except the ginger ale in a blender on fast speed for about 10 seconds. Pour into a tall glass filled with crushed ice and top up with ginger ale.

248 BAJAN SUN

There is certainly a feeling of warm tropical sunshine to this cocktail.

SERVES 1

1 measure white rum
1 measure mandarin brandy
1 measure fresh orange juice
1 measure pineapple juice
splash of grenadine
ice
fresh pineapple slice and a
   cherry, to decorate

Shake all the liquid ingredients well over ice. Pour into a tall glass filled with ice and dress with a slice of pineapple and a cherry.

249 SPACE ODYSSEY

Remember those coloured cherries? Well, here is one reason to keep some in the cupboard – they are a lot of fun in cocktails!

SERVES 1

1 measure golden rum
2 dashes Angostura bitters
ice
coloured cherries
ginger beer

Mix the rum and bitters in a highball glass filled with ice and coloured cherries. Top up with ginger beer to taste.

250
TAMARA'S TIPPLE

The dark secrets at the bottom of this glass add rich sweetness, so you shouldn't need to add too much cola.

SERVES 1

2 measures dark rum
1 measure crème de cacao
ice
cola
lemon slices

Mix the first two ingredients in a tall glass filled with ice. Top up with a little cola and finish with slices of lemon.

252
PALM BEACH

If it's been a long time since your last holiday, conjure up the blue skies of Florida and the rolling surf with this sunny cocktail.

SERVES 1

1 measure white rum
1 measure gin
1 measure pineapple juice
cracked ice

Shake the rum, gin and pineapple juice vigorously over ice until well frosted. Strain into a chilled glass.

251
GRAND BAHAMA

An unusually restrained tropical cocktail, with none of the usual flamboyance added by pineapple and coconut.

SERVES 1

1 measure white rum
1/2 measure brandy
1/2 measure triple sec
1 measure lime juice
ice
lime slice, to decorate

Shake the liquid ingredients vigorously over ice until well frosted. Strain into a chilled cocktail glass and dress with a slice of lime.

253
OCEAN BREEZE

It's a breeze to make and as colourful as the whipped-up ocean on an early morning. Just don't dilute it too much.

SERVES 1

1 measure white rum
1 measure amaretto
1/2 measure blue curaçao
1/2 measure pineapple juice
crushed ice
soda water

Shake the white rum, amaretto, blue curaçao and pineapple juice together over ice. Pour into a tall glass and top up with soda water to taste.

254
CUBAN SPECIAL (see right-hand page for picture)

A light and sweet offering from the tropical island.

SERVES 1

2 measures rum
1 measure lime juice
1 tbsp pineapple juice
1 tsp triple sec
ice
pineapple wedges, to decorate

Pour the rum, lime juice, pineapple juice and triple sec over ice and shake until well frosted. Strain into a chilled cocktail glass and dress with pineapple wedges.

255
CUBA LIBRA

The 1960s and 1970s saw a meteoric rise in the popularity of this simple long drink.

SERVES 1

cracked ice
2 measures white rum
cola
lime wedge, to decorate

Half fill a highball glass with cracked ice. Pour the rum over the ice and top up with cola. Stir gently and dress with a wedge of lime.

256
OLD SOAK

Sit back and relax with a seriously warming mix of flavours from the Deep South.

SERVES 1

2 measures golden rum
1 measure Southern Comfort
1 measure ginger syrup
cracked ice
soda water

Stir the first three ingredients over ice in a chilled tumbler or large wine glass. Top up with soda water to taste.

257 TIGER'S MILK

The addition of milk gives a flavour of innocence, but be warned, this one has a real bite!

SERVES 1

2 measures golden rum
1 1/2 measures brandy
1 tsp sugar syrup
1/2 cup milk
crushed ice
ground cinnamon and a
    cinnamon stick, to decorate

Blend the rum, brandy, sugar syrup and milk with crushed ice until combined. Pour into a chilled wine glass. Sprinkle with ground cinnamon and serve with a cinnamon stick as a stirrer.

258 SANTA CRUZ DAISY

Traditionally Daisies were made with raspberry syrup, but any good sugar or fruit syrup will produce a delicate sweetness.

SERVES 1

3 dashes sugar syrup
1 tsp curaçao
juice 1/2 small lemon
2 measures rum
crushed ice
soda water

Shake the first four ingredients well over ice and strain into a tumbler or highball glass. Top up with soda water.

259 DARK & STORMY

Golden rum has a mellow, slightly milder taste, but you could use dark rum here for a really stormy mix.

SERVES 1

2 measures golden rum
1 measure lime juice
1/2 measure sugar syrup
ice
ginger beer
lime slice and lime peel twist,
    to decorate

Shake the first three ingredients over ice until well frosted. Strain into a chilled highball glass and top up with ginger beer to taste. Dress with a lime slice and a twist of lime.

260 DRAGON LADY

It might be thought to be the same colour as the fiery breath of the female of the species.

SERVES 1

1 measure golden rum
1 measure orange juice
dash white curaçao
dash grenadine
ice
bitter lemon, chilled
orange slice
orange peel twist, to
    decorate

Stir the first four ingredients well over ice, strain into an ice-filled highball glass and top up with bitter lemon. Add a slice of orange and dress with an orange twist.

261
NIRVANA

It may not be possible to obtain a perfect state of harmony and bliss through a cocktail, but this has to be the next best thing.

SERVES 1

2 measures dark rum
1/2 measure grenadine
1/2 measure tamarind syrup
1 tsp sugar syrup
cracked ice
grapefruit juice

Shake the rum, grenadine, tamarind syrup and sugar syrup vigorously over ice until well frosted. Half fill a chilled glass with cracked ice and strain the cocktail over them. Top up with grapefruit juice.

263
BANANA COLADA

You'll need more than a straw to drink (eat) this with.

SERVES 1

crushed ice
2 measures white rum
4 measures pineapple juice
1 measure Malibu
1 banana, peeled and sliced

Mix some crushed ice in a blender with the liquid ingredients and the banana. Blend until smooth, then pour, without straining, into a tall chilled tumbler.

262
AMIGOS PIÑA COLADA

A Piña Colada is usually made with light rum – this dark rum version will quickly turn your drinking partners into friends.

SERVES 4

crushed ice
1/2 cup rum
1 cup pineapple juice
5 measures coconut cream
2 measures dark rum
2 measures single cream
pineapple wedges and
    cocktail cherries, to decorate

Mix some crushed ice in a blender with the liquid ingredients. Blend until smooth. Pour, without straining, into tall chilled tumblers and dress with pineapple wedges and cocktail cherries.

264
STRAWBERRY COLADA

Designed for all those strawberry lovers among you.

SERVES 1

crushed ice cubes
3 measures golden rum
4 measures pineapple juice
1 measure coconut cream
6 hulled strawberries
pineapple wedges and
    strawberries, to decorate

Mix some crushed ice in a blender with the liquid ingredients and the strawberries. Blend until smooth, then pour, without straining, into a tall chilled tumbler. Dress with pineapple wedges and strawberries.

265 WHITE LION

White around the edges, but definitely red-blooded.

SERVES 1

cracked ice
dash Angostura bitters
dash grenadine
2 measures white rum
1 measure lemon juice
1 tsp sugar syrup

Shake some cracked ice in a cocktail shaker with the liquid ingredients until a frost forms. Strain into a chilled cocktail glass.

267 BLACK WIDOW

Not as wicked as its name suggests, but if you are feeling adventurous, you could take it straight, on the rocks!

SERVES 1

2/3 measure dark rum
1/3 measure Southern Comfort
juice 1/2 lime
dash curaçao
ice
soda water
lime peel twist, to decorate

Shake the rum, Southern Comfort, lime juice and curaçao well together over ice and strain into a chilled tumbler. Top up with soda water to taste and dress with a twist of lime peel.

266 PARADISE FIZZ

This lovely long drink is also great made with gin and should be poured over lots of ice to enjoy it really cold.

SERVES 1

1 measure white rum
juice 1/2 lime
1 tsp icing sugar
1/2 measure Midori
1/2 egg white
ice
soda water
lime peel shreds, to decorate

Shake the first five ingredients over ice until well frosted. Strain into an ice-filled long glass and top up with soda water to taste. Sprinkle with shreds of lime peel.

268 RUM 'N' CURRANT

This old-fashioned drink is making a comeback, drunk either short or long.

SERVES 1

1 measure dark rum
1/2 measure blackcurrant cordial
ice
lemonade

Mix the rum and blackcurrant cordial over ice in a tumbler. Top up with lemonade to taste.

269 CARIBBEAN BLUES

The cool crystal blue cocktail invites you to think of Caribbean sea and sand, and enjoy this tropical mix.

SERVES 1

1 measure white rum
1/2 measure blue curaçao
good squeeze lime juice
1/4 measure sugar syrup
ice
soda water
3 frozen lime slices, to decorate

Mix the first four ingredients in a large cocktail glass with a few ice cubes. Top up with soda water to taste and dress with the frozen slices of lime.

271 PINEAPPLE PLANTER'S PUNCH

A traditional punch with a tropical touch.

SERVES 1

1 measure white rum
1 measure pineapple juice
juice of 1/2 lime
1/2 measure white curaçao
dash maraschino
ice
fruit slices, to decorate

Mix the liquid ingredients together and serve in a highball glass with ice. Dress with fruit slices.

270 ORANGE PLANTER'S PUNCH

Whoever thought of adding orange to the original deserves a campaign medal.

SERVES 1

1 measure rum
1 measure orange curaçao
2 dashes Angostura bitters
1 tsp grenadine
juice of 1 1/2 limes
ice, to serve

Mix the liquid ingredients together and serve in a highball glass with ice.

272 PLANTATION PUNCH

The original, made, naturally, with Southern Comfort.

SERVES 1

2 measures dark rum
1 measure Southern Comfort
1 measure lemon juice
ice
1 tsp brown sugar
sparkling water
1 tsp ruby port

Shake the rum, Southern Comfort and lemon juice vigorously over ice with the brown sugar until well frosted. Strain into a tall, chilled glass and fill, almost to the rim, with sparkling water. Float the port on top by pouring it gently over the back of a teaspoon.

273
PLANTER'S COCKTAIL

Lighter and more delicate than the original, it still manages to pack a punch.

SERVES 1

1 measure rum
juice of ¹/₂ lime
1 tsp sugar syrup
dash Angostura bitters

Mix the ingredients together and pour into a cocktail glass.

275
PLANTER'S TEA

It may look as dainty as a cup of tea, but there the similarity comes to an alcoholic end.

SERVES 1

2 measures strong black tea
2 measures dark rum
1 cup orange juice
¹/₂ cup fresh lemon juice
orange slices, to decorate

Mix the liquid ingredients together. Heat, sweeten to taste and dress with orange slices.

274
PLANTER'S PUNCH REFRESHER

On a really hot evening, the classic punch needs to lose some sweetness and become a seriously cool drink.

SERVES 1

2 measures rum
2 measures lime juice
1–2 tsp grenadine
dash Angostura bitters
soda water
ice

Mix the first four ingredients together and pour into a highball glass. Top up with soda water and serve with ice.

276
PLANTER'S PUNCH

Derived from a Hindi word meaning five, punch is so called because, traditionally, it contained five ingredients.

SERVES 1

2 measures white rum
2 measures dark rum
1 measure lemon juice
1 measure lime juice
1 tsp sugar syrup
¹/₄ tsp triple sec
dash grenadine
cracked ice
sparkling water
fruit slices, to decorate

Shake the white rum, dark rum, lemon juice, lime juice, sugar syrup, triple sec and grenadine vigorously over ice until well frosted. Half fill a tall chilled tumbler or Collins glass with cracked ice and strain the cocktail over it. Top up with sparkling water and stir gently. Dress with fruit slices.

277
SAN PAULO

Golden rum brings out the sweetness of the tomatoes, giving this cocktail a warm fruitiness quite different from its look alike, the Bloody Mary.

SERVES 1

1 measure golden rum
good squeeze lime juice
2 measures tomato juice
dash Tabasco sauce
celery salt
pepper
ice

Stir the first six ingredients together well over ice and strain into an ice-filled highball glass.

279
SAILOR'S RUM PUNCH

Sail in the West Indies and you will come back with this classic recipe in your pocket.

SERVES 1

1 part lemon or lime juice
2 parts honey or sugar syrup
3 parts strong rum
few shakes of Angostura bitters
4 parts weak, chilled fruit juice
ice
fruit pieces, to serve

Mix the first four ingredients together in advance, chill, and allow the flavours to develop for a while. To serve, mix in the fruit juice, and pour into a highball glass with a little more ice. Serve with fruit.

278
CALYPSO STING

There is definitely a sting in the tail of this one, so enjoy with caution.

SERVES 1

1 measure dark rum
1 measure Malibu
1/2 measure orange curaçao
1/2 measure orange juice
dash fresh lime juice
ice
tonic water
Angostura bitters
cherry and a slice of lime, to decorate

Shake the first five ingredients well over ice. Pour into a highball glass and top up with tonic water. Finish with a drop or two of Angostura bitters, and dress with a cherry and a lime slice.

280
RUM DAISY

Fresh as a daisy and certainly lighter than a Sailor's Rum Punch.

SERVES 1

2 measures golden rum
1 measure lemon juice
1 tsp sugar syrup
1/2 tsp grenadine
cracked ice
orange slice, to decorate

Pour the liquid ingredients over ice and shake until well frosted. Half fill a small, chilled tumbler with cracked ice and strain the cocktail over it. Dress with an orange slice.

281 VIRGIN'S PRAYER

What exactly is she praying for? And will this help?

SERVES 1

1 measure white rum
1 measure dark rum
1 measure Kahlúa
1 tsp lemon juice
2 tsp orange juice
ice
lime slices, to decorate

Shake the liquid ingredients over ice until well frosted. Strain into a small, chilled tumbler and dress with slices of lime.

282 POLYNESIA

Get into the rhythm and let your hair down with the assistance of a few of these.

SERVES 1

2 measures white rum
2 measures passion fruit juice
1 measure lime juice
1 egg white
cracked ice
dash Angostura bitters

Shake the rum, passion fruit juice, lime juice and egg white over cracked ice with a dash of Angostura bitters until well frosted. Strain into a chilled cocktail glass.

283 POLYNESIAN SOUR

A tropical sour that actually bears little relation to the original whisky version.

SERVES 1

crushed ice
2 measures light rum
1/2 measure guava juice
1/2 measure lemon juice
1/2 measure orange juice

Mix all the ingredients in a blender until smooth. Pour into a chilled cocktail glass.

284 FIREMAN'S SOUR

It may help him up the ladder – but do you want him to put out your fire?

SERVES 1

2 measures white rum
1 1/2 measures lime juice
1 tbsp grenadine
1 tsp sugar syrup
ice
cocktail cherry, to decorate

Shake the liquid ingredients over ice until well frosted. Strain into a cocktail glass and dress with a cocktail cherry.

285
BLUE HAWAIIAN

An eye-catching drink with a tropical flavour. Be flamboyant with the fruit finish if you like – certainly on special occasions – or just leave this drink to stand out from the crowd.

SERVES 1

ice
2 measures Bacardi rum
1/2 measure blue curaçao
1 measure pineapple juice
1/2 measure coconut cream
pineapple wedge, to decorate

Place a handful of ice in the cocktail shaker and pour in the liquid ingredients. Shake vigorously over ice and strain into a wine goblet. Dress with a small wedge of pineapple.

286
THE BACARDI COCKTAIL

White rum, synonymous with the name Bacardi, is the base of many well-known cocktails. This one, of course, must be made with Bacardi.

SERVES 1

2 measures Bacardi rum
2 tsp fresh lime juice
dash grenadine
icing sugar or sugar syrup, to taste
ice

Shake the first four ingredients over ice until well frosted. Strain into a shallow cocktail glass. Drink with a straw.

287
BACARDI CRUSTA

Experienced cocktail makers will know that absinthe is an extra strong spirit – making this cocktail especially daring.

SERVES 1

1/2 measure lime juice
1 tsp granulated sugar
1 tsp absinthe
1 1/2 measures white rum
ice
lime slice, to decorate

Rub a little lime juice around the rim of a cocktail glass and dip into the sugar. Set aside to harden. Stir the rest of the lime juice with the absinthe and rum over ice until well frosted. Strain into the glass and dress with a slice of lime.

288
ACAPULCO

Originally, this was always rum-based and did not include any fruit juice. Nowadays, it is increasingly made with tequila, since this has become better known outside its native Mexico.

SERVES 1

2 measures white rum
1/2 measure triple sec
1/2 measure lime juice
1 tsp sugar syrup
1 egg white
cracked ice
fresh mint sprig, to decorate

Shake the first five ingredients vigorously over ice until frosted. Half fill a chilled highball glass with cracked ice and strain the cocktail over it. Dress with a mint sprig.

289
CASABLANCA

Named after the movie in 1942 and most probably enjoyed by its hero, the inimitable Humphrey Bogart.

SERVES 1

3 measures white rum
4 measures pineapple juice
2 measures coconut cream
2 scoops crushed ice
pineapple wedge, to decorate

Shake all the ingredients except the fruit together over ice and strain into a large cocktail glass with more ice, if you like. Dress with pineapple.

290
CUBA SPECIAL

This is short, strong and sweet. Serve with plenty of ice to enhance all the flavours and sip slowly.

SERVES 1

1¹/2 measures white rum
1¹/2 measures pineapple juice
juice of ¹/2 fresh lime
1 measure Cointreau
crushed ice
fresh cherries and pineapple
    wedge, to decorate

Shake all the ingredients except the fruit together over ice until well frosted. Pour into a chilled cocktail glass or tumbler and dress with cherries and a piece of pineapple.

291
BISHOP

It is strange how men of the cloth have gained a reputation for being enthusiastic about the good material things in life. Even Rudyard Kipling wrote about smuggling 'brandy for the parson'. It goes to show that spirituality is no barrier to spirits.

SERVES 1

dash lemon juice
cracked ice
1 measure white rum
1 tsp red wine
pinch icing sugar

Splash the lemon juice over the ice, pour in the rum and wine and add a pinch of sugar. Shake vigorously until frosted. Strain into a chilled wine glass.

292
PARISIAN
BLONDE

A surprising number of cocktails include cream. This dreamy mixture is creamy, smooth and very sophisticated.

SERVES 1

1 measure dark rum
1 measure orange curaçao
1 measure cream
ice
orange peel twist, to
    decorate

Shake the liquid ingredients well over ice and strain into a chilled cocktail glass. Dress with orange peel.

293
JOSIAH'S BAY FLOAT

Designed for two to share, this is a wonderful cocktail for a special occasion in the summer. For the more prosaic, serve in tall, chilled tumblers, rather than a pineapple shell.

SERVES 2

2 measures golden rum
1 measure Galliano
2 measures pineapple juice
1 measure lime juice
4 tsp sugar syrup
cracked ice
champagne
lime and lemon slices and
    cocktail cherries, to decorate
scooped-out pineapple shell,
    to serve

Shake the rum, Galliano, pineapple juice, lime juice and sugar syrup vigorously over ice until well frosted. Strain into the pineapple shell, top up with champagne and stir gently. Dress with lime and lemon slices and cocktail cherries and serve.

294
RAIL-ROADSTER

Carefully decorate the rim well in advance for a really good effect.

SERVES 1

1 tsp fine zest of lime
1 tsp icing sugar
1 1/2 measures white rum
1/2 measure Galliano
1 measure lime juice
crushed ice
dry ginger ale

Mix the lime zest and sugar together. Rub the rim of a glass with a little rum, then dip it into the sugar to coat thoroughly. Set aside to dry. Shake all the remaining ingredients except the ginger ale together with the crushed ice until well chilled. Pour into the glass and top up with a little ginger ale to taste.

295
CINDERELLA

If the fairytale heroine had been knocking back cocktails until the clock struck midnight, it's hardly surprising that she forgot the time and lost her shoe on the way home.

SERVES 1

3 measures white rum
1 measure white port
1 measure lemon juice
1 tsp sugar syrup
cracked ice
1 egg white

Shake the rum, port, lemon juice and sugar syrup over ice with the egg white until well frosted. Strain into a chilled glass.

296
HAWKSBILL SPECIAL

A smooth banana concoction with plenty of mellow West Indian character.

SERVES 1

1 small ripe banana
1 measure white rum
1/2 measure Galliano
1/2 measure crème de banane
freshly squeezed juice of
    1/2 lime
crushed ice

Mix all the ingredients quickly in a blender until smooth. Pour into a chilled glass with extra ice.

297

BANANA DAIQUIRI

Who doesn't like a daiquiri? This was one of the first party cocktails to be made in a blender. Short but lethal.

SERVES 1

2 measures white rum
1/2 measure triple sec
1/2 measure lime juice
1/2 measure single cream
1 tsp sugar syrup
1/4 banana, peeled and sliced

Blend the ingredients until smooth, then pour the mixture, without straining, into a chilled tumbler.

298

DERBY DAIQUIRI

You could happily drink this until you drop – and that may not take too long!

SERVES 1

2 measures white rum
1 measure orange juice
1/2 measure triple sec
1/2 measure lime juice
ice
lime peel, to decorate

Blend the liquid ingredients with ice until smooth, then pour, without straining, into a chilled cocktail glass and dress with lime peel.

299

PASSIONATE DAIQUIRI

This may look demure, but will probably bring some passion into your life.

SERVES 1

2 measures white rum
1 measure lime juice
1/2 measure passion fruit syrup
ice
cocktail cherry, to decorate

Pour the liquid ingredients over ice and shake vigorously until well frosted. Strain into a chilled cocktail glass and dress with a cocktail cherry.

300

PEACH DAIQUIRI

Daiquiris made with soft fruit are the original alcoholic smoothies – to be handled with care!

SERVES 1

2 measures white rum
1 measure lime juice
1/2 tsp sugar syrup
1/2 peach, peeled, stoned and chopped

Blend the ingredients together until smooth, then pour, without straining, into a chilled tumbler.

301 DAIQUIRI

Daiquiri is a town in Cuba, where this drink was said to have been invented in the early part of the twentieth century. A businessman had run out of imported gin and so had to make do with the local drink – rum – which, at that time, was often of unreliable quality.

SERVES 1

2 measures white rum
3/4 measure lime juice
1/2 tsp sugar syrup
cracked ice

Pour the rum, lime juice and sugar syrup over ice and shake vigorously until well frosted. Strain into a chilled cocktail glass.

302 FROZEN DAIQUIRI

One of the great classic cocktails, the Daiquiri has moved on. It's not just mixed with fresh fruit or unusual ingredients, it's entered the twenty-first century with a whole new future as slushes take on a leading role in fashionable cocktail bars.

SERVES 1

crushed ice
2 measures white rum
1 measure lime juice
1 tsp sugar syrup
lime slice, to decorate

Mix the crushed ice, rum, lime juice and sugar syrup in a small blender until slushy. Pour into a chilled champagne flute and dress with a lime slice.

303 FROZEN PEACH DAIQUIRI

Perfect for cooling down on hot summer days.

SERVES 1

crushed ice
2 measures white rum
1 measure lime juice
1 tsp sugar syrup
1/2 peach, peeled, stoned and chopped
peach slice, to decorate

Mix crushed ice in a blender with the next four ingredients until slushy. Pour into a chilled cocktail glass and dress with a peach slice.

304 FROZEN PINEAPPLE DAIQUIRI

This elegantly dressed version would be good on hot nights.

SERVES 1

crushed ice
2 measures white rum
1 measure lime juice
1/2 tsp pineapple syrup
55 g/2 oz finely chopped fresh pineapple
pineapple wedges, to decorate

Mix crushed ice in a blender with the next four ingredients until slushy. Pour into a chilled cocktail glass. Dress with some pineapple wedges.

305 FROZEN STRAWBERRY DAIQUIRI

This was the first, and the classic, frozen daiquiri recipe with soft fruit added.

SERVES 1

crushed ice
2 measures white rum
1 measure lime juice
1 tsp sugar syrup
7 strawberries

Mix crushed ice cubes in a blender with the liquid ingredients and 6 strawberries, until slushy. Pour into a chilled cocktail glass and dress with the remaining strawberry.

307 XYZ

Ice cool, this beautifully simple cocktail is very refreshing – one is never enough!

SERVES 1

1/2 measure fresh lemon juice
1/2 measure white rum
1/2 measure Cointreau
cracked ice
lime slice, to decorate

Shake all the liquid ingredients together over ice until well frosted. Strain into a chilled cocktail glass and dress with a slice of lime.

306 FOX TROT

Such a quick and easy cocktail should be made and enjoyed more often, just like the old-fashioned dance itself!

SERVES 1

juice of 1/2 lemon or 1 lime
2 dashes orange curaçao
2 measures white rum
ice
orange peel, to decorate

Shake the first three ingredients well over ice and strain into a cocktail glass. Add more ice if you like and dress with a strand of orange peel.

308 PALM BREEZE

Grate and strain a little fresh pineapple flesh to make real juice. The flavour will be much nicer – although perhaps not quite as sweet.

SERVES 1

1 measure white rum
1 measure gin
2–3 measures pineapple juice
ice
fresh pineapple slice, to decorate

Shake the first three ingredients well over ice and strain into a cocktail glass. Dress with a slice of fresh pineapple.

309 PEACH DREAMER

Orange juice with a dangerous kick and a tantalizing pink ripple.

SERVES 1

1 measure white rum
1 measure peach schnapps
3 measures fresh orange juice
ice cubes and crushed ice
1 measure grenadine

Shake the first three ingredients well over ice and pour on to crushed ice in a chilled cocktail glass. Slowly pour a little grenadine into the glass before serving.

310 RUM SWIZZLE

Cocktails were originally blended with swizzle sticks until the glass became frosted – hard work on the arms!

SERVES 1

2 measures dark rum
1 measure fresh lime juice
1/2 measure sugar syrup
2–3 dashes Angostura bitters
55 g/2 oz crushed ice, plus extra, to taste

Blend all the ingredients slowly in a blender until frothy and part frozen. Pour into an iced tumbler with more ice to taste. Serve with a swizzle stick.

311 CONTRARY MARY

The type of rum makes all the difference to any cocktail, but especially here, where the result should be soft, not knockout! So use a white or golden rum.

SERVES 1

1 1/2 measures light rum
1 1/2 measures pineapple juice
2 dashes grenadine
1 dash maraschino
ice
cherries, to decorate

Shake the liquid ingredients well together and strain into a cocktail glass. Add ice to taste and dress with cherries.

312 ST. LUCY SMASH

This tastes wonderful and smells like a tropical island.

SERVES 1

1 segment lime
2 measures golden rum
1/2 measure raspberry liqueur
1 measure apple juice
few mint leaves, crushed
ice
raspberries and slices of lime, to decorate

Rub lime around the rim of an old-fashioned tumbler, then chill it. Shake the next four ingredients over ice. Pour into the chilled tumbler and add ice to taste. Dress with raspberries and slices of lime.

313 TONGUE TWISTER

Light or golden rum has a subtler taste than the dark rum, so it doesn't mask other liqueur flavours.

SERVES 1

1 measure light rum
1/2 measure coconut cream liqueur
1/2 measure orange curaçao
1 measure lemon juice
ice
grated nutmeg, to decorate

Shake the first four ingredients well over ice. Strain into a chilled cocktail glass and sprinkle with grated nutmeg.

314 SHANGHAI

Dark rum, with its stronger, sweeter taste, perfectly suits the dryness of the anise-flavoured pastis.

SERVES 1

4 measures dark rum
1 measure pastis
3 measures lemon juice
2 dashes grenadine
cracked ice
lemon slice and maraschino cherry, to decorate

Shake all the liquid ingredients together over ice until well frosted. Strain into a chilled glass and dress with a slice of lemon and a cherry.

315 APRICOT LADY

The mellow flavour of this cocktail is matched by its rich golden colour, with all the fragrance of a tropical sunrise.

SERVES 1

2 measures golden rum
2 measures apricot brandy
1 measure fresh lime juice
3 dashes orange curaçao
1 tsp egg white
crushed ice
apricot slice

Blend all the ingredients except the fruit in a blender until slushy. Strain into a chilled glass. Dress with a slice of apricot and drink with a straw.

316 GREEN DEVIL

This mix of blue curaçao and orange juice produces a truly wicked shade of green – but a great taste!

SERVES 1

lime juice
icing sugar
1 measure light rum
1/2 measure blue curaçao
1 measure orange juice
ice
lime slice, to decorate

Dip the rim of a large cocktail glass into lime juice and then into sugar to create sugar frosting. Set aside to dry. Shake the liquid ingredients well over ice. Pour into the frosted glass and dress with a slice of lime.

317
THE DEVIL

It doesn't taste as wicked as it sounds, but it has got a black streak in it that you may want to change to something sweeter, like a twist of fruit.

SERVES 1

1 measure dark rum
1/2 measure red vermouth
ice
black olive, to decorate

Stir the rum and vermouth together over ice. Strain into a chilled cocktail glass and dress with a black olive.

319
BOSTON SIDECAR

This is the version of the sidecar developed for the seemingly sedate residents of Boston.

SERVES 1

1 1/2 measures white rum
1/2 measure brandy
1/2 measure triple sec
1/2 measure lemon juice
ice
orange peel twist,
   to decorate

Pour the liquid ingredients over ice and shake vigorously until well frosted. Strain into a chilled cocktail glass and dress with a twist of orange peel.

318
JAMAICA JOE

Rich and pungent Jamaica rum will mix surprisingly well with the sweetness of the Tia Maria and advocaat (an egg-and-brandy liqueur).

SERVES 1

1 measure Jamaica rum
1 measure Tia Maria
1 measure advocaat
cracked ice
dash grenadine
nutmeg, for dusting

Shake the rum, Tia Maria and advocaat together over ice until well frosted. Add the grenadine. Pour into a chilled cocktail glass and dust lightly with freshly grated nutmeg.

320
RUM COBBLER

This is, quite simply, every bit as refreshing as it looks.

SERVES 1

1 tsp icing sugar
2 measures sparkling water
cracked ice
2 measures white rum
lime slice and orange slice,
   to decorate

Put the sugar into a chilled goblet. Add the sparkling water and stir until the sugar has dissolved. Fill the glass with ice and pour in the rum. Stir well and dress with a lime slice and an orange slice.

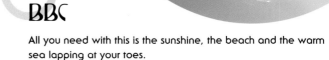

321
KOKOLOKO

For a stunning party effect, quickly dip the rim of the glass first in one of the liqueurs, then into a mixture of cocoa and icing sugar.

SERVES 1

cocoa powder
icing sugar
1 measure coconut cream
1 measure coconut rum
1 measure crème de cacao
1 measure milk
cracked ice

Frost the rim of the glass using a little liqueur, cocoa and sugar. Set aside to dry. Mix the liquid ingredients together and pour over ice in a tumbler.

322
BEACH BUM

Like puréed mango on the rocks, this cocktail is fruit with a kick.

SERVES 1

1 measure dark rum
1 measure peach brandy
1 measure lime juice
flesh of half mango
ice
lime slice, to decorate

Blend the first four ingredients in a blender at a slow speed for about 10 seconds. Pour into a large glass filled with ice and dress with a slice of lime.

323
BBC

All you need with this is the sunshine, the beach and the warm sea lapping at your toes.

SERVES 1

1/2 ripe banana
1 measure dark rum
1 measure Bailey's Irish Cream
1/2 measure coconut cream
crushed ice

Reserve a slice or two of banana and blend all the ingredients together in a blender until smooth. Pour into a large chilled cocktail glass and dress with the reserved banana slices.

324
COCO ROCO

To set the scene – serve this coconut cocktail in a real coconut shell.

SERVES 1

2 measures fresh coconut
  juice
1/2 measure white rum
1/2 measure apricot brandy
1/2 measure coconut milk
crushed ice

Blend all the ingredients in a blender for about 5 seconds. Serve in a coconut shell or chilled tumbler and drink through a straw.

325
BOLO

A popular eighteenth-century cocktail celebrating the new abundance of citrus fruits.

SERVES 1

1 egg white
1–2 tsp icing sugar
pinch allspice, plus extra to decorate
juice of 1/4 lemon or lime
juice of 1/2 orange
1 measure white rum
ice

Dip the rim of the glass into egg white and then into a mixture of allspice and sugar. Allow to dry before filling the glass. Shake the lemon juice, orange juice and rum together with the remaining sugar until the sugar has dissolved. Pour over ice into the cocktail glass and sprinkle a little allspice on top.

326
HURRICANE

This flamboyant cocktail is synonymous with Pat O'Brien's Bar in the New Orleans French Quarter. A popular drink with the tourists because if you managed to drink it all, you could take your glass home.

SERVES 1

ice
4 measures dark rum
1 measure lemon juice
2 measures sweet fruit cocktail or juice (passion fruit and orange are the usual)
soda water
orange slices and cherries, to decorate

Fill a tall cocktail glass or highball glass with ice. Shake the rum, lemon juice and sweet fruit cocktail until well combined and pour into the chilled glass. Top up with soda water and dress with orange slices and cherries.

327
BRAZILIAN BATIDA

Cachaça is also known as Brazilian firewater and is a local white rum, somewhat stronger than the norm.

SERVES 1

2 measures cachaça or white rum
1/2 measure strawberry syrup
few strawberries
crushed ice

Blend the first three ingredients in a blender for a few seconds until frothy. Pour into a glass with the crushed ice.

328
KIWI KRUSH

Crushed with plenty of ice, this fruity combination quickly makes an adult slush. Enjoy before it goes past its best.

SERVES 1

2 kiwi fruit, peeled
2 measures light rum
1/2 measure melon liqueur
2 measures grapefruit juice
crushed ice

Reserve a slice of kiwi fruit. Blend all the remaining ingredients in a blender on a slow speed until slushy. Pour into a large glass, and dress with the slice of kiwi fruit.

329 ZOMBIE (see right-hand page for picture)

The individual ingredients of this cocktail vary considerably from one recipe to another, but all Zombies contain a mixture of white, golden and dark rum in a range of proportions.

SERVES 1

2 measures dark rum
2 measures white rum
1 measure golden rum
1 measure triple sec
1 measure lime juice
1 measure orange juice
1 measure pineapple juice
1 measure guava juice
1 tbsp grenadine
1 tbsp orgeat syrup
1 tsp Pernod
crushed ice
fresh mint and pineapple
    wedges, to decorate

Shake all the liquid ingredients together over crushed ice until well combined and frosted. Pour without straining into a chilled glass. Dress with the mint and wedges of pineapple.

330 BIG CITY MIST

Served over lots of ice, this is a long refreshing concoction.

SERVES 1

1 measure Irish Mist
1 measure dark rum
2 measures passion fruit juice
1 measure pink grapefruit juice
dash grenadine
ice

Shake the liquid ingredients together over ice. Pour into a long glass filled with ice and dress with a stirrer.

331 BEAUTIFUL DREAMER

Coconut cream is used in many cocktails, but, because it separates in the container, it will often need to be beaten or blended before using.

SERVES 1

2 measures white rum
1 measure coconut cream,
    beaten until creamy
1 measure guava juice
1 measure pineapple juice
ice
melon or guava slices,
    to decorate

Shake the first four ingredients well over ice. Pour into a large cocktail glass and dress with a slice of fruit.

332
TROPICAL FRUIT PUNCH

This exotic-looking cocktail is simplicity itself and can be varied with different fruit juices. Top with lavish amounts of fruit for a festive effect and add ginger ale to make a great long drink.

SERVES 6

1 small ripe mango
4 tbsp lime juice
1 tsp finely grated fresh ginger
1 tbsp light brown sugar
1.2 litres/2 pints orange juice
1.2 litres/2 pints pineapple juice
90 ml/3 fl oz rum
crushed ice
fruit slices, to decorate

Blend or process the mango with the lime juice, ginger and sugar until smooth. Add the orange juice, pineapple juice and the rum and process again for a few seconds until smooth. Divide the crushed ice between six glasses and pour the punch over. Dress with some fruit slices.

334
YELLOW BIRD

This really is best made with fresh sweet ripe pineapple, so you will just have to make a jug and invite around some friends.

SERVES 1

1 ripe pineapple
3 measures dark rum
2 measures triple sec
2 measures Galliano
1 measure lime juice
ice cubes
pineapple leaves, to decorate

Blend the pineapple for 30 seconds in a blender, add the next four ingredients, and blend for another 10–20 seconds. Pour into a large cocktail glass filled with ice and dress with pineapple leaves.

333
STRAWBERRIES & CREAM

This becomes thick and icy, almost like a sorbet or slush, so don't leave it sitting around to melt.

SERVES 1

1 measure light rum, iced
1 measure chilled grapefruit juice
1 measure double cream
5–6 large strawberries, hulled
  (save one to serve)
55 g/2 oz crushed ice

Blend all the ingredients together in a blender for 10–15 seconds. Pour into a chilled cocktail glass and finish with the remaining strawberry.

335
ZOMBIE PRINCE

This is lighter and more refreshing than the original Zombie, replacing the cherry brandy with grapefruit juice.

SERVES 1

dash Angostura bitters
ice
1 measure white rum
1 measure golden rum
1 measure dark rum
1/2 measure lemon juice
1/2 measure orange juice
1/2 measure grapefruit juice
1 tsp brown sugar

Splash Angostura bitters over ice in a mixing glass, pour in all the liquid ingredients and add the sugar. Stir to mix well, then strain into a tall chilled tumbler.

336 RUM COOLER

The characteristic sweetness and perfume of rum blends with so many exotic fruits – make this one with mango and lychee, as an alternative.

SERVES 1

2 ice cubes
juice of 1 lime
1¹/₂ measures rum
1¹/₂ measures pineapple juice
1 medium-ripe banana, cut into chunks
cracked ice
lime peel twist, to decorate

Blend the first five ingredients in a blender for about 1 minute or until smooth. Pour over ice into a chilled glass and finish with a twist of peel.

337 ZOMBIE BOY

Basically the same as the parent zombie, with a couple of subtle differences.

SERVES 1

crushed ice
2 measures dark rum
2 measures white rum
1 measure golden rum
1 measure triple sec
1 measure lemon juice
1 measure orange juice
1 measure pineapple juice
1 measure mango nectar
1 tbsp grenadine
1 tbsp orgeat
1 tsp Pernod
fresh mint sprigs and pineapple wedges, to decorate

Put the ice in a blender with the liquid ingredients. Blend until smooth. Pour, without straining, into chilled Collins glasses and dress with mint and wedges of pineapple.

338 GUMDROP MARTINI

This goes strangely well with gumdrops, hence the odd name.

SERVES 1

lemon wedge
icing sugar
2 measures lemon rum
1 measure vodka
¹/₂ measure Southern Comfort
¹/₂ measure lemon juice
¹/₂ tsp dry vermouth
ice

Rub the rim of a chilled cocktail glass with a wedge of lemon, then dip in a saucer of sugar to frost. Shake the liquid ingredients vigorously over ice until well frosted. Strain into the prepared glass.

339 GOLD COFFEE

Far richer than iced coffee, with cream and topped with sweet passion fruit.

SERVES 1

1 measure dark rum
1 measure curaçao
3 measures strong cold black coffee
ice cubes
1 scoop vanilla ice cream
2 tsp strained passion fruit sauce

Blend the first three ingredients in a blender with some ice cubes until slushy. Pour into a chilled glass, add the ice cream, and spoon over the passion fruit sauce.

340
MYSTERIOUS

Dark rum and coffee could hide many a mysterious combination. This combination is sweet and slightly orangey, perfect for after dinner.

SERVES 1

1 measure dark rum
1 measure orange curaçao
1/2 measure coffee liqueur
1/2 measure fresh orange juice
ice
1 tbsp double cream, to decorate

Shake the liquid ingredients over ice until well frosted. Strain into a chilled cocktail glass and top with cream.

341
GRETNA GREEN

Light and frothy and wonderfully iced, this is a great drink for a warm summer afternoon.

SERVES 1

1 measure light rum
1/2 measure crème de menthe
1 measure pineapple juice
1 measure coconut ice cream or sorbet
mint chocolate sticks, to decorate

Blend the first four ingredients in a blender for 10–20 seconds or until partly frozen. Pour into a chilled cocktail glass and dress with mint chocolate sticks.

342
SENSATIONS

This certainly has something for all the senses – huge taste, rich creamy texture and the zingy aroma of lime, and, of course, it should be ice cold.

SERVES 1

1 measure Sambuca
1 measure light rum
1 measure lime juice
1 measure cream
crushed ice
flower or petals, to decorate

Blend the first five ingredients slowly in a blender for about 10 seconds, until thick and slushy. Pour into a chilled glass and dress with a flower.

343
WEDDING BOWL

This stunning punch will get the guests guessing what is in it!

SERVES 24

1 kg/2.2 lb canned pineapple chunks
225 ml/8 fl oz pineapple juice
225 ml/8 fl oz lemon juice
2 measures sugar syrup
freshly grated nutmeg
1 bottle light rum
ice
1 kg/2.2 lb sliced strawberries
2–3 bottles soda water

Blend the first five ingredients with half the rum in a blender on slow speed until smooth. Chill for 24 hours or overnight. When ready to serve, pour into a punch bowl filled with ice and add the rest of the rum, the strawberries and the soda water. Serve immediately.

344
MANGO FREEZE

These can be made in advance and would be great served in carefully hollowed-out orange shells.

SERVES 4

6 measures golden rum
4 measures mango juice
4 measures fresh orange juice
1 measure sugar syrup
good squeeze lemon juice
1 egg white
ice
lemonade

Blend the first six ingredients together in a blender with ice until frothy and frozen. Pour into frozen glasses or containers and top up with lemonade to taste.

345
POLAR BEAR

Although you can use prepared passion fruit juice in this recipe, you only need a little, so hunt down the fresh fruit and enjoy the fun of these striking black seeds.

SERVES 1

2 measures light rum
2 measures advocaat
juice of 1 passion fruit, strained, seeds reserved to decorate
crushed ice
lemonade

Blend the rum, advocaat and most of the passion fruit juice with ice in a blender for about 10 seconds until thick and frothy. Pour into a glass filled with ice and top up with lemonade to taste. Finally, swirl the remaining passion fruit juice, with the reserved seeds, on top of the ice before serving.

346
CHOCOLATE ORANGE TODDY

Rich and soothing – just what you need to help ease away the stresses of the day.

SERVES 4

85 g/3 oz orange-flavoured plain chocolate, broken into squares
600 ml/1 pint milk
3 tbsp rum
2 tbsp double cream
cinnamon sticks, to serve

Place the chocolate in a small saucepan with the milk. Heat over a low heat until just boiling, stirring continuously. Remove from the heat and stir in the rum. Pour into heatproof cups and swirl the cream over the top. Serve with cinnamon sticks.

347
HAYDEN'S MILK FLOAT

An irresistible meld of perfect partners – rum, cherry, cream and chocolate – this cocktail is almost too good to be true.

SERVES 1

2 measures white rum
1 measure kirsch
1 measure white crème de cacao
1 measure single cream
cracked ice cubes
grated chocolate
cocktail cherry, to decorate

Shake the rum, kirsch, crème de cacao and cream vigorously over ice until well frosted. Strain into a chilled highball glass. Sprinkle with grated chocolate and dress with a cocktail cherry.

348
CHOCOLATE EGG NOG

The perfect pick-me-up on a cold winter's night, this delicious drink will get the taste buds tingling.

SERVES 8

8 egg yolks
200 g/7 oz sugar
1 litre/1³/4 pints milk
225 g/8 oz plain chocolate, grated
150 ml/5 fl oz dark rum

Beat the egg yolks with the sugar until thickened. Pour the milk into a large saucepan, add the grated chocolate and bring just to the boil. Remove from the heat and gradually beat in the egg yolk mixture. Stir in the rum and pour into heatproof glasses.

349
CHOCOLATE CREAM FIZZ

This is a seriously rich version of a fizz with ice cream added – it's certainly not for dieters!

SERVES 1

1 measure white rum
¹/2 measure chocolate mint liqueur
generous dash crème de menthe
dash lemon juice
scoop chocolate mint ice cream
soda water
flaked white chocolate, to decorate

Blend the first five ingredients in a blender on slow speed. Pour into an iced glass, top up with soda water to fizz and dress with flaked white chocolate.

350
TOM & JERRY

You really should have a Tom and Jerry mug to serve this in, but your favourite will probably do just as well.

SERVES 1

1 measure Jamaican rum
1 measure brandy
1 egg, lightly beaten into 90 ml/3 fl oz milk
sugar, to taste

Gently stir all the ingredients together while warming the milk through (do not heat too much or the egg will separate). Serve immediately in heatproof glasses.

351
RUM NOGGIN

Noggin is the old-fashioned word for a small mug and also for sharing a drink. What better way to send winter guests off into the night?

SERVES 8

6 eggs
4–5 tsp icing sugar
freshly grated nutmeg, plus extra for sprinkling
475 ml/16 fl oz dark rum
1.2 litres/2 pints milk, warmed

Blend the eggs in a punch bowl with the sugar and a little nutmeg. Whisk in the rum and gradually stir in the milk. Warm through gently and serve in small heatproof glasses, sprinkled with nutmeg.

352 THE REAL THING

This is one way to make your own cream liqueur at home. If you can find strong rum, bottle it and keep in the refrigerator.

SERVES 4
300 ml/10 fl oz sweetened condensed milk
150 ml/5 fl oz rum
3 eggs
1/2 tsp vanilla extract
few drops lime juice
crushed ice
Angostura bitters

Blend the first five ingredients in a blender until smooth and creamy. Serve poured over crushed ice with a few drops of Angostura bitters as a delicious after-dinner treat.

353 EYE-OPENER

Living up to its name, this cocktail has a serious kick and will make a worthwhile breakfast on certain occasions.

SERVES 1
1 measure rum
2 dashes crème de noyaux
2 dashes absinthe
2 dashes curaçao
1 egg yolk
1 tsp icing sugar
ice

Shake the first six ingredients well over ice and strain into a cocktail glass.

354 RUM TODDY

Be aware that warming alcohol always makes it seem that little bit stronger.

SERVES 1
1 measure rum or brandy
water and sugar, to taste
orange peel twist

Warm the rum with an equal quantity of water, and add sugar to taste. Add the peel and serve in a heatproof glass.

355 ORANGE RUM SHRUB

If you ever find yourself in possession of extra strong rum, this is the time to use it to good advantage. It will keep really well and makes a superb long drink.

SERVES 24
2 litres/3 1/2 pints fresh orange juice
225 g/8 oz sugar
6 litres/5 quarts dark rum
ice
soda water, to taste

Mix the first three ingredients together in a large jug. Store in bottles in a cool dark place for 6 weeks. To serve, strain into chilled long glasses filled with ice and top up with soda water to taste.

WHISKY

Whisky has taken on a new lease of life with the increasing popularity of whisky cocktails. For a dancing drink, try a Highland Fling to get those flavours really flying. Or if a genteel southern belle is more to your taste, try the Scarlett O'Hara, to put a rosy glow in those cheeks.

356
MANHATTAN

Said to have been invented by Sir Winston Churchill's American mother, Jennie, the Manhattan is one of many cocktails named after places in New York.

SERVES 1
dash Angostura bitters
3 measures rye whisky
1 measure sweet vermouth
cracked ice
cocktail cherry, to decorate

Shake the liquids over cracked ice and mix well. Strain into a chilled glass and decorate with a cherry.

358
WHISKY SOUR

Originating in the American South and using some of the best American whisky, this classic can also be made with vodka, gin or other spirits.

SERVES 1
1 measure lemon or lime juice
2 measures blended whisky
1 tsp icing sugar or sugar syrup
ice
lime or lemon slice and
   maraschino cherry, to
   decorate

Shake the lemon juice, whisky, and sugar well over ice and strain into a cocktail glass. Dress with a slice of lime and a cherry.

357
OLD FASHIONED

So ubiquitous is this cocktail that a small straight-sided tumbler is known as an old-fashioned glass. It is a perfect illustration of the saying, 'Sometimes the old ones are the best.'

SERVES 1
1 sugar cube
dash Angostura bitters
1 tsp water
2 measures bourbon
cracked ice
orange peel twist, to decorate

Place the sugar cube in a small chilled old-fashioned glass. Add the bitters and water. Mash with a spoon until the sugar has dissolved, then pour in the bourbon and stir. Add ice and dress with a twist of orange peel.

359
WHISKY SOUR WOBBLY SHOT

A new twist on a classic cocktail for a new generation of cocktail drinkers, but be careful to keep children away from the refrigerator.

SERVES 8
1 packet lemon jelly
125 ml/4 fl oz hot water
225 ml/8 fl oz bourbon

Place the jelly in a large heatproof measuring jug. Pour in the hot water and stir until the gelatin has dissolved. Leave to cool, then stir in the bourbon to make up to 475 ml/17 fl oz. Divide between eight shot glasses and chill until set.

360 MINT COOLER

Whisky and mint is a great after-dinner combination, but as a long drink with soda water it is delicious at almost any time of the day.

SERVES 1

2 measures whisky
ice
3 dashes crème de menthe
soda water, to taste

Pour the whisky over ice in a chilled tumbler and stir in the crème de menthe. Top up with soda water to taste.

361 GREEN DIMPLES

Originating from the days of Haig Dimple whisky and flavoured with another old favourite – the herb-based green Chartreuse.

SERVES 1

1/2 measure whisky
1/2 measure apple juice
good dash green Chartreuse
ice
soda water
mint sprig, to decorate

Stir the first three ingredients over ice and strain into an ice-filled highball glass. Top up with soda water and dress with a sprig of mint.

362 FROZEN MINT JULEP

Even cooler than the original Mint Julep.

SERVES 1

crushed ice
2 measures bourbon
1 measure lemon juice
1 measure sugar syrup
6 fresh mint leaves

Put crushed ice into a blender or food processor. Add the remaining ingredients and blend at low speed until slushy. Pour into a small chilled glass.

363 JOCOSE JULEP

More than a plain julep, this will really improve the mood.

SERVES 1

crushed ice
3 measures bourbon
1 measure green crème de menthe
1 1/2 measures lime juice
1 tsp sugar syrup
6 fresh mint leaves
sparkling water

Put some crushed ice into a blender. Pour the liquid ingredients over the ice. Add 5 mint leaves. Process until smooth. Fill a chilled tumbler with ice and pour in the cocktail. Top up with sparkling water and stir gently. Dress with a mint leaf.

364
MINT JULEP

A julep is simply a mixed drink sweetened with syrup. The Mint Julep is the traditional drink of the Kentucky Derby.

SERVES 1

leaves from 1 fresh mint
   sprig, plus an extra sprig,
   to decorate
1 tbsp sugar syrup
crushed ice
3 measures bourbon

Put the mint leaves and sugar syrup into a small chilled glass and mash with a teaspoon. Add ice and stir before adding the bourbon. Dress with a sprig of mint.

366
ON THE FENCE

It's the Angostura bitters that are sitting on the fence here – on the top waiting for that final mix when you take the first sip.

SERVES 1

1 measure whisky
ice
cider
2 dashes Angostura bitters

Stir the whisky with ice in a tall glass. Top up with cider to taste and finish with a few dashes of Angostura bitters.

365
BRUNO

Whisky and vermouth are a popular mix, but the addition of the banana liqueur adds a very unusual and exciting touch.

SERVES 1

1 measure whisky
1/2 measure red vermouth
1/2 measure crème de banane
ice
ginger ale
banana slices, to decorate

Stir the first three ingredients together and pour into a tumbler full of ice. Top up with ginger ale and dress with a few slices of banana.

367
BROOKLYN

This mix gives an unusually bitter-sweet cocktail when finished off with the more unusual Amer Picon bitters.

SERVES 1

1 measure rye whisky
1/2 measure sweet vermouth
dash maraschino
dash Amer Picon or
   Angostura bitters
ice
cocktail cherry, to decorate

Stir the liquid ingredients in a mixing glass with ice to chill, then strain into a chilled cocktail glass. Add a cocktail cherry to finish.

368
FRENCH KISS

A luscious lipstick-red marriage of Kentucky bourbon with apricot and pomegranate.

SERVES 1

2 measures bourbon
1 measure apricot liqueur
2 tsp grenadine
1 tsp lemon juice
ice

Shake the liquid ingredients vigorously over ice until well frosted. Strain into a chilled cocktail glass.

370
OUT OF THE GLEN

Raspberries have a dominant fresh tang and mix well with stronger spirits.

SERVES 1

1/2 measure Scotch whisky
1/3 measure brandy
juice of 1/2 lemon
2 dashes sugar syrup
4 dashes raspberry syrup
1/2 egg white
ice
soda water, to taste

Shake the first six ingredients together over ice until well frosted. Strain into a highball glass filled with ice and top up with soda water to taste.

369
BLOOD &
SAND

Cherry brandy is a full-flavoured liqueur. You could use brandy instead, but do not expect as punchy a cocktail.

SERVES 1

1 measure Scotch whisky
1 measure cherry brandy
1 measure red vermouth
ice
orange juice

Shake the first three ingredients over ice until frosted. Strain into a medium-sized glass and top up with orange juice.

371
OH! HENRY!

Whisky lovers enjoy this variation when they want something a little sweeter and deeper.

SERVES 1

1 measure Benedictine
1 measure whisky
ice
ginger ale, to taste

Stir the Benedictine and whisky gently in a medium tumbler with ice. Top up with ginger ale to taste.

ELK'S OWN (see right-hand page for picture)

This would be the perfect accompaniment to some star-gazing under a clear night sky.

SERVES 1

2 measures rye whisky
1 measure ruby port
1/2 measure lemon juice
1 tsp sugar syrup
1 egg white
ice
star fruit slice, to decorate

Shake the first five ingredients vigorously over ice until well frosted. Strain into a chilled cocktail glass and dress with a slice of star fruit.

ISOBELLA

Quite a cocktail of spirits in one glass, so add soda water to mellow the flavours.

SERVES 1

1/2 measure whisky
1/4 measure brandy
1/4 measure red vermouth
1/8 measure Galliano
1/8 measure mandarin liqueur
ice
juice of 1 orange
chilled soda water
orange peel strip, to decorate

Shake the first five ingredients over ice until well frosted. Strain into a chilled cocktail glass. Dress with a strip of orange peel.

MAMMY

The peel of any citrus fruit has the most pungent and aromatic flavour, but use a zester or fine peeler so you leave the bitter white pith on the fruit.

SERVES 1

juice and zest of 1 lime
2 measures whisky
ice
ginger ale
lime peel strips, to decorate

Remove some long shreds of lime zest. Stir the lime juice and whisky over ice in a highball glass and top up with ginger ale. Dress with lime peel.

375 BLACK WATCH

An unusual version of whisky and soda that makes a great drink for any time of day or evening.

SERVES 1

2/3 measure Scotch whisky
1/3 measure Kahlúa or coffee
   liqueur
ice
soda water

Mix the whisky and Kahlúa with a few lumps of ice in a large tumbler. Top up with soda water to taste.

377 THE CHAMPION

Four great drinks blended in one has to produce a champion cocktail – try it for yourself and see!

SERVES 1

1/2 measure dry vermouth
1/2 measure Scotch whisky
1/4 measure Benedictine
1/4 measure white curaçao
ice
soda water

Shake the first four ingredients over ice until well frosted. Strain into a small tumbler filled with ice and top up with soda water.

376 THAI COCKTAIL SLING

A Thai-style version of a classic cocktail – a long drink with a strong kick of whisky.

SERVES 1

1 measure whisky
1/2 measure cherry brandy
1/2 measure orange-flavoured
   liqueur
1/2 measure lime juice
1 tsp jaggery
dash Angostura bitters
crushed ice
2 ice cubes
125 ml/4 fl oz pineapple juice
pineapple wedge, to decorate

Shake the first six ingredients well over ice until frosted. Place the ice cubes in a large glass. Pour the cocktail over and top up with the pineapple juice. Dress with a pineapple wedge.

378 MIAMI BEACH

A cool, dry, mouth-puckering combination – the perfect antidote to the sometimes hot and humid Miami weather.

SERVES 1

2 measures Scotch whisky
1 1/2 measures dry vermouth
2 measures pink grapefruit
   juice
ice
orange peel strip, to decorate

Shake the liquid ingredients vigorously over the ice until well frosted, then strain into a chilled cocktail glass. Dress with a strip of orange peel.

379
LIME SWIZZLE

Lime juice and zest are both sharp and very aromatic, so don't allow them to overpower the soft sweetness of the Drambuie.

SERVES 1

1 1/2 measures Drambuie
1/4 tsp finely grated zest of lime
1 tsp icing sugar
few drops lime juice
ice
soda water

Rub the rim of a large glass with Drambuie. Mix the lime zest and sugar and dip the glass rim in this. Stir all the ingredients, including the remaining sugar and zest, together in the glass. Top up with soda water.

380
MINT SUNRISE

A splash of cool enjoyment as the sun comes up after a night of partying.

SERVES 1

1 1/2 measures Scotch whisky
1/2 measure brandy
1/2 measure white curaçao
cracked ice
fresh mint sprig, to decorate

Pour the liquid ingredients over cracked ice in a chilled tumbler and stir gently. Dress with a fresh mint sprig.

381
SOUTHERN ORANGE

For a party, prepare lots of ice cubes with pieces of fruit in them to add a little glamour, and rim the glasses, too.

SERVES 12

6 measures Southern Comfort
6 measures gin
6 measures orange curaçao
6 measures orange juice
ice cubes
ginger ale

Mix the first four ingredients together well and chill until required. When ready to serve pour measures into chilled tumblers or glasses filled with ice cubes and top up with ginger ale.

382
THE APPLE TEASER

The flavour of apple comes through gently, giving a soft fruitiness to these liqueurs.

SERVES 1

1/3 measure whisky
1/3 measure amaretto
1/3 measure Calvados
dash grenadine
1 measure apple juice
ice
soda water
apple slice, to decorate

Shake the first five ingredients together over ice until well frosted. Strain into a highball glass filled with ice and top up with a little soda water. Dress with a slice of apple.

383 TRIXIE DIXIE

Because there is lots of fruit and fruit juice in this cocktail, you may not want to add much soda water, just ice well and offer soda water to taste.

SERVES 4

3 measures gin
6 measures Southern Comfort
3 measures lime juice
4 slices fresh pineapple
ice
soda water, to taste
pineapple slices, to decorate

Blend the first four ingredients in the blender on low speed until creamed and frothy. To serve, pour into ice-filled glasses and top up with the soda water to taste. Dress with slices of pineapple.

384 SAMBA

You could make this one short and strong if you prefer a good kick of whisky.

SERVES 1

1/2 measure Scotch whisky
1/4 measure golden rum
1/4 measure sweet red vermouth
1/8 measure apricot brandy
soda water, to taste
maraschino cherry, to decorate

Mix the first four ingredients in a large tumbler and top up with soda water to taste. Dress with a cherry.

385 KENTUCKY ORANGE BLOSSOM

Whisky and orange – unexpected, but simply delicious!

SERVES 1

2 measures bourbon
1 measure orange juice
1/2 measure triple sec
ice
orange slice, to decorate

Shake the liquid ingredients vigorously over ice until well frosted. Strain into a chilled cocktail glass and dress with a slice of orange.

386 WALLIS SIMPSON

Tall, cool and calculated to be a success at all the important parties of the social calendar.

SERVES 1

1 measure Southern Comfort
1 tsp icing sugar
dash Angostura bitters
chilled champagne

Pour the Southern Comfort into a chilled champagne flute, add the sugar and stir well until dissolved. Add a dash Angostura bitters and top up with chilled champagne.

387
ITALIAN STALLION

What you get when you mix Southern charm with Italian cool.

SERVES 1

ice
dash Angostura bitters
2 measures bourbon
1 measure Campari
1/2 measure sweet vermouth
lemon peel twist,
   to decorate

Put 4–6 ice cubes into a mixing glass. Add the bitters and pour in the bourbon, Campari and vermouth. Stir well to mix, then strain into a chilled cocktail glass and dress with a twist of lemon peel.

389
LOCH LOMOND

Sugar syrup was used long before we had mixers, such as ginger beer or tonic, so this may be where the idea stemmed from.

SERVES 1

1 1/2 measures Scotch whisky
1 measure sugar syrup
3 dashes Angostura bitters
ice

Shake the first three ingredients well over ice and strain into a cocktail glass.

388
AFFINITY

Some cocktails need to be stirred, not shaken. Use a large glass with space for lots of ice to cool the cocktail quickly. Then strain immediately to avoid diluting the flavours.

SERVES 1

1 measure Scotch whisky
1/2 measure dry vermouth
1/2 measure red vermouth
2 dashes Angostura bitters
few ice cubes

Pour the liquid ingredients, in the order in which they are listed, over ice in a mixing glass. Stir with a long-handled spoon. Strain into a chilled cocktail glass.

390
BEADLESTONE

A strange name for a straightforward cocktail that is perfect in its simplicity.

SERVES 1

cracked ice
2 measures Scotch whisky
1 1/2 measures dry vermouth

Put some cracked ice into a mixing glass and pour the whisky and vermouth over the ice. Stir well to mix and strain into a chilled cocktail glass.

391
FLYING SCOTSMAN

This sits low in the glass, so there's no danger of losing any when the bar sways with the motion of the train.

SERVES 1

crushed ice
dash Angostura bitters
2 measures Scotch whisky
1 measure sweet vermouth
1/4 tsp sugar syrup

Put some crushed ice into a blender, dash Angostura bitters over the ice, and add the whisky, vermouth and sugar syrup. Blend until slushy and pour into a small chilled tumbler.

392
THISTLE

Nobody knows how this got its name, as it's smooth and not at all prickly.

SERVES 1

cracked ice
dash Angostura bitters
2 measures Scotch whisky
1 1/2 measures sweet vermouth

Put some cracked ice into a mixing glass. Dash Angostura bitters over the ice and pour in the whisky and vermouth. Stir well to mix and strain into a chilled cocktail glass.

393
BARBICAN

For a really stunning effect prepare these ice cubes well in advance. Simply put the black seeds from the passion fruit in a little lemon water and freeze overnight in an ice tray.

SERVES 1

2 measures Scotch whisky
1/4 measure Drambuie
1/2 passion fruit, strained to separate the seeds from the juice
ice
passion fruit seeds frozen in an ice cube, to decorate

Shake the whisky, Drambuie and passion fruit juice over ice until well chilled. Strain into a chilled cocktail glass. Dress with a passion fruit ice cube.

394
HIGHLAND FLING

Blended whisky is best suited to cocktails – single malts should always be drunk neat or with a little added water. However, a throat-burning blend of whisky will make a mixture closer to rocket fuel than a cocktail and no amount of additions will help.

SERVES 1

cracked ice
dash Angostura bitters
2 measures Scotch whisky
1 measure sweet vermouth
cocktail olive, to decorate

Put cracked ice into a mixing glass. Dash Angostura bitters over the ice. Pour in the whisky and vermouth. Stir well to mix and strain into a chilled glass. Dress with a cocktail olive.

395
ROBBIE BURNS

This is named after Scotland's national poet, whose birthday is dutifully celebrated every 25 January.

SERVES 1

1/2 measure sweet vermouth
1/2 measure Scotch whisky
1/4 measure Benedictine
finely grated lemon zest

Shake the liquids together gently and pour into a small unchilled liqueur glass or tiny tumbler. Sprinkle with a little zest.

397
GODFATHER

Amaretto is an Italian liqueur, so perhaps the inspiration for this cocktail comes from Don Corleone, the protagonist in Mario Puzo's famous book.

SERVES 1

cracked ice
2 measures Scotch whisky
1 measure amaretto

Fill a chilled highball glass with cracked ice. Pour in the whisky and amaretto and stir to mix.

396
RUSTY NAIL

One of the great classic cocktails, so simple and very popular. It must be served on the rocks.

SERVES 1

cracked ice
1 measure Scotch whisky
1 measure Drambuie

Fill an old-fashioned glass half full with ice. Pour in the whisky and Drambuie and stir well.

398
THE ACROBAT

Dry cider is not often used in cocktails, which is a pity as it is a great way to add length with a little strength to a drink.

SERVES 1

2 measures whisky
1 measure Cointreau
1 measure lime juice
ice
dry cider
lime wedge, to decorate

Mix the first three ingredients over ice until frosted. Strain into an ice-filled long glass and top up with cider. Dress with a wedge of lime.

399 HIGHLAND COOLER

Whisky packed with other tastes – ginger, lemon and bitters – is a great long drink.

SERVES 1

1 tsp icing sugar
juice of $^1/_2$ lemon
2 dashes Angostura bitters
2 measures Scotch whisky
ice
ginger ale

Stir the first four ingredients together over ice in a chilled tumbler. Top up with ginger ale to taste.

401 NEW YORKER

New York's favourite whisky has seen the creation of many great cocktails – this is one of the quickest and best.

SERVES 1

2 measures Jack Daniels
$^1/_2$ measure fresh lime juice
$^1/_2$ measure grenadine
ice
orange peel twist, to decorate

Shake the first three ingredients over ice well until frosted. Pour into a chilled cocktail glass and dress with an orange peel twist.

400 WHISKY SLING

A serious sling – no soda water required to dilute the alcohol.

SERVES 1

1 tsp icing sugar
1 measure lemon juice
1 tsp water
2 measures American blended whiskey
ice
orange slice, to decorate

In a mixing glass, stir the sugar with the lemon juice and water until the sugar has dissolved. Pour in the whiskey and stir to mix. Half fill a small chilled tumbler with ice and strain the cocktail over it. Dress with a slice of orange.

402 ARTILLERY PUNCH

Ideal for a party's alcohol arsenal.

SERVES 15

1$^1/_3$ bottles bourbon
1$^1/_3$ bottles red wine
2 litres/3$^1/_2$ pints strong black tea
475 ml/16 fl oz dark rum
225 ml/8 fl oz gin
225 ml/8 fl oz apricot brandy
4 measures lemon juice
4 measures lime juice
4 tbsp sugar syrup
large block of ice
orange slices, to decorate

Pour the first nine ingredients into a large bowl. Refrigerate for 2 hours. To serve, place a large block of ice in a punch bowl. Pour the punch over the ice and dress with orange slices.

403
ALHAMBRA

Even the smallest amount of apricot brandy adds an aromatic fruity finish to this full-bodied cocktail.

SERVES 1

1/2 measure Scotch whisky
1/2 measure golden rum
1/4 measure sweet vermouth
1/8 measure apricot brandy
ice cubes
fresh cherry, to decorate

Mix the first four ingredients together in a mixing glass with ice. Strain into a medium-sized tumbler filled with ice and dress with a cherry.

404
TWIN PEAKS

Bourbon, named after a county in Kentucky, must be made from at least 51 per cent corn mash and is the country's most popular whisky. It forms the base of many more cocktails than its Scottish cousin.

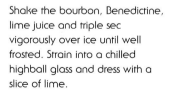

SERVES 1

2 measures bourbon
1 measure Benedictine
1 measure lime juice
dash triple sec
cracked ice
lime slice, to decorate

Shake the bourbon, Benedictine, lime juice and triple sec vigorously over ice until well frosted. Strain into a chilled highball glass and dress with a slice of lime.

405
WHITE WHISKY

Bourbon fans may think this is a waste of good bourbon, but try this mix first – the result is different and a winner.

SERVES 1

1 measure bourbon
2 dashes white crème de menthe
2 dashes white curaçao
1 dash Angostura bitters
1 dash sugar syrup
ice cubes
mint leaves, to decorate

Shake the liquid ingredients over ice until frosted and strain into a chilled cocktail glass. Dress with mint.

406
WHISKY COCKTAIL

If they'd been lucky enough to have these, the Confederate troops would have been fired up to railroad the Yankees.

SERVES 1

2 measures bourbon
1 measure Southern Comfort
1 measure orange juice
dash triple sec
ice
orange slice, to decorate

Shake the liquid ingredients vigorously over ice until well frosted. Strain into a chilled cocktail glass. Dress with a slice of orange.

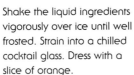

407 LONG GONE

This is one to mellow out with after the party guests have long gone.

SERVES 1

2 measures bourbon
1 measure Drambuie
1 measure orange juice
dash orange bitters
ice
orange slice, to decorate

Shake the liquid ingredients vigorously over ice until well frosted. Strain into a chilled cocktail glass. Dress with a slice of orange.

408 QUEEN OF MEMPHIS

Perhaps she got to Tennessee by way of Japan? Whatever the story, she added a treasure of the East to one of the South.

SERVES 1

2 measures bourbon
1 measure Midori
1 measure peach juice,
dash maraschino
ice
melon wedge, to decorate

Shake the liquid ingredients vigorously over ice until well frosted. Strain into a chilled cocktail glass and dress with a wedge of melon.

409 WILD WOMEN

Trashy already – or made that way by too many of these dangerous drinks?

SERVES 1

2 measures bourbon
1 measure Pernod
1 measure apple juice
dash Angostura bitters
ice
apple slice, to decorate

Shake the liquid ingredients vigorously over ice until well frosted. Strain into a chilled cocktail glass and dress with a slice of apple.

410 PERRY HIGHBALL

Pear drinks are softer and mellower in flavour than apple and even the bubbly perries are unlike cider, but great in this mix.

SERVES 1

2 measures whisky
ice
perry

Pour the whisky over ice in a highball glass and top up with perry.

411
BLACK SHRUB

Bourbon has its own distinctive flavour, which is warm, rich and oaky.

SERVES 1

½ measure bourbon
½ measure sloe gin
ice
fresh cherry, to decorate

Stir the liquid ingredients together with ice. Strain into a chilled cocktail glass and dress with a cherry.

412
WEDDING BELLS

How many marriage proposals have been encouraged by the consumption of a few of these?

SERVES 1

cracked ice
dash orange bitters
2 measures rye whisky
1 measure triple sec
2 measures Lillet
strip of orange peel,
   to decorate

Put some cracked ice into a mixing glass. Dash orange bitters over the ice and pour in the whisky, triple sec and Lillet. Stir well to mix, then strain into a chilled cocktail glass and dress with orange peel.

413
HIGHLAND RAIDER

This is a unique blend of three great Scottish drinks. Finish them off with a few fresh raspberries and you have a really great mix.

SERVES 1

1 measure Drambuie
1 measure whisky
1 measure Glayva
ice
soda water
raspberries, to decorate

Stir the first three ingredients over ice until well chilled. Strain into a tall glass or tumbler with more ice and top up with soda water to taste. Dress with raspberries.

414
WHISKY RICKEY

Following in the footsteps of its gin-based cousin, it substitutes whisky for gin, as the name suggests.

SERVES 1

2 measures whisky
1 measure lime juice
cracked ice
soda water
lime slice, to decorate

Pour the whisky and lime juice over the ice into a chilled highball glass. Top up with soda water. Stir gently to mix and dress with a slice of lime.

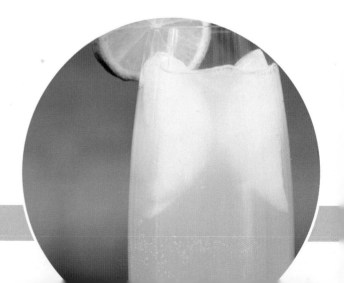

415
BLACKBERRY FREEZE

This cocktail should be really cold, and adding the frozen berries is a useful and attractive idea.

SERVES 1

1 measure bourbon
1 measure dry vermouth
1/4 measure lemon juice
1/4 measure blackberry liqueur
ice cubes
few frozen blackberries,
    to decorate

Shake all the liquid ingredients well together over ice until frosted. Strain into a cocktail glass and float in a few frozen blackberries.

416
DANDY

The fruit flavour added at the end is what gives this rich combination a special touch.

SERVES 1

1/2 measure rye whisky
1/2 measure Dubonnet
dash Angostura bitters
3 dashes cassis
ice
few frozen berries, to decorate

Mix the ingredients with ice and strain into an iced shot glass. Dress with berries.

417
MAPLE LEAF

One might expect a drink named for the national emblem of Canada to feature Canadian Club whisky, but it owes its title to the maple syrup used as an ingredient.

SERVES 1

2 measures bourbon
1 measure lemon juice
1 tsp maple syrup
crushed ice

Shake the liquid ingredients together over ice until well frosted. Strain into a cocktail glass.

418
OLD PAL

This bitter-sweet yet mellow concoction will make everyone an old pal.

SERVES 1

2 measures rye whisky
ice
1 1/2 measures Campari
1 measure sweet vermouth

Pour the whisky over ice in a shaker with the Campari and vermouth. Shake vigorously until well frosted, then strain into a chilled cocktail glass.

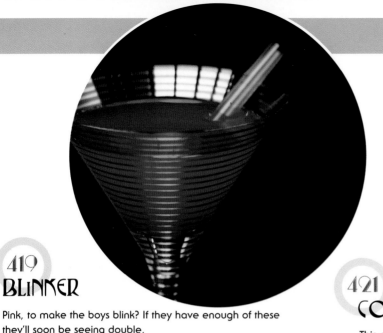

419
BLINKER

Pink, to make the boys blink? If they have enough of these they'll soon be seeing double.

SERVES 1

2 measures rye whisky
2¹/₂ measures grapefruit juice
1 tsp grenadine
ice

Shake the liquid ingredients vigorously over ice until well frosted. Strain into a chilled cocktail glass.

421
COMMODORE

This classic cocktail is short and sharp, with a good strong kick that will be sure to wake you up.

SERVES 1

4 measures rye whisky
1 measure fresh lime juice
2 dashes orange bitters
sugar, to taste
ice
lime peel strip, to decorate

Shake the first four ingredients together over ice until well frosted. Strain into a small tumbler or cocktail glass and dress with a strip of lime peel.

420
SAZERAC

Regarded by many people of New Orleans as the best cocktail in the world! Make it with cognac instead of rye for a truly spectacular drink.

SERVES 1

ice cubes
1 tsp sugar syrup or granulated sugar
3 dashes Angostura bitters
2 measures rye whisky
¹/₂ tsp anise
lemon peel strip

Fill a tumbler or cocktail glass with ice cubes to chill well. Mix the sugar syrup, bitters and whisky until well blended. Empty the ice out of the glass, swirl the anise around the inside of the glass to coat lightly, and drain off any excess. Pour in the whisky mix. Rub the strip of lemon peel along the rim, then add to the glass.

422
THE ALGONQUIN

Style and sophistication are the key to this drink from the famous Algonquin Hotel in New York.

SERVES 1

¹/₂ measure rye whisky
¹/₂ measure dry vermouth
¹/₄ measure pineapple juice
ice cubes

Shake the liquid ingredients over ice until frosted. Strain into an ice-filled old-fashioned glass.

423
KLONDIKE COOLER

Designed for cooling down with when Gold Fever had finally run its course.

SERVES 1

1/2 tsp icing sugar
1 measure ginger ale
2 measures blended whisky
cracked ice
sparkling water
lemon peel twist, to decorate

Put the sugar into a tall chilled tumbler and add the ginger ale. Stir until the sugar has dissolved, then fill the glass with cracked ice. Pour the whisky over the ice and top up with sparkling water. Stir gently to mix and dress with a twist of lemon peel.

424
OK CORRAL

This is probably what the folks down at the OK Corral would have put their fists around if they could have got hold of the ingredients.

SERVES 1

2 measures rye whisky
1 measure grapefruit juice
1 tsp orgeat
ice

Pour the liquid ingredients over ice and shake vigorously until well frosted. Strain into a chilled cocktail glass.

425
COWBOY

In movies, cowboys drink their rye straight, often pulling the cork out of the bottle with their teeth. It is certainly difficult to imagine John Wayne or Clint Eastwood sipping delicately from a chilled cocktail glass.

SERVES 1

3 measures rye whisky
2 tbsp single cream
cracked ice

Pour the whisky and cream over ice and shake vigorously until well frosted. Strain into a chilled glass.

426
BACCARAT

Cocktails have always been enjoyed at casinos and go hand in hand with the atmosphere of risk and gambling!

SERVES 1

1 measure Jack Daniels
1/2 measure Dubonnet
2 dashes cassis
ice

Shake the liquid ingredients vigorously over ice until frosted. Strain into a chilled cocktail glass.

427
VIEUX CARRÉ

Originating in the old town of New Orleans, this is a mean cocktail for serious occasions.

SERVES 1

1 measure rye whisky
1 measure cognac
1 measure sweet vermouth or martini
4 dashes Angostura or Peychauds bitters
1 tsp Benedictine
ice

Mix the liquid ingredients in a cocktail shaker or tall glass. Pour into a small ice-filled tumbler or cocktail glass.

429
IRISH EYES

Not all Irish eyes are green, but this will certainly cause them to smile, whatever their colour.

SERVES 1

cracked ice
2 measures Irish whiskey
1/2 measure green Chartreuse

Put some cracked ice into a mixing glass. Pour the whiskey and Chartreuse over the ice. Stir well. Strain into a chilled glass.

428
COLLEEN

One that is definitely for the girls!

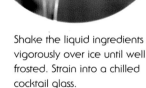

SERVES 1

2 measures Irish whiskey
1 measure Irish Mist
1 measure triple sec
1 tsp lemon juice
ice

Shake the liquid ingredients vigorously over ice until well frosted. Strain into a chilled cocktail glass.

430
SHILLELAGH

Not to be attempted with anything except Irish whiskey.

SERVES 1

2 measures Irish whiskey
1 measure dry sherry
1 tsp golden rum
1 tsp lemon juice
pinch of icing sugar
ice
cocktail cherry, to decorate

Shake the first five ingredients vigorously over ice until well frosted. Strain into a chilled cocktail glass and dress with a cherry.

431
IRISH SHILLELAGH

A shillelagh is a wooden cudgel, traditionally made from blackthorn. Undoubtedly, this is a cocktail that hits the spot.

SERVES 1

crushed ice
2 measures Irish whiskey
1 measure lemon juice
1/2 measure sloe gin
1/2 measure white rum
1/2 tsp sugar syrup
1/2 peach, peeled, stoned and finely chopped
2 raspberries, to decorate

Put the crushed ice into a blender and add the whiskey, lemon juice, sloe gin, rum, sugar syrup and peach. Blend until smooth. Pour into a small chilled glass and dress with raspberries.

432
SHAMROCK

Whether or not St. Patrick was the inventor of Irish whiskey, this drink is a favourite on his feast day, 17th March.

SERVES 1

1 measure Irish whiskey
1 measure dry vermouth
3 dashes green Chartreuse
3 dashes crème de menthe
cracked ice

Stir all the ingredients together in a mixing glass until well frosted. Strain into a chilled cocktail glass.

433
ASHLEY WILKES

A fine upstanding Southern cocktail, just like the man of Scarlett O'Hara's dreams.

SERVES 1

3 fresh mint sprigs, plus extra to decorate
1 tsp sugar
dash lime juice
cracked ice
2 measures bourbon
1 measure peach brandy

Crush the mint and place in a chilled tumbler. Add the sugar, lime juice and some cracked ice. Pour in the bourbon and peach brandy and stir to mix. Dress with a fresh sprig of mint.

434
RHETT BUTLER

When Margaret Mitchell wrote her civil war epic, *Gone With the Wind,* she created an enduring romantic hero in Rhett Butler. His debonair charm and devil-may-care attitude were brought to life by the heart-throb film star Clark Gable.

SERVES 1

2 measures Southern Comfort
1/2 measure clear curaçao
1/2 measure lime juice
1 tsp lemon juice
cracked ice
lemon peel twist, to decorate

Shake the Southern Comfort, curaçao, lime juice and lemon juice vigorously over ice until well frosted. Strain into a chilled cocktail glass and dress with a twist of lemon peel.

435
SCARLETT O'HARA

Appropriately a rich red colour with the warm undertones of Southern Comfort.

SERVES 1

cranberry ice cubes
2 measures Southern Comfort
2 measures cranberry juice
1 measure lime juice
ice

Prepare a few ice cubes with cranberries frozen in them. Shake the next three ingredients well over ice, then strain into a chilled cocktail glass. Finish with a cranberry ice cube.

437
BOSTON SOUR

Another, slightly frothier variation on the original theme.

SERVES 1

1 measure lemon or lime juice
2 measures blended whisky
1 tsp sugar syrup
1 egg white
ice
lemon slice and cocktail cherry, to decorate

Shake the ingredients over ice and strain into a cocktail glass. Dress with a lemon slice and a cocktail cherry.

436
BOURBON SOUR

This variation on the Whisky Sour substitutes bourbon for the blended whisky.

SERVES 1

1 measure lemon juice
2 measures bourbon
1 tsp sugar syrup
ice
lemon slice, to decorate

Shake the lemon juice, bourbon and sugar syrup well over ice and strain into a cocktail glass. Dress with a lemon slice.

438
19TH GREEN

Whiskey with a kick, perfect for cold wet days and ideal for carrying undiluted in a hip flask to help you keep your head down!

SERVES 1

1 1/2 measures Irish whiskey
1 measure green curaçao
ice
dry ginger ale

Stir the whiskey and curaçao in a tumbler with the ice. Top up with some ginger ale.

439 MOUNT ETNA

Not surprisingly, this is a fairly explosive cocktail. It may not work first time but if it does, handle with care!

SERVES 1

2 measures whisky
2 measures pure orange juice
shell of 1/2 lime, squeezed empty
1 1/2 measures Cointreau

Mix the whisky and orange juice in a heatproof glass. Soak the lime shell in the Cointreau in a small saucepan for about 10 minutes. Warm the Cointreau carefully over a low heat. Hold the lime shell in a large spoon, fill it with Cointreau, and ignite carefully. Lower immediately into the glass. Allow the flames to finish and the glass to cool before drinking.

441 WHISKY CRUSTA

Tumblers and old-fashioned glasses are not often crusted but it works well with a short strong drink in a spacious glass.

SERVES 1

1/2 tsp icing sugar
1/2 measure lemon juice
1 measure whisky
1 tsp sugar syrup
1 tsp maraschino
dash orange bitters
orange slice, to decorate

Rub the rim of an old-fashioned glass with some of the lemon juice and then dip in sugar. Stir the liquid ingredients over ice and strain into the crusted glass. Dress with a slice of orange.

440 TARTAN BREEZE

This will put some fire in your sporran, ready for real Scottish Highland ice and winds.

SERVES 1

1 1/2 measures Scotch whisky
1/2 measure apricot brandy
1 measure orange juice
dash Angostura bitters
ice cubes

Shake the liquid ingredients well together over ice. Strain into a large cocktail glass with more ice.

442 MILLIONAIRE COCKTAIL

This cool one won't cost a million, but it could make you feel like a millionaire!

SERVES 1

2/3 measure bourbon
1/3 measure Cointreau
2 dashes grenadine
1 egg white
ice

Shake the first four ingredients over ice and strain into a cocktail glass.

443
MILLIONAIRE MIX

Not reserved for those wealthy enough to belong to the millionaire's club, this is luxurious enough for the wannabees.

SERVES 1

1 measure rye whisky
1/2 measure grenadine
1/2 measure curaçao
1/2 egg white
ice
dash Pernod

Shake the first four ingredients well over ice. Strain into a small wine glass and add a dash Pernod at the last minute.

444
TNT

Deceptively short and simple, this could prove to be an explosive combination!

SERVES 1

cracked ice
1 measure Pernod
I measure rye whisky

Put some cracked ice into a mixing glass. Pour the Pernod and whisky over the ice and stir well to mix. Strain into a chilled cocktail glass.

445
WHISKY SANGAREE

A touch of rich red port trickles through this cocktail.

SERVES 1

cracked ice
2 measures bourbon
1 tsp sugar syrup
soda water
1 tbsp ruby port
freshly grated nutmeg,
  to decorate

Put cracked ice into a chilled tumbler. Pour over the bourbon and sugar syrup and top up with soda water. Stir gently to mix, then float the port on top. Sprinkle with freshly grated nutmeg.

446
SCOTCH SANGAREE

Not really a true sangaree, but one that can be made with ingredients that are readily available in Scotland.

SERVES 1

1 tsp clear honey
sparkling water
cracked ice
2 measures Scotch whisky
twist of lemon and freshly
  grated nutmeg, to decorate

Put the honey in a chilled tumbler with a little sparkling water. Stir until dissolved. Add some ice and the whisky and top up with sparkling water. Stir gently, then dress with a lemon twist and sprinkle with freshly grated nutmeg.

447

MQS (Mary Queen of Scots; see right-hand page for picture)

If they'd had cocktails in the sixteenth century, this one would have been fit for a queen.

SERVES 1

lemon wedge
icing sugar
cracked ice
2 measures Scotch whisky
1 measure Drambuie
1 measure green Chartreuse

Rub the rim of a chilled cocktail glass with the lemon, then dip in sugar to frost. Put some cracked ice into a mixing glass. Pour the whisky, Drambuie and Chartreuse over the ice and stir to mix. Strain into the prepared glass.

448

BOURBON COBBLER

Really smooth, as only a cocktail made with Southern Comfort can be.

SERVES 1

1 tsp icing sugar
dash lemon juice
2 measures bourbon
1 measure Southern Comfort
soda water
cracked ice
peach slice, to decorate

Put the sugar into a tall, chilled glass and dash lemon juice over it. Add some cracked ice and pour in the bourbon and Southern Comfort. Top up with soda water and stir to mix. Dress with a slice of peach.

449

SHERRY NIGHTS

Sherry is not often used in cocktails – perhaps there was never any to spare. Now, however, it is drunk less often neat and more often mixed in intriguing combinations, such as this one.

SERVES 1

1 dash egg white or fruit juice
icing sugar
1 tsp finely grated orange zest
1 measure medium sherry
1/2 measure whisky
1 measure orange juice
2 dashes orange curaçao
ice cubes

Dip the rim of a medium-sized cocktail glass into a little beaten egg white, then into a mixture of sugar and orange zest. Set aside until dry. Blend the remaining ingredients together in a blender for 10 seconds. Pour into the prepared cocktail glass with more ice.

450
PINK ALMOND

This warm and fuzzy cocktail is perfect after a hard day.

SERVES 1

2 measures blended American whiskey
1 measure amaretto
1/2 measure crème de noyaux
1/2 measure cherry brandy
1 measure lemon juice
ice
lemon slice, to decorate

Shake the whiskey, amaretto, crème de noyaux, cherry brandy and lemon juice vigorously over ice until well frosted. Strain into a chilled goblet and dress with a slice of lemon.

452
PRINCE CHARMING

The perfect drink after a cold, windy day in the countryside.

SERVES 1

1/2 measure Drambuie
1/2 measure cognac
1/2 measure fresh lemon juice
ice

Stir the liquid ingredients together over ice until really cold. Strain into an iced cocktail glass.

451
SPARKLING DIAMOND

This is a crazy combination of liqueurs, but it works surprisingly well once you've added the lemon. Extra crushed ice at the last minute brings out all the separate flavours.

SERVES 1

1/4 measure peppermint schnapps
1/4 measure white crème de cacao
1/4 measure Southern Comfort
1/4 measure lemon juice
crushed ice

Shake all the liquid ingredients over ice until frosted. Strain into a chilled shot glass and add a small spoonful of crushed ice.

453
COCONUT BREEZE

This cocktail uses clear or white coconut liqueur, but if you can't find it, a creamy coconut liqueur will make a good replacement.

SERVES 1

1 measure coconut liqueur
1/2 measure Drambuie
2 measures pawpaw juice
few ice cubes
lime slice, to decorate

Shake the liquid ingredients well over ice until well frosted. Pour into a chilled cocktail glass and dress with a slice of lime.

454 HALLEY'S COMFORT

Here's one to send you straight into orbit!

SERVES 1
cracked ice
2 measures Southern Comfort
2 measures peach schnapps
sparkling water
lemon slice, to decorate

Half fill a tall chilled tumbler with cracked ice. Pour the Southern Comfort and peach schnapps over the ice and top up with sparkling water. Stir gently and dress with a slice of lemon.

456 PEACH COMFORT

You could use nectarine or even apricot instead of peach.

SERVES 1
2 measures bourbon
1 measure Southern Comfort
2 measures peach juice
juice 1/2 lemon
2 dashes dry vermouth
1/2 small ripe peach, peeled, plus 1 slice to decorate
crushed ice

Blend together all the ingredients in a blender until smooth. Strain into an ice-filled highball glass and dress with a slice of peach.

455 SOUTHERN PEACH

This really is peachy – smooth and deliciously creamy, too. What's not to like?

SERVES 1
1 measure Southern Comfort
1 measure peach brandy
1 measure single cream
dash Angostura bitters
cracked ice
peach slice, to decorate

Shake the Southern Comfort, peach brandy and cream with a dash Angostura bitters vigorously over cracked ice until well frosted. Strain the mixture into a chilled cocktail glass. Dress with a slice of peach.

457 STRAWBERRY KISS

Whisky and strawberries make a great partnership, well worth remembering next time you need to add a lift to your bowl of berries.

SERVES 1
1 measure Jack Daniels
1 measure strawberry syrup
3 strawberries
crushed ice
single cream

Blend the first four ingredients in a blender on low speed for about 10 seconds. Pour into a chilled fluted glass and gently float the cream on top.

458
BOURBON FOG

If you like iced coffee, you will love this drink. Serve it at a summer party or barbecue and have everything ready in advance to add the ice cream at the last minute.

SERVES 10

1 litre/1³/4 pints strong black coffee, ice cold
1 litre/1³/4 pints vanilla ice cream
1 litre/1³/4 pints bourbon

Gently blend all the ingredients together in a large punch bowl. When smooth and frothy, serve in little mugs or small chilled glasses.

459
AFTER NINE

There is certainly no need to serve chocolate after dinner to anyone who is enjoying this rich cocktail.

SERVES 1

1 measure whisky
1 measure mint chocolate liqueur
1 measure cream
ice
grated chocolate, for sprinkling

Stir or whisk all the liquid ingredients together briefly with a little ice. Strain into a cocktail glass and sprinkle with grated chocolate.

460
A SCOTCH COCKTAIL

Just the drink to warm a lady's heart, especially after being outdoors on a cold winter's day.

SERVES 1

2 measures Scotch whisky
1 measure cream
1 measure honey

Mix all the ingredients well in a warmed glass and leave to cool. Add a spoon to mix.

461
HAIR OF THE DOG

This well-known expression – a tot of whatever gave you the hangover – is in fact a popular Scottish 'morning after' tipple!

SERVES 1

1 measure Scotch whisky
1¹/2 measures single cream
¹/2 measure clear honey
ice

Gently mix the whisky, cream and honey together. Pour into a cocktail glass over ice and serve.

462
BOILER-MAKER

Originally, boilermaker was American slang for a shot of whisky, followed by a beer chaser. This version is marginally more sophisticated, but every bit as lethal.

SERVES 1

1 cup pale ale
1 1/2 measures bourbon or rye whisky

Pour the beer into a chilled beer glass or tankard. Pour the bourbon into a chilled shot glass. Gently submerge the shot glass into the beer.

464
SCOTTISH NIGHTCAP

You should certainly sleep well after a glass or two of this surprisingly good concoction.

SERVES 1

1 1/4 cups pale ale
1 tsp cocoa powder
4 tbsp Scotch whisky
2 small egg yolks
2 tsp sugar

Heat the ale with the cocoa and the whisky until almost boiling. Whisk the egg yolks with the sugar and then gradually whisk into the hot ale. Serve in heatproof glasses.

463
THE GREEN MAN

The colour is most unusual and doesn't look as though it might contain whisky, but it makes an excellent drink.

SERVES 1

1 measure Irish whiskey
1/2 measure blue curaçao
1 measure fresh lemon juice
dash egg white
ice cubes

Shake the first four ingredients with a little ice until well frosted. Pour into a medium-sized tumbler or glass and top up with more ice.

465
IRISH COW

Although pure and innocent looking, this cow has a kick!

SERVES 1

225 ml/8 fl oz milk
2 measures Irish whiskey
1 tsp icing sugar

Heat the milk in a small saucepan to just below boiling point. Remove from the heat and pour into a warmed punch glass. Pour in the whisky and sugar. Stir until the sugar has dissolved.

466
BOURBON MILK PUNCH
(see right-hand page for picture)

With so many healthy ingredients, this could almost be good for you – but watch out for that bourbon kick!

SERVES 1

2 measures bourbon
3 measures milk
1 tsp clear honey
dash vanilla extract
ice
freshly grated nutmeg,
    to decorate

Shake the bourbon, milk, honey and vanilla extract over ice until well frosted. Strain into a chilled tumbler and sprinkle with freshly grated nutmeg.

467
CHOCORANGE CHILLER

Rimming the glass with cocoa adds a dramatic touch.

SERVES 1

1/2 tsp cocoa powder
1/2 tsp icing sugar
3 measures Drambuie
juice of 1 orange
150 ml/5 fl oz sparkling water
few drops Angostura bitters
2–3 ice cubes
chocolate flakes, to decorate

Mix the cocoa and sugar together. Rub the rim of the glass with Drambuie, then dip into the cocoa mixture. Set aside until dry. Mix the orange juice, Drambuie and sparkling water. Put the ice and a few drops of bitters in the bottom of the glass, pour on the orange fizz and dress with chocolate flakes.

468
PINK HEATHER

The sparkling sophistication of this cocktail will transport you a million miles away from its Scottish highland origins.

SERVES 1

1 measure Scotch whisky
1 measure strawberry liqueur
chilled sparkling wine
fresh strawberry, to decorate

Pour the whisky and the strawberry liqueur into a chilled champagne flute. Top up with chilled sparkling wine. Dress with a strawberry.

TEQUILA

Tequila instantly conjures an image of fun, frolics and wild parties. If you want to spice up your cocktail repertoire, what could be more perfect than this Latino liquid? Why not try the fruity warmth of the famous Tequila Sunrise, or a classic Margarita, certain to be a hit with any cocktail crowd.

469
MARGARITA

This cocktail, invented in 1942 in Mexico, is a more civilized version of the original way to drink tequila – a lick of salt from the back of your hand, a suck of lime juice and a shot of tequila!

SERVES 1

lime wedge
coarse salt
cracked ice
3 measures white tequila
1 measure triple sec
2 measures lime juice
lime wedge, to decorate

Rub the rim of a chilled cocktail glass with the lime wedge and then dip in salt to frost. Put the ice cubes into a cocktail shaker. Pour over the liquid ingredients. Shake vigorously until a frost forms. Strain into the prepared glass and dress with a lime wedge.

470
TEQUILA
SLAMMER

Slammers are also known as shooters. The idea is that you pour the ingredients directly into the glass, without stirring. Cover the glass with one hand to prevent spillage, slam it onto a table to mix, and drink the cocktail down in one!

SERVES 1

1 measure chilled white tequila
1 measure lemon juice
chilled sparkling wine

Put the tequila and lemon juice into a chilled glass. Top up with sparkling wine. Cover the glass with your hand and slam.

471
TEQUILA
SUNRISE

This is one cocktail you shouldn't rush when making, otherwise you will spoil the attractive sunrise effect as the grenadine slowly spreads through the orange juice.

SERVES 1

2 parts silver tequila
cracked ice
orange juice
1 measure grenadine

Pour the tequila over ice in a chilled highball glass and top up with orange juice. Stir well to mix. Slowly pour in the grenadine.

472
HUATUSCO
WHAMMER

To be authentic, this cocktail should be filled up with that world-famous brand of cola, but you can use other brands if you prefer.

SERVES 1

1 measure white tequila
1/2 measure white rum
1/2 measure vodka
1/2 measure gin
1/2 measure triple sec
1 measure lemon juice
1/2 tsp sugar syrup
cracked ice
chilled cola

Shake the tequila, rum, vodka, gin, triple sec, lemon juice and sugar syrup vigorously over ice until well frosted. Fill a chilled Collins glass with cracked ice and strain the cocktail over them. Top up with cola and stir.

473
BLINDING SUNRISE

Have enough of these and you'll appreciate the true meaning of a blinding sunrise!

SERVES 1

1 measure white tequila
1 measure vodka
3 measures orange juice
1 tsp triple sec
cracked ice
1 measure grenadine
orange slices, to decorate

Shake the tequila, vodka, orange juice and triple sec vigorously over ice until well frosted. Half fill a tumbler with cracked ice and strain the cocktail over. Slowly pour the grenadine over and dress with orange slices.

474
BIRD OF PARADISO

Dressed artistically with wedges of orange, this really does look as exotic as a bird of paradise.

SERVES 1

1 1/2 measures white tequila
1/2 measure white crème de cacao
1/2 measure Galliano
1 measure orange juice
1/2 measure single cream
cracked ice
orange wedges, to decorate

Shake the liquid ingredients vigorously over cracked ice until well frosted. Strain into a chilled wine glass. Dress with orange wedges.

475
BUTTAFUOCO

The clear and tranquil appearance masks a fiery combination.

SERVES 1

2 measures white tequila
1/2 measure Galliano
1/2 measure cherry brandy
1/2 measure lemon juice
cracked ice
soda water
cocktail cherries, to decorate

Shake the tequila, Galliano, cherry brandy and lemon juice vigorously over ice until well frosted. Half fill a tumbler with cracked ice and strain the cocktail over it. Top up with soda water and dress with cocktail cherries.

476
CHANGUIRONGO

A simple cocktail with a surprisingly complicated name.

SERVES 1

cracked ice
2 measures white tequila
ginger ale
lime slice, to decorate

Half fill a tall chilled tumbler with cracked ice. Pour in the tequila and top up with ginger ale. Stir gently and dress with a lime slice.

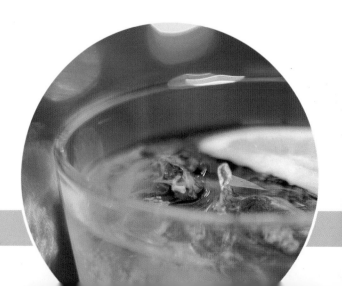

477
MAGNA CARTA

This should be added to the cocktail maker's charter as an example of the perfect cocktail.

SERVES 1

lime wedge
icing sugar
2 measures white tequila
1 measure triple sec
ice
chilled sparkling wine

Rub the rim of a wine glass with the lime, then dip in the sugar to frost. Stir the tequila and triple sec over ice in a mixing glass. Strain into the prepared glass and top up with sparkling wine.

478
TEQUILA FIZZ

Ginger ale provides the fabulous fizzy finish.

SERVES 1

3 measures white tequila
1 measure grenadine
1 measure lime juice
1 egg white
cracked ice
ginger ale

Shake the first four ingredients vigorously over ice until well frosted. Half fill a chilled tumbler with ice and strain the cocktail over. Top up with ginger ale.

479
ROYAL MATADOR

You won't even need a glass for this tropical-looking delight.

SERVES 2

1 pineapple, flesh removed and shell reserved
crushed ice
4 measures golden tequila
1¹/₂ measures framboise
2 measures lime juice
1 tbsp amaretto
star fruit slice, to decorate

Put the pineapple flesh in a blender and purée. Add the ice and the liquid ingredients. Blend until slushy, then pour into the pineapple shell. Dress with a star fruit slice.

480
MEXICOLA

Tequila goes surprisingly well with cola – you can make this as long a drink as you like.

SERVES 1

cracked ice
2 measures tequila
1 measure lime juice
cola
lime slice, to decorate

Half fill a tall chilled tumbler with cracked ice. Pour the tequila and the lime juice over the ice and top up with cola. Stir gently and dress with a lime slice.

461
ZIPPER

This shooter gets its name from an unusual, not to say louche, method of serving it, but tastes just as good served more conventionally.

SERVES 1
crushed ice
1 measure tequila
1/2 measure Grand Marnier
1/2 measure single cream

Put the crushed ice into a cocktail shaker and pour in the tequila, Grand Marnier and cream. Close the shaker and shake vigorously for 10–20 seconds, until the outside of the shaker is misted. Strain into a shot glass.

483
ROSITA

A rosy Italian twist for the Mexican tipple.

SERVES 1
ice
2 measures Campari
2 measures white tequila
1/2 measure dry vermouth
1/2 measure sweet vermouth
lime peel twist, to decorate

Put some ice into a mixing glass. Pour over the Campari, tequila, dry vermouth and sweet vermouth. Stir well to mix, then strain into a small chilled tumbler and dress with a twist of lime.

482
TEQUINI

A delicious tequila twist on the classic martini. Serve with a twist of lime instead of lemon, for the traditional tequila and lime pairing.

SERVES 1
3 measures white tequila
1/2 measure dry vermouth
cracked ice
dash Angostura bitters
lemon twist, to decorate

Pour the tequila and vermouth over cracked ice into a mixing glass. Add a dash Angostura bitters and stir well. Strain into a chilled cocktail glass and dress with a twist of lemon.

484
MARGARITA SHOT

Frosting the glasses with salt pays homage to the original non-jelly cocktail recipe of 1942.

SERVES 8
1/2 lime, cut into wedges
2 tbsp fine salt
1 packet lime jelly
1 cup hot water
4 tbsp Cointreau
225 ml/8 fl oz tequila

Rub the rims of eight shot glasses with lime, then dip in salt. Place the jelly in a large heatproof measuring jug. Add the hot water and stir until the jelly has dissolved. Leave to cool, then stir in the Cointreau and tequila to make up to 475 ml/16 fl oz. Divide between the prepared glasses and chill until set.

485

SHADY LADY (see right-hand page for picture)

This lady certainly puts the others in the shade!

SERVES 1

3 measures tequila
1 measure apple brandy
1 measure cranberry juice
dash lime juice
ice

Shake the liquid ingredients over ice until well frosted. Strain into a chilled cocktail glass.

486

COWGIRL'S PRAYER

One to linger over while she prays for a handsome cowboy to come along.

SERVES 1

2 measures golden tequila
1 measure lime juice
ice
lemonade
lime slices, to decorate

Pour the tequila and lime juice over ice into a tall tumbler and top up with lemonade. Stir gently and dress with slices of lime.

487

EL DIABLO

One or two Diablos and you will certainly feel a bit of a devil, but one or two too many and you will feel like the very devil!

SERVES 1

cracked ice
2–3 lime peel strips
1 measure lime juice
3 measures white tequila
1 measure cassis

Fill a small chilled glass with ice, add the lime peel, lime juice, tequila and cassis. Stir well.

488
JUAN COLLINS

Elegant and seductive, in a Mexican kind of way.

SERVES 1

cracked ice
2 measures white tequila
1 measure lemon juice
1 tsp sugar syrup
sparkling mineral water
orange wedges, to decorate

Half fill a chilled tumbler with cracked ice and pour in the tequila, lemon juice and sugar syrup. Top up with mineral water and stir gently. Dress with orange wedges.

490
SUBMARINO

The name of this cocktail comes from the highly unusual method of preparation.

SERVES 1

1 cup Mexican beer
2 measures white tequila

Pour the beer into a chilled beer glass or tankard. Pour the tequila into a chilled shot glass, then gently submerge the shot glass in the beer.

489
TEQUILA SHOT

According to custom, this is the only way to drink neat tequila.

SERVES 1

1 measure gold tequila
pinch salt
lime wedge

Pour the tequila into a shot glass. Put the salt at the base of your thumb, between your thumb and index finger. Hold the lime wedge in the same hand. Hold the shot in the other hand. Lick the salt, down the tequila and suck the lime.

491
JACK FROST

It looks dramatic and icy cold, but it tastes delicious and has enough kick to warm you up despite the cool blue colour.

SERVES 1

3/4 measure blue curaçao, iced
icing sugar
1 measure chilled tequila
2 measures chilled cream
1/2 cup crushed ice

Dip the rim of a medium-sized cocktail glass in the curaçao, shake off any excess and dip immediately in sugar. Set aside in a cold place to dry and set. Shake the rest of the curaçao and the tequila and cream over ice until well frosted. Pour carefully into the glass.

492
NAVAJO TRAIL

Probably a bit too refined a drink to indulge in while roughing it on the trail. Wait until you're safely back home.

SERVES 4
2 measures white tequila
1 measure triple sec
1 measure lime juice
1 measure cranberry juice
ice

Pour the liquid ingredients over ice and shake vigorously until well frosted. Strain into a chilled cocktail glass.

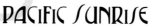

494
PACIFIC SUNRISE

It's the blue curaçao that gives this cocktail its stunning colour and the inspiration for its name.

SERVES 1
1 measure white tequila
1 measure blue curaçao
1 measure lime juice
dash bitters
ice

Shake the liquid ingredients vigorously over ice until well frosted. Strain into a chilled cocktail glass.

493
GINGER ALE FIZZ

The tart fruitiness of tequila is not often appreciated neat, but it is great with many of the sweetened and fuller-flavoured mixers.

SERVES 1
2 measures tequila
1/2 measure grenadine
5–6 measures dry ginger ale
crushed ice

Shake the tequila, grenadine and half the ginger ale over ice until slushy and frosted. Pour into a chilled tall glass and top up with ginger ale to taste.

495
TEQUILA MOCKINGBIRD

In spite of the horrible literary pun in the name, this popular cocktail is fast becoming a modern classic.

SERVES 1
2 measures white tequila
1 measure white crème de menthe
1 measure fresh lime juice
cracked ice

Shake the tequila, crème de menthe and lime juice vigorously over ice until well frosted. Strain into a chilled highball glass.

496
THE BLUES

This bright cocktail would be very sweet if it weren't for the lemon juice, so be careful with the balance of the ingredients the first time you make it.

SERVES 1

1½ measures tequila
½ measure maraschino
½ measure blue curaçao
½ measure lemon juice
ice cubes
bitter lemon

Shake the tequila, maraschino, curaçao and lemon juice well together over ice until frosted. Strain into a tumbler and top up with bitter lemon.

498
KICKING BULL

Don't dilute with too much ice until you have tried this very interesting mix.

SERVES 1

1 measure tequila
1 measure rye whisky
1 measure Kahlúa
ice

Stir all the ingredients briskly in a large tumbler full of ice.

497
WILD NIGHT OUT

Tequila has a reputation for being an extraordinarily potent spirit, but most commercially exported brands are the same strength as other spirits, such as gin or whisky. 'Home-grown' tequila or its close relative, mescal, may be another matter.

SERVES 1

3 measures white tequila
2 measures cranberry juice
1 measure lime juice
cracked ice
soda water

Shake the first three ingredients vigorously over ice until well frosted. Half fill a chilled highball glass with cracked ice and strain the cocktail over them. Add soda water to taste.

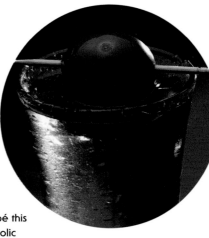

499
BOMB SQUAD

You could probably flambé this drink, but enjoy the alcoholic tomatoes first.

SERVES 1

1 measure tequila
1 measure whisky
1 measure vodka
few drops Tabasco sauce
ice
2 cherry tomatoes soaked in vodka, to decorate

Mix the first four ingredients together and pour into an iced shot or cocktail glass. Add an ice cube and dress with the vodka-soaked tomatoes on toothpicks.

500
TEQUILA STEELER

Rich creamy coconut helps to smooth this fiery combination, but don't be fooled by the soft baby pink colour!

SERVES 1

1 measure tequila
1/2 measure white rum
1/2 measure vodka
1/4 measure coconut cream
dash lime juice
few drops grenadine
ice
flower, to decorate

Shake the first six ingredients well together over ice. Pour into a chilled glass and dress with a flower.

501
BRAVE BULL

Spain's historical association with Mexico have left many legacies – not least a taste for bullfighting – although whether this cocktail is named in tribute to the bull or because it makes the drinker brave is anyone's guess.

SERVES 1

2 measures white tequila
1 measure Tia Maria
cracked ice
lemon peel twist, to decorate

Pour the tequila and Tia Maria over cracked ice in a mixing glass and stir well to mix. Strain into a chilled goblet and dress with lemon peel.

502
JARANA

Tequila has the reputation of being fiery, but it can be tempered and it is great mixed with pineapple.

SERVES 1

2 measures tequila
2 tsp sugar
ice
pineapple juice
lime wedge, to decorate

Mix the tequila and sugar over ice in a tall glass. Top up with pineapple juice and dress with a lime wedge.

503
MAD DOG

You will soon be in the doghouse if you have too many of these. You can make it longer with plenty of ice.

SERVES 1

1 measure white tequila
1 measure crème de banane
1 measure white crème de cacao
1/2 measure lime juice
cracked ice
lime and banana slices and a cocktail cherry, to decorate

Shake the first four ingredients vigorously over ice until well frosted. Strain into a chilled cocktail glass and dress with a lime slice, banana slice and a cocktail cherry.

504
TEQUILA COCKTAIL
(see right-hand page for picture)

What could be more straightforward than the original Tequila Cocktail, clear and simple?

SERVES 1

cracked ice
2 measures tequila
1 tbsp cranberry juice

Put cracked ice into a cocktail shaker with the liquid ingredients. Shake vigorously until well frosted, then strain into a chilled cocktail glass.

505
STRAWBERRY FAYRE

Poured over crushed ice, this becomes a delicious long cocktail, but you could top it up with soda water too.

SERVES 1

1 measure tequila
3 strawberries
1 tbsp cranberry juice
1/2 measure single cream
2 grinds pepper
crushed ice

Blend the first five ingredients in a blender for 10–15 seconds, until smooth. Pour into a long glass full of crushed ice.

506
CAROLINA

Some cocktails, such as this, require the mellow flavour of the golden, aged tequilas.

SERVES 1

3 measures golden tequila
1 tsp grenadine
1 tsp vanilla extract
1 measure single cream
cracked ice
1 egg white
cinnamon
cocktail cherry, to decorate

Pour the tequila, grenadine, vanilla extract and cream over ice in a shaker and add the egg white. Shake vigorously until frosted. Strain into a chilled cocktail glass. Sprinkle with cinnamon and dress with a cocktail cherry.

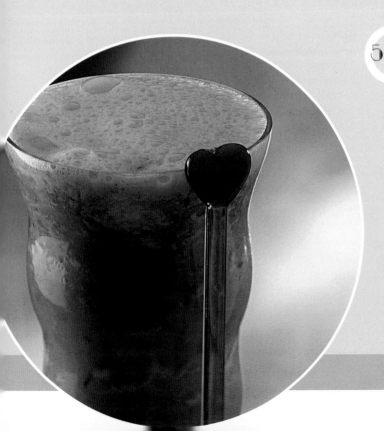

BRANDY

Warming, rich and indulgent, brandy adds a tantalizing texture to your cocktail creations. Try the Hungarian Coffee or a Coffee Time as a post-prandial treat. After a day at the office or out on the sports field you can treat yourself to a Hot Brandy Chocolate or a Nightcap Flip. There is a cocktail here for every occasion.

507
PINK LADY

Pretty in pink – they say! But this really is a truly great-tasting easy-drinking cocktail.

SERVES 1

1 measure brandy
1 measure Cointreau
1/2 measure lemon juice
dash grenadine
ice
mandarin peel, to decorate

Shake all the ingredients well over ice until frosted and strain into a chilled tall cocktail glass with a cube of ice. Dress with a piece of mandarin peel.

508
BRANDY SOUR

That classic of the American South, the Whisky Sour, lends itself to being made with other spirits, in this case, brandy.

SERVES 1

1 measure lemon or lime juice
2 1/2 measures brandy
1 tsp icing sugar or sugar syrup
ice
lime slice and maraschino cherry, to decorate

Shake the lemon juice, brandy and sugar well over ice and strain into a cocktail glass. Dress with a lime slice and a cherry.

509
SIDECAR

Cointreau is the best-known brand of the orange-flavoured liqueur, or you could use triple sec, which is drier and stronger than curaçao and is always colourless.

SERVES 1

cracked ice
2 measures brandy
1 measure triple sec
1 measure lemon juice
orange peel twist,
    to decorate

Put some cracked ice into a cocktail shaker. Pour the brandy, triple sec and lemon juice over ice and shake vigorously until a frost forms. Strain into a chilled glass and dress with a twist of orange peel.

510
SWEET SINGAPORE SLING

Try this for a delicate taste of Asian sweet and sour.

SERVES 1

1 measure gin
2 measures cherry brandy
dash lemon juice
cracked ice
soda water
cocktail cherry, to decorate

Shake the first three ingredients vigorously over ice until well frosted. Half fill a chilled tumbler with cracked ice and strain in the cocktail. Top up with soda water and decorate with a cherry.

511 MULE'S HIND LEG

This will soon have you talking the proverbial hind leg off the mule.

SERVES 1

2 measures brandy
1 measure triple sec
1 measure lemon juice
cracked ice
orange peel twist, to decorate

Shake the liquid ingredients vigorously over ice until well frosted. Pour into a chilled cocktail glass. Dress with a twist of orange peel.

513 BRANDY CUBAN

A cool touch of lime adds a touch of Havana to this cocktail.

SERVES 1

1 1/2 measures brandy
1/2 measure lime juice
ice
cola
lime wedge, to decorate

Pour the brandy and lime juice into a tumbler half filled with ice. Top up with cola and stir gently. Dress with a wedge of lime.

512 BRANDY JULEP

Still minty, but this time made with brandy.

SERVES 1

2 measures brandy
1 tsp sugar syrup
4 fresh mint leaves
cracked ice

Shake the brandy, sugar syrup and mint vigorously over ice until well frosted. Strain into a chilled cocktail glass.

514 CUBAN

You could make this more meaningful by having it in the company of a fine Cuban.

SERVES 1

2 measures brandy
1 measure apricot brandy
1 measure lime juice
1 tsp white rum
ice

Pour the liquid ingredients over ice and shake vigorously until well frosted. Strain into a chilled cocktail glass.

515 AMBROSIA

Truly a cocktail worthy of the gods – although first you have to find your gods!

SERVES 1

1¹/2 measures brandy
1¹/2 measures apple brandy
¹/2 tsp raspberry syrup
ice
chilled champagne
fresh raspberry, to decorate

Shake the brandy, apple brandy and raspberry syrup vigorously over ice until well frosted. Strain into a chilled wine glass. Top up with chilled champagne and dress with a raspberry.

516 HEAVENLY

With three different kinds of brandy and some delicious fruity flavours, this will take you heavenwards.

SERVES 1

cracked ice
1¹/2 measures brandy
¹/2 measure cherry brandy
¹/2 measure plum brandy
maraschino cherries,
   to decorate

Put the ice in a mixing glass. Pour the liquid ingredients over the ice and stir well to mix. Strain into a chilled cocktail glass and dress with cherries.

517 PARADISE

This fruity combination is truly heavenly, with just a hint of sharpness to prevent it from becoming sickly sweet.

SERVES 1

cracked ice
1 measure gin
¹/2 measure apricot brandy
¹/2 measure freshly squeezed
   orange juice
dash lemon juice

Put the ice in a cocktail shaker and pour in the gin, apricot brandy, orange juice and lemon juice. Close the shaker and shake vigorously for 10–20 seconds, until the outside of the shaker is misted. Strain into a tumbler.

518 CHERRY COLA

Don't be fooled by the innocent name – this is a respectably alcoholic cocktail.

SERVES 1

cracked ice
2 measures cherry brandy
1 measure lemon juice
cola
lemon slice, to decorate

Half fill a tall chilled tumbler with cracked ice. Pour the cherry brandy and lemon juice over the ice. Top up with cola, stir gently, and dress with a slice of lemon.

519
NAPOLEON

These two rich fruity liqueurs mix well and make a great long cocktail.

SERVES 1

1 measure Mandarine
   Napoléon
1 measure cherry brandy
ice
lemonade

Pour the liqueurs into a highball glass filled with ice. Stir gently and then gradually top up with lemonade.

521
STARS & STRIPES

You'll need a steady hand for this, otherwise your stripes will become zig-zags.

SERVES 1

$^{3}/_{4}$ measure chilled cherry
   brandy
$^{3}/_{4}$ measure chilled blue
   curaçao
$1^{1}/_{2}$ measures chilled light
   cream

Pour the cherry brandy into a chilled shot glass. With a steady hand, gently pour in the curaçao to make a second layer and, finally, gently pour in the cream.

520
LE TRIOMPHE

This is fruity and very refreshing, and you can make it longer still by adding soda water or crushed ice.

SERVES 1

1 measure cognac
$^{3}/_{4}$ measure Grand Marnier
$^{3}/_{4}$ measure pineapple juice
$^{1}/_{2}$ measure grapefruit juice
good splash grenadine
ice
fresh cherry, to decorate

Shake the first five ingredients together over ice. When well chilled and mixed, strain into a long glass, top up with ice, and dress with a cherry.

522
STAR-BANGLED SPANNER

It is probably fortunate that after getting your tongue around a couple, your hand will become too unsteady to pour more.

SERVES 1

$^{1}/_{2}$ measure chilled green
   Chartreuse
$^{1}/_{2}$ measure chilled triple sec
$^{1}/_{2}$ measure chilled cherry
   brandy
$^{1}/_{2}$ measure chilled yellow
   Chartreuse
$^{1}/_{2}$ measure chilled blue
   curaçao
$^{1}/_{2}$ measure chilled crème
   de violette
$^{1}/_{2}$ measure chilled brandy

Pour the green Chartreuse into a chilled flute, then, with a steady hand, gently pour in the triple sec to make a second layer. Add the cherry brandy to make a third, the yellow Chartreuse to make a fourth, the crème de violette to make a fifth and the curaçao to make a sixth. Float the brandy on top.

523
BELLADORA

If you love the kick of mint in your cocktails, add more to this one, varying it to taste for each drinker.

SERVES 1

3/4 measure cognac
3/4 measure Cointreau
3/4 measure grapefruit juice
ice
tonic water
2 tsp crème de menthe

Shake the first three ingredients together over ice until well frosted. Strain into a chilled tall glass and top up with tonic water. Pour in the crème de menthe at the end.

524
AZURE

The blue curaçao added at the end of mixing this cocktail certainly produces a stunning effect.

SERVES 1

1 1/4 measures cognac
3/4 measure Cointreau
3/4 measure lemon juice
ice
3 measures bitter lemon or
   to taste
1 tbsp blue curaçao
lime slice, to decorate

Shake the first three ingredients over ice until frosted. Strain into a chilled wine glass or large cocktail glass and mix in the bitter lemon. Carefully pour the curaçao down the side of the glass and leave to stand for 1–2 minutes to settle. Dress with a slice of lime.

525
WIDOW'S KISS

With a name like that it has to be daring – and it is – until you add the soda water!

SERVES 1

1/2 measure Benedictine
1/2 measure Chartreuse
1 measure Calvados
ice
soda water
Angostura bitters, to taste

Pour the liqueurs into a highball glass filled with ice. Stir once, top up with soda water, and add Angostura bitters to taste.

526
ANTOINETTE

For a light sparkling drink on any occasion, this is a lovely mix. Add more Calvados to taste and freshen it up with extra lemon or lime juice.

SERVES 1

1 1/2 measures Calvados
1/2 measure fresh lemon
   juice
1/2 measure syrup de
   gomme
ice
sparkling cider
strip of apple peel, to
   decorate

Shake the first three ingredients over ice until frosted. Strain into a highball or tall cocktail glass and top up with sparkling cider to taste. Dress with apple peel.

527
COUNTRY COUSIN COLLINS

The apple brandy brings a rustic charm to this drink.

SERVES 1
2 measures apple brandy
1 measure lemon juice
1/2 tsp sugar syrup
crushed ice
dash orange bitters
sparkling water
lemon slices, to decorate

Blend the apple brandy, lemon juice and sugar syrup with crushed ice and a dash orange bitters at a medium speed for 10 seconds. Pour into a chilled tumbler and top up with sparkling water. Stir gently and dress with slices of lemon.

528
RED RED ROSE

'A rose by any other name...' This pretty cocktail is truly a thing of beauty and a joy for ever.

SERVES 1
1 1/2 measures brandy
1 tsp grenadine
1/2 tsp Pernod
1/2 fresh peach, peeled and mashed
cracked ice
sparkling wine
slice of fresh peach, to decorate

Shake the brandy, grenadine, Pernod and peach vigorously over ice until frosted. Strain into a chilled wine goblet and top up with sparkling wine. Stir gently, then dress with a peach slice.

529
SANGAREE

Like Sangria, the name of this cocktail is derived from the Spanish word for blood, and it was originally made with wine.

SERVES 1
cracked ice
2 measures brandy
1 measure sugar syrup
soda water
1 tsp port
pinch of freshly grated nutmeg

Put some cracked ice into a chilled highball glass. Pour over the brandy and sugar syrup, then top up with soda water. Stir gently to mix. Float the port on top by pouring it gently over the back of a teaspoon and sprinkle with grated nutmeg.

530
ARCHIPELAGO

A colourful selection of flavours and fruits from many places is topped with a layer of cream, almost like fruit salad and cream in a bowl.

SERVES 1
cracked ice
1 1/4 measures cognac
3/4 measure kiwi juice or syrup
1/4 measure mandarin liqueur
1/4 measure chocolate liqueur
ice
1 tbsp single cream
slice of kiwi fruit, to decorate

Stir all the ingredients except the cream and fruit in a chilled mixing glass and strain into a cocktail glass. Carefully pour the cream in a layer over the top. Dress with a kiwi slice.

531
CHESHIRE CAT

Deliciously enigmatic, this will make you grin from ear to ear!

SERVES 1

1 measure brandy
1 measure sweet vermouth
1 measure orange juice
cracked ice
chilled champagne

Pour the brandy, vermouth and orange juice over cracked ice in a mixing glass. Stir well, then strain into a chilled flute and top up with chilled champagne.

532
NAPOLEON CHAMPAGNE

The silky-textured mandarin-flavoured liqueur was created in Belgium in honour of the creator of the famous put-down.

SERVES 1

1 measure Mandarine
  Napoléon
1 measure Campari
1 measure brandy
ice
chilled champagne

Pour the Mandarine Napoléon, Campari and brandy over ice and stir well. Strain into a chilled champagne flute and top up with chilled champagne.

533
SHERWOOD

Enjoy this rich fruit and cream cocktail after lunch or dinner, or even in place of dessert, as it is sweet.

SERVES 1

$1/2$ measure chilled Cointreau
$1/2$ measure chilled Benedictine
$3/4$ measure fraise de bois
ice
$3/4$ measure cream
strawberry slice, to decorate

Stir the Cointreau, Benedictine and fraise in a mixing glass with a little ice. Strain into an iced cocktail glass and float a layer of cream gently on the top. Dress with a slice of strawberry.

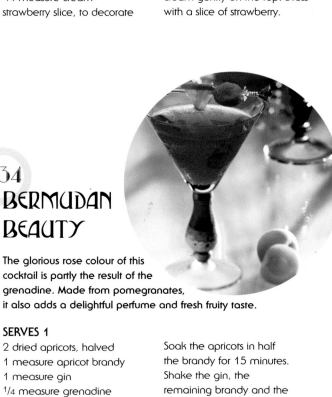

534
BERMUDAN BEAUTY

The glorious rose colour of this cocktail is partly the result of the grenadine. Made from pomegranates, it also adds a delightful perfume and fresh fruity taste.

SERVES 1

2 dried apricots, halved
1 measure apricot brandy
1 measure gin
$1/4$ measure grenadine
ice
soda water

Soak the apricots in half the brandy for 15 minutes. Shake the gin, the remaining brandy and the grenadine over ice until well frosted. Strain into a tall cocktail glass and top up with a little soda water. Add the apricots and the last few drops of brandy.

535
PINADORA

Try this lovely pineapple and melon blend when you want to get back into that holiday mood.

SERVES 1

1 measure brandy
1/3 measure Midori
1/3 measure white rum
1/5 measure crème de menthe
ice
chilled pineapple juice
chilled soda water
melon slice, to decorate

Shake the first four ingredients together well over ice. Strain into a highball glass, add the pineapple and top up with soda water to taste. Dress with a slice of melon.

536
SLEEPY AFTERNOON

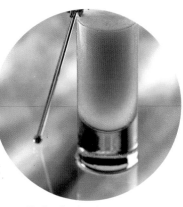

For lazy Sunday afternoons in the sun, try this long and very fruity drink.

SERVES 1

1 measure cognac
1/2 measure Benedictine
1/2 measure pineapple juice
1/4 measure lemon juice
ice
ginger ale
lemon peel, to decorate

Shake the first four ingredients well over ice. Strain into a long glass and top up with ginger ale. Dress with lemon peel.

537
SLEEPY HEAD

As its name implies, this is a lovely bedtime soother, so there is no need to ice it.

SERVES 1

2 measures brandy
orange peel strip
3–4 mint leaves
ginger ale

Stir the brandy, orange peel and mint together in a medium-sized tumbler. Top up with ginger ale to taste.

538
HORSE'S NECK

This refreshing drink can also be made with gin or with bourbon, adding a couple of dashes of Angostura bitters. The same name is also used for a brandy and champagne pick-me-up.

SERVES 1

lemon peel twist
ice cubes
1 measure brandy
dry ginger ale

Drop the lemon peel twist into a tall glass and anchor it with ice cubes. Pour in the brandy and top up with ginger ale.

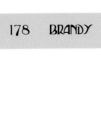

539

RIKKI-TIKKI-TAVI

A little bit of this, a little bit of that – it all adds up to a long cool drink.

SERVES 1

1 sugar cube
dash Angostura bitters
1 tsp brandy
1 tsp white curaçao
chilled champagne

Put the sugar cube into a chilled flute and dash the bitters over it until red but still intact. Pour in the brandy and curaçao and top up with chilled champagne.

541

POUSSE-CAFÉ

A pousse-café is a layered cocktail of many different coloured liqueurs. It is crucial to ice all the liqueurs first.

SERVES 1

¼ measure grenadine
¼ measure crème de menthe
¼ measure Galliano
¼ measure kümmel
¼ measure Benedictine

Ice all the liqueurs and a tall shot, elgin or pousse-café glass. Carefully pour the liqueurs over a spoon into the glass. Leave to stand for a few minutes to settle.

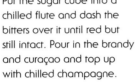

540

SUMMERTIME PUNCH

With a kick of Italian brandy and a few sprigs of basil, you will soon be transported to the Tuscan hills.

SERVES 2

90 ml/3 fl oz dry white wine
3 measures Tuaca or Italian
    brandy
squeeze of lemon, lime and
    orange juice
ice
citrus fruit slices
few basil sprigs
soda water

Shake the first three ingredients well over ice. Pour into a jug with the fruit and basil sprigs. Pour into glasses and top up with soda water.

542

APPLE BLOSSOM

It may not be the colour of apple blossom, but it tastes deliciously light and fresh.

SERVES 1

2 measures brandy
1½ measures apple juice
½ tsp lemon juice
ice
lemon slice, to decorate

Pour the brandy, apple juice and lemon juice over ice in a mixing glass and stir well. Half fill a small chilled tumbler with ice and strain the cocktail over it. Dress with a slice of lemon.

543
CHERRY KITSCH

This is a velvety smooth cocktail, fruity but with a rich brandy undertone. A touch of maraschino liqueur added at the end would be good too.

SERVES 1
1 measure cherry brandy
2 measures pineapple juice
1/2 measure kirsch
1 egg white
crushed ice
frozen maraschino cherry, to
    decorate

Shake the cherry brandy, pineapple juice, kirsch and egg white well over ice until frosted. Pour into a chilled tall thin glass and top with a frozen maraschino cherry.

544
GINGER & BRANDY MIX

Don't waste your best Calvados in this mix – apple brandy will be fine.

SERVES 1
2 measures apple brandy
2 measures port
juice of 1 orange
ginger ale
ice

Stir the first three ingredients in a chilled highball glass until frosted. Fill up with ginger ale and ice.

545
MRS. FITZHERBERT

Sweet and pretty, like its namesake, the elegant mistress of the Prince Regent.

SERVES 1
1 measure white port
1 measure cherry brandy
ice

Pour the port and cherry brandy over ice in a mixing glass. Stir to mix. Strain into a chilled cocktail glass.

546
GODDAUGHTER

An unusual one, with its mixture of apple, almond and cinnamon – more apple pie than cocktail!

SERVES 1
crushed ice
2 measures apple brandy
1 measure amaretto
1 tsp apple sauce
ground cinnamon,
    to decorate

Put some crushed ice into a blender and add the apple brandy, amaretto and apple sauce. Blend until smooth, then pour the mixture, without straining, into a chilled goblet. Sprinkle with ground cinnamon.

547
AMERICAN ROLLS-ROYCE

A seriously smooth all-American classic.

SERVES 1

2 measures brandy
2 measures orange juice
1 measure triple sec
ice

Shake the liquid ingredients over ice until well frosted. Strain into a chilled glass.

548
BRANDY OLD FASHIONED

The Old Fashioned is yet another old favourite that can be adapted to other spirits – in this case, brandy.

SERVES 1

1 sugar cube
dash Angostura bitters
1 tsp water
3 measures brandy
cracked ice
lemon peel twist, to
    decorate

Place the sugar cube in a small chilled old-fashioned glass and add the bitters and water. Mash with a spoon until the sugar has dissolved, then pour in the brandy and stir. Add ice and dress with a twist of lemon.

549
APPLE RUM RICKEY

With apple brandy and rum instead of gin, this has a fruity appeal.

SERVES 1

1 measure apple brandy
1/2 measure white rum
1/2 measure lime juice
cracked ice
sparkling water
lime slice, to decorate

Shake the apple brandy, rum and lime juice vigorously over ice until well frosted. Half fill a chilled tumbler with ice and strain the cocktail over it. Top up with sparkling water and dress with a lime slice.

550
THE DIGGER

This refreshing mix of citrus flavours has quite a kick, so add plenty of crushed ice.

SERVES 1

2 measures brandy
1 measure Van der Hum or
    orange liqueur
1 measure sugar syrup
3–4 grapefruit segments
crushed ice
long grapefruit peel twist,
    to decorate

Blend all the ingredients except the peel in a blender for 10–15 seconds. Pour into a medium-sized cocktail glass with extra ice. Dress with grapefruit peel.

551
DIAMOND BEAUTY

This sumptuous drink packs a punch, so beware of indulging in too many beauties – appreciate them slowly.

SERVES 1

1 measure brandy
1 measure dry vermouth
1 measure grenadine
1 measure orange juice
dash white crème de menthe
ice
2–3 dashes port

Shake the first five ingredients together over ice until well frosted. Strain into a chilled cocktail glass and gently add the port so that it floats on top.

552
EXOTIC MILLIONAIRE

This is full of subtle flavours, ranging from bitter almonds to orange flower water. A taste sensation!

SERVES 1

1 measure brandy
1/5 measure orgeat
1/5 measure orange curaçao
1/5 measure crème de noyaux
2 dashes Angostura bitters
ice
mint sprig, to decorate

Shake the liquid ingredients over ice. Strain into cocktail glass. Dress with a mint sprig.

553
FIRST NIGHT

A rich and warming concoction, ideal for calming the nerves before a first night – or to celebrate after the performance.

SERVES 1

2 measures brandy
1 measure Van der Hum
1 measure Tia Maria
1 tsp cream
ice
grated chocolate, to decorate

Shake the liquid ingredients together over ice. Strain into a chilled cocktail glass and dress with a little grated chocolate.

554
MILLIONAIRE

There are many versions of this cocktail, mainly dependent on the unusual contents of your cocktail cabinet.

SERVES 1

2/3 measure apricot brandy
2/3 measure sloe gin
2/3 measure Jamaican rum
dash grenadine
juice 1/2 lemon or lime
ice
blueberries, to decorate

Shake all the liquid ingredients well over ice and strain into an ice-filled cocktail glass. Add a few blueberries and serve.

555 ROLLER-COASTER

Perhaps not the cocktail to use your best vintage brandy in, as there are so many things added.

SERVES 1

2 dashes fresh lemon juice
icing sugar
orange peel twist
ice
1 measure brandy
1/2 measure dry orange curaçao
3 dashes maraschino
1 dash Angostura bitters

Rub the rim of the glass with lemon juice and then dip it into sugar. Leave to dry. Place the twist of orange peel in the bottom of the glass and top up with ice. Stir the next three ingredients in a small glass of ice and strain into the prepared glass. Dash with the bitters at the last moment.

556 SMOOTHING THE EDGES

It would probably be unwise to investigate the provenance of this oddly named cocktail – perhaps it is so called because it creates a pleasantly warm glow in the cockles of the heart.

SERVES 1

dash triple sec
cracked ice
1 measure brandy
1 measure Madeira

Dash triple sec over cracked ice in a mixing glass. Pour in the brandy and Madeira. Stir well to mix, then strain into a chilled cocktail glass.

557 ADAM'S APPLE

Applejack in the US, Calvados in France, and apple brandy as a generic term – whatever you call it, it provides a delicious fruit flavour and a tempting aroma to this cocktail.

SERVES 1

2 measures apple brandy
1 measure gin
1 measure dry vermouth
dash yellow Chartreuse
ice

Pour the liquid ingredients over ice in a mixing glass. Stir well and strain into a chilled glass.

558 CORPSE REVIVER

Not a morning-after reviver, more an end-of-a-hectic-day pick-me-up and one to get you in the mood for a party!

SERVES 1

cracked ice
2 measures brandy
1 measure apple brandy
1 measure sweet vermouth

Put the cracked ice into a mixing glass. Pour the brandy, apple brandy and vermouth over the ice. Stir gently to mix. Strain into a chilled cocktail glass.

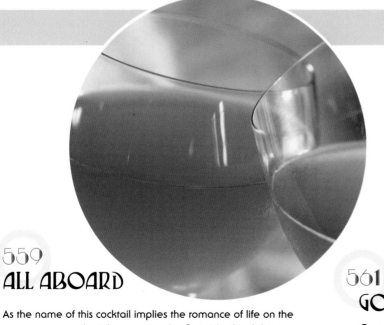

559
ALL ABOARD

As the name of this cocktail implies the romance of life on the ocean wave, make it for two people. Certainly, this delicious concoction is as smooth as a calm sea.

SERVES 2
cracked ice
4 measures brandy
3 measures white rum
1 measure clear curaçao
1 measure lemon juice

Put the cracked ice into a cocktail shaker. Pour the brandy, rum, curaçao and lemon juice over and shake vigorously until frosted. Strain into two chilled wine goblets.

561
GOLDEN MEDALLION

Orange juice and Galliano bring out the rich fruitiness of the brandy.

SERVES 1
1 measure brandy
1 measure Galliano
1 measure fresh orange juice
dash egg white
cracked ice
orange peel twist, to decorate

Shake the first four ingredients together over ice until well frosted. Strain into a cocktail glass. Dress with a twist of orange peel.

560
BRASILICA

This bright, cheerful little cocktail has a serious kick disguised by fresh fruity flavours.

SERVES 1
1/2 measure brandy
1/4 measure port
1 measure orange juice
ice
1/2 measure framboise or a
  few drops raspberry syrup

Shake the brandy, port and orange juice well over ice. Pour into a chilled glass and then slowly pour in the framboise so that some sits at the bottom of the glass.

562
ANTONIO

This is mint with power! Serve it on the rocks to lessen the blow, or sip slowly and leisurely.

SERVES 1
1/3 measure brandy
1/3 measure gin
1/6 measure maraschino
1/6 measure crème de menthe
ice

Chill a small cocktail glass. Mix the liquid ingredients together over ice and strain into the chilled glass. Add more ice to taste.

563

BUD (Brandy, Vermouth and Dubonnet)
(see right-hand page for picture)

This is one of those no-nonsense straightforward cocktails with no fancy liqueurs. Simply delicious!

SERVES 1

cracked ice
1 measure brandy
1 measure dry vermouth
1 measure Dubonnet

Put some cracked ice into a mixing glass. Pour the brandy, dry vermouth and Dubonnet over the ice. Stir to mix and strain into a chilled cocktail glass.

564

MOONRAKER

A powerful mix, this cocktail is more likely to fire you into orbit than to reduce you to trying to rake the moon's reflection out of a pond.

SERVES 1

cracked ice
dash Pernod
1 measure brandy
1 measure peach brandy
1 measure quinquina

Put the cracked ice into a mixing glass. Dash Pernod over the ice and pour in the brandy, peach brandy and quinquina. Stir well to mix, then strain into a chilled highball glass.

565

BRANDY ALEXANDER

A lovely creamy concoction that is popular as an after-dinner cocktail. The original was the Alexander, a gin-based drink.

SERVES 1

1 measure brandy
1 measure dark crème de
   cacao
1 measure double cream
ice
grated nutmeg, to decorate

Shake the brandy, crème de cacao and cream vigorously over ice until well frosted. Strain into a chilled cocktail glass and dress with a sprinkling of grated nutmeg.

566
B & B

Although elaborate concoctions are great fun to mix –
and drink – some of the best cocktails are the simplest.
B & B – brandy and Benedictine – couldn't be easier, but it
has a superbly subtle flavour.

SERVES 1

1 measure brandy
1 measure Benedictine
cracked ice

Pour the brandy and
Benedictine over the ice in
a mixing glass and stir to
mix. Strain into a chilled
cocktail glass.

567
FBR

A number of cocktails are known simply by initials. In this case,
FBR stands for Frozen Brandy and Rum. Others seem to be
obscure and, in one or two instances, slightly naughty.

SERVES 1

crushed ice
2 measures brandy
1¹/2 measures white rum
1 tbsp lemon juice
1 tsp sugar syrup
1 egg white

Put the crushed ice, brandy,
rum, lemon juice, sugar
syrup and egg white into a
blender. Blend until slushy
and pour into a chilled
highball glass.

568
TUSCAN DESSERT

Italian brandies have their own character and delicious flavour,
like this Tuscan speciality.

SERVES 1

2 measures Tuaca brandy
4 measures apple juice
¹/2 measure lemon juice
1 tsp brown sugar
ice
pinch ground cinnamon,
   to decorate

Shake the first four ingredients
well over ice and strain into a
chilled tumbler. Add more ice to
taste and sprinkle with cinnamon.

569
PRINCESS

No particular princess is
specified, although a number
of other cocktails are named
after queens and princes. Perhaps
drinking this makes everyone feel like royalty.

SERVES 1

2 tsp chilled single cream
1 tsp icing sugar
2 measures chilled apricot
   brandy

Pour the cream into a tiny
bowl and stir in the sugar.
Pour the apricot brandy into
a chilled liqueur glass and
float the sweetened cream
on top by pouring it over the
back of a teaspoon.

570 GOLDEN GALLEON

The deep yellows of Galliano and passion fruit make sure this cocktail has a rich golden colour and a good fruity flavour.

SERVES 1

1 measure brandy
1 measure Galliano
1 measure passion fruit juice
dash lemon juice
ice cubes

Stir all the liquid ingredients together well in a mixing glass. Strain into an ice-filled tumbler and add a stirrer.

571 BRANDY COCKTAIL

No fancy name, no fancy history – just plain and simple, exactly what it says it is.

SERVES 1

cracked ice
dash Angostura bitters
2 measures brandy
1/2 tsp sugar syrup
lemon slice, to decorate

Put cracked ice into a cocktail shaker with a dash Angostura bitters, the brandy and the sugar syrup. Shake vigorously until well frosted, then strain into a chilled cocktail glass and dress with a slice of lemon.

572 CLASSIC COCKTAIL

It cannot lay claim to being the first or even the only classic, but it has all the characteristic hallmarks of sophistication associated with cocktails.

SERVES 1

lemon wedge
1 tsp icing sugar
2 measures brandy
1/2 measure clear curaçao
1/2 measure maraschino
1/2 measure lemon juice
cracked ice
lemon peel twist, to decorate

Rub the rim of a chilled cocktail glass with the lemon wedge and then dip in the sugar to frost. Shake the brandy, curaçao, maraschino and lemon juice vigorously over ice until well frosted. Strain into the glass and dress with a twist of lemon peel.

573 SANTA MARIA

This combination is sharp and sweet, so serve well iced or over ice if you like to soften the sharpness.

SERVES 1

1 measure brandy
1 measure triple sec
1 measure lemon juice
ice
orange peel twist, to decorate

Shake the liquid ingredients together over ice until frosted. Pour into a chilled cocktail glass and dress with a twist of orange peel.

574 CAESARINI

Eggs are often used in cocktails, the yolks to enrich and give thickness to the drink, and the whisked-up whites to give a stunning frothy effect.

SERVES 1

1¹/2 measures brandy
¹/2 measure orange curaçao
1 egg yolk
2 dashes grenadine
ice

Shake the liquid ingredients well over ice and strain into a medium-sized cocktail glass.

575 A.J.

For all those A.J.s out there who thought they'd inspired a cocktail – this one is named for the brandy.

SERVES 1

1¹/2 measures applejack or
   apple brandy
1 measure grapefruit juice
ice

Shake the applejack and grapefruit juice vigorously over ice until well frosted. Strain into a chilled cocktail glass.

576 CHERRY BRANDY FIX

A fix is quick and easy to prepare directly in the glass. Be sure to use plenty of ice for best effect.

SERVES 1

1 tsp icing sugar
1 tsp water
juice of ¹/2 lemon
¹/2 measure cherry brandy
1 measure brandy
ice
lemon slice, to decorate

Mix the sugar and water in the bottom of a small tumbler. Stir in the lemon juice and brandies. Fill up with ice and stir slowly. Dress with a slice of lemon.

577 CHERRY BLOSSOM

Cherry blossom is used to make a pretty, pink scented liqueur in Japan. This is not so subtle or scented, but well worth trying.

SERVES 1

²/3 measure brandy
³/5 measure cherry brandy
dash grenadine
dash curaçao
dash lemon juice
ice

Shake the liquid ingredients together over ice and strain into a cocktail glass.

578
HUNTSMAN

If you're in need of Dutch courage, this will do the trick, and revive you at the end of the day too.

SERVES 1

2 measures cognac
cracked ice
splash Benedictine
soda water, to taste

Stir the cognac over ice in an old-fashioned tumbler until well chilled. Add the Benedictine and soda water to taste.

579
BRANDY COBBLER

A perfect concoction, perfectly assembled together.

SERVES 1

1 tsp icing sugar
3 measures sparkling water
cracked ice
2 measures brandy
lemon slice and cocktail cherry,
   to decorate

Put the sugar into a small chilled tumbler and add the sparkling water. Stir until the sugar has dissolved, then fill the glass with cracked ice. Pour in the brandy and stir well. Dress with a lemon slice and a cocktail cherry.

580
REMBRANDT

A quick and simple drink to rival Kir any day. It may be too sweet for some, so a drop of lemon juice will help.

SERVES 1

lemon juice
icing sugar
1/2 measure apricot brandy
1 glass dry white wine, chilled

Dip the rim of a wine glass into a little lemon juice, then into the sugar. Set aside to dry. Pour the brandy into the bottom of the glass and add lemon juice to taste. Top up with wine so the brandy swirls around the glass.

581
BEAGLE

It's strange to think that this could just as easily have been called a Snoopy, if the famous beagle had predated it.

SERVES 1

cracked ice
dash kümmel
dash lemon juice
2 measures brandy
1 measure cranberry juice

Put cracked ice into a mixing glass. Dash kümmel and lemon juice over the ice and pour in the brandy and cranberry juice. Stir well to mix and strain into a chilled cocktail glass.

582
KISS KISS

Kissing will probably be on your mind after a few of these sweet offerings.

SERVES 1
cracked ice 1 measure cherry
  brandy
1 measure gin
1 measure sweet vermouth
cocktail cherry, to decorate

Put some cracked ice into a mixing glass. Pour the cherry brandy, gin and vermouth over the ice. Stir well, then strain into a chilled cocktail glass. Dress with a cocktail cherry.

583
HONEYMOON

The traditional nuptial journey is so called because the first month of marriage was thought to be sweet. If you are sick of the sight of champagne following the wedding, why not share this sweet concoction?

SERVES 2
4 measures apple brandy
2 measures Benedictine
2 measures lemon juice
2 tsp triple sec
cracked ice

Shake the brandy, Benedictine, lemon juice and triple sec vigorously over ice until well frosted. Strain into two chilled cocktail glasses.

584
WHITE COSMOPOLITAN

Nothing like its pink cousin the Cosmopolitan, for this is far more fruity, and instead of vodka, it is based on a punchy lemon-flavoured Italian liqueur.

SERVES 1
1¹/2 measures limoncello
¹/2 measure Cointreau
1 measure white cranberry and
  grape juice
ice
dash orange bitters
few red cranberries,
  to decorate

Shake the limoncello, Cointreau and cranberry and grape juice over ice until well frosted. Strain into a chilled glass. Add the bitters and dress with cranberries.

585
PANDA

Slivovitz is a colourless plum brandy, usually made from Mirabelle plums. It is often drunk straight but can add a fruity note to cocktails. You can use apricot, peach or cherry brandy in its place if it is not available, but the cocktail will be a different colour.

SERVES 1
1 measure slivovitz
1 measure apple brandy
1 measure gin
1 measure orange juice
cracked ice
dash sugar syrup

Shake the slivovitz, apple brandy, gin and orange juice vigorously over ice with a dash sugar syrup until well frosted. Strain into a chilled cocktail glass.

586
PINK WHISKERS

Drinkers of this luscious pink drink will really be the cat's whiskers.

SERVES 1

2 measures apricot brandy
1 measure dry vermouth
2 measures orange juice
dash grenadine
ice

Shake the liquid ingredients vigorously over ice until well frosted. Strain the mixture into a chilled cocktail glass.

588
FUZZCAAT

Advocaat features in many adventurous Dutch cocktails.

SERVES 1

1 measure brandy
1/2 measure advocaat
1/2 measure peach brandy
flesh of 1/2 ripe peach, peeled
dash lime cordial
crushed ice
lemonade
orange slice, to decorate

In a blender, blend the first five ingredients over ice until slushy and well frosted. Pour into a tall glass with more ice, add the lemonade to taste, and dress with a slice of orange.

587
DEAUVILLE PASSION

Deauville was elegant, extravagant and very fashionable during the cocktail era early last century and no doubt many great cocktails were created there.

SERVES 1

1³/4 measures cognac
1¹/4 measures apricot curaçao
1¹/4 measures passion fruit
   juice
ice
bitter lemon, to taste
mint leaves, to decorate

Shake the cognac, apricot curaçao and passion fruit juice over ice until well frosted. Strain into a chilled glass, top up with bitter lemon to taste and dress with mint.

589
AUTUMNAL APPLE CUP

Perfect for late summer and hot weather entertaining in the garden, so have all the ingredients well chilled in advance.

SERVES 6

juice of 3 small oranges
5–6 measures Calvados
few drops vanilla extract
3 cups chilled apple juice
   or cider
ice
apple slices, to serve

Mix the first four ingredients in a jug and top up with plenty of ice. Serve each glass with a slice of apple. For a longer drink, add sparkling water, or an apple-flavoured water, to taste.

590 ATOMIC

Deliciously flavoured with orange and mandarin, but topped with fraise and kiwi fruit, this eerie-looking drink tastes wonderful.

SERVES 1

1¼ measures cognac
¾ measure Grand Marnier
¼ measure blue curaçao
ice
3 measures exotic fruit juice
1 tsp fraise
kiwi fruit slice, to decorate

Shake the first three ingredients together over ice until frosted. Strain into a chilled highball glass and top up with fruit juice. Float in a few drops of fraise and dress with a slice of kiwi fruit.

592 ROYAL WEDDING

Serve these to give any occasion a royal air.

SERVES 1

1 measure kirsch
1 measure peach brandy
1 measure orange juice
ice

Shake the ingredients vigorously over ice until well frosted. Strain into a chilled cocktail glass.

591 TAIPAN NECTAR

A luxurious combination that has no dangerous bite, just super-cool smoothness.

SERVES 1

2 measures brandy
1 measure apricot brandy
1 measure mango nectar
4 cubes ripe mango
crushed ice
any combination of fruit, to decorate

Blend the first five ingredients in a blender for 20 seconds, until thick and frothy. Pour into a large cocktail glass and dress with fruit.

593 CREAM DREAM

This certainly is smooth and creamy, and the Grand Marnier adds a special hint of orange sweetness.

SERVES 1

1 measure Grand Marnier
1 measure vodka
ice
1 measure whipped cream
orange peel strip,
    to decorate

Shake the first two ingredients over ice until frosted. Strain into an iced martini glass and gently spoon on the whipped cream. Dress with a strip of orange peel.

594
THE INVIGORATOR

This enriched version of iced coffee would be great for a Sunday morning brunch. Give it plenty of time to chill to be at its best.

SERVES 1
1 egg
300 ml/10 fl oz strong black
   coffee (cold)
2 measures brandy
1 measure port
sugar
ice

Beat the egg in a cocktail shaker. Add the coffee, brandy, port, and sugar to taste. Shake with a little ice until frothy and pour into a large goblet or wine glass, with more ice if you like.

596
BANANA SMOOTH

For an after-dinner drink, this is a delicious mix. Crème de banane has very rich overtones but it is balanced by the cognac.

SERVES 1
1¼ measures cognac
1¼ measures crème de
   banane
ice
1–2 tbsp chilled cream
mint leaves, to decorate

Mix the first two ingredients with ice in a mixing glass. Strain into a chilled cocktail glass. Carefully pour in the cream over the back of a spoon to form a layer. Dress with mint leaves.

595
REDCURRANT SHRUB

This cocktail is one for bottling when you have a glut of fruit, ready to enjoy later in the year. You could make it with blackcurrants too.

SERVES 20
900 g/2 lb redcurrants, crushed
1.3 kg/2 lb 8 oz sugar
brandy or rum, to taste
soda water or lemonade
ice
fresh redcurrants, to decorate

Press the redcurrants through muslin. Stir the juice and sugar in a saucepan until the sugar has dissolved, then bring to the boil and boil gently for 8–10 minutes, spooning off the foam occasionally. Leave to cool and add brandy to taste. Bottle and leave to mature for 5–6 weeks. To serve, dilute with soda water and add ice. Dress with some fresh redcurrants.

597
EGGNOG

The perfect lift when recovering and a marvellous energy boost when you are feeling a little bit under the weather.

SERVES 1
1 egg
1 tbsp icing sugar
2 measures brandy
milk, warm or cooling
freshly grated nutmeg,
   to decorate

Whisk the first three ingredients together, strain into a tall glass and top up with milk. Sprinkle with the nutmeg.

598

HUNGARIAN COFFEE

(see right-hand page for picture)

Arguably hotter and sweeter than the Irish variety, this will really hit the spot on a cold day.

SERVES 1

2½ measures strong hot coffee
1½ measures brandy
1 tbsp grated chocolate
1 tsbp whipped cream
cinnamon stick, to serve

Pour the coffee and brandy into an Irish coffee glass, stir in the grated chocolate, top with whipped cream, and serve with a cinnamon stick.

599

THE REVIVER

There are many cocktails designed to revive after a heavy night of drinking. This is the one that most people say really works, but that's up to you.

SERVES 1

1/3 measure brandy
1/3 Fernet Branca
1/3 measure crème de menthe
ice

Shake the liquids well over ice until frosted. Strain into a cocktail glass and drink as quickly as possible.

600

GLACIER

A dark and rich combination of liqueurs like this needs to be well iced before being topped with a whirl of soft cream.

SERVES 1

2 measures brandy
1 measure crème de cacao
1/2 measure framboise
roughly crushed ice
whipped cream

Mix the first three ingredients together in a mixing glass over ice. Pour into a chilled cocktail glass and top with a little whipped cream.

601 COFFEE DI SARONNO

This could send anyone to sleep after a good dinner, so you had better make the coffee nice and strong.

SERVES 1

1 measure brandy
1/2 measure Amaretto di
   Saronno
1 cup espresso coffee
sugar, to taste

Warm the brandy and Amaretto in a small cup in a saucepan of hot water. Pour into a warmed brandy glass and top up with coffee. Sweeten to taste.

603 LA BAMBA

A glorious combination that needs to be well iced because it can be too rich for some.

SERVES 1

1 1/4 measures cognac
1 measure coffee liqueur
1/2 measure Malibu
ice

Stir the liquid ingredients in a mixing glass with ice. Strain into a small chilled glass.

602 BLACK MAGIC

Drinking your after-dinner cognac with a touch of chocolate and orange is a bit like enjoying liqueur chocolates in a glass!

SERVES 1

1 1/4 measures cognac
1/2 measure chocolate liqueur
3/4 measure mandarin liqueur
ice
1 tbsp cream
chocolate flakes, to decorate

Stir the first three ingredients over ice in a mixing glass. Strain into a chilled cocktail glass and carefully float the cream on top. Dress with chocolate flakes.

604 DARK SECRETS

The hidden secret is, of course, all the rich liqueurs and brandy wrapped up in thick cream.

SERVES 1

1 1/4 measures cognac
3/4 measure amaretto
3/4 measure coffee liqueur
1–2 tbsp double cream
ice
toasted flaked almonds, to
   decorate

Stir all the ingredients except the almonds rapidly in a mixing glass full of ice. Strain into an iced liqueur glass and dress with toasted almonds.

605
MIDNIGHT COWBOY

You have to be a cola lover to want to do this to your brandy! But perhaps at midnight anything goes.

SERVES 1

1 measure brandy
1/2 measure coffee liqueur
1/2 measure cream, chilled
crushed ice
cola

Slowly blend together the brandy, coffee liqueur, cream and ice in a blender until frothy. Pour into a chilled long glass. Top up with cola.

607
ORANGE DAWN

Not quite a breakfast-time drink, but it would make a very good 'morning after' tempter.

SERVES 1

1/2 measure Galliano
1/2 measure brandy
1/2 measure orange juice
1/2 egg white
crushed ice
glacé orange peel,
   to decorate

Blend all the ingredients except the peel in a blender until well frosted. Pour into a chilled cocktail glass and dress with a twist of glacé orange peel.

606
STINGER

Aptly named, this is a refreshing, clean-tasting cocktail to tantalize the taste buds and make you sit up and take notice. However, bear in mind that it packs a punch and if you have too many, you are likely to keel over.

SERVES 1

2 measures brandy
1 measure white crème
   de menthe
cracked ice

Pour the brandy and crème de menthe over ice and shake vigorously until well frosted. Strain into a chilled highball glass.

608
HOT BRANDY CHOCOLATE

Brandy and chocolate have a natural affinity, as this delicious drink demonstrates.

SERVES 4

1 litre/1³/4 pints milk
115 g/4 oz plain chocolate,
   broken into pieces
2 tbsp sugar
5 tbsp brandy
6 tbsp whipped cream
grated nutmeg, to decorate

Bring the milk to the boil in a saucepan, then remove from the heat. Add the chocolate and sugar and stir over a low heat until the chocolate has melted. Pour into four heatproof glasses. Pour the brandy over a spoon on the top of each. Finish with a swirl of cream and some nutmeg.

609
UNDER MILK WOOD

This is a punchy mixture made smooth and mellow with the addition of cream and chocolate, definitely for after dinner.

SERVES 1

³/4 measure cognac
³/4 measure white crème de cacao
¹/2 measure cream
1 measure Grand Marnier
ice
pinch of cocoa powder

Stir all the liquid ingredients in a mixing glass with ice. Strain into a chilled glass and sprinkle with cocoa powder.

611
NAPOLEON'S NIGHTCAP

Instead of hot chocolate, he favoured a chocolate-laced brandy with a hint of banana. Daring and extravagant!

SERVES 1

1¹/4 measures cognac
1 measure dark crème de cacao
¹/4 measure crème de banane
ice
1 tbsp cream

Stir the cognac, crème de cacao and crème de banane in a mixing glass with ice. Strain into a chilled glass and spoon on a layer of cream.

610
SWISS SILK

Creamy smooth and icy, laced with brandy – and with a hint of cherries, this is a summer special.

SERVES 2

1 measure cherry liqueur
1 measure brandy
1 scoop vanilla ice cream
crushed ice
2 maraschino cherries, to decorate

Blend all the ingredients except the cherries in a blender until smooth and then pour into sundae glasses or large cocktail glasses. Dress with maraschino cherries.

612
THUNDER-BOLT

If names are anything to go by, this should wake you up – and it's designed to make you feel better.

SERVES 1

¹/2 measure cognac
1 egg yolk
¹/2 measure fresh orange juice
ice
1–2 drops Angostura bitters

Whisk together the cognac and egg yolk and add the fresh orange juice. Strain into a small cocktail glass with ice and top with a few drops of Angostura bitters.

613
NOCTURNE

There's no need to be nocturnal to enjoy this delicious mix, just a little daring.

SERVES 1

1¼ measures cognac
pinch cinnamon
a little icing sugar
¾ measure crème de noyaux
¼ measure crème de cacao
ice
3 coffee beans, to decorate

Rub the rim of a chilled cocktail glass with a little cognac. Mix the cinnamon and sugar and dip the rim into this. Stir the three liquids in a mixing glass with ice and strain into the chilled glass. Float three coffee beans on top to dress.

615
BANANA BOMBER

This cocktail is as dazzling as it is delicious and gloriously addictive. Try it with white crème de cacao and a layer of cream too – equally irresistible!

SERVES 1

1 measure crème de banane
1 measure brandy

Pour the banana liqueur gently into a shot glass. Gently pour in the brandy over the back of a teaspoon, being careful not to allow the layers to mix.

614
COFFEE TIME

This is a luxurious coffee for any after-dinner occasion. Have plenty ready, as it will go down very well.

SERVES 1

1 measure coconut liqueur
1 measure coffee liqueur
1 measure brandy
freshly brewed hot coffee
whipped sweetened cream

Mix the liqueurs and brandy in a heatproof glass or mug. Pour in the fresh coffee and top with a spoonful of whipped cream.

616
FANCY FREE

The key to this layered drink is to ice both the liqueurs and the glass. If it does seem to mix on impact, give it a little time to settle and form its layers again.

SERVES 1

⅓ measure iced cherry brandy
⅓ measure iced Cointreau
⅓ measure iced apricot
  liqueur

Pour the three liqueurs in order of listing over the back of a spoon into an iced tall shot glass so that they form coloured layers.

617

NIGHTCAP FLIP (see right-hand page for picture)

A flip always contains egg so this makes for a soothing and interesting nightcap, even if it is a strange colour.

SERVES 1

¹/₃ measure brandy
¹/₃ measure anisette
¹/₃ measure blue curaçao
1 egg yolk
ice
maraschino cherry, to decorate

Shake the first four ingredients well over ice and then strain into a cocktail glass. Dress with a maraschino cherry.

618

GLÖGG

This hot punch will soon get the party going with a swing.

SERVES 20

1 bottle red wine
1 bottle medium sherry
3–4 tbsp sugar
¹/₂ bottle brandy
dash Angostura bitters
raisins and unsalted almonds,
   to decorate

Heat all the ingredients except the raisins and almonds together until the sugar is dissolved and the mixture is piping hot. Pour into heatproof cups or mugs with a few nuts and raisins in the bottom.

619

GINGER BEER

Not as tame as its British namesake, which is simply ginger-flavoured beer.

SERVES 1

1 cup pale ale
2 measures ginger brandy

Pour the ale into a chilled beer glass or tankard, then pour in the ginger brandy.

BUBBLES

Classic champagne cocktails have been a popular choice for centuries. Now it's easy to bring the elegance of champagne to your own social calendar – just let the bubbles do the work. Have a bubbly birthday to remember, indulge in a fruity Mimosa or follow in Bogie's footsteps by creating a Casablanca-style French 75.

620 CHAMPAGNE COCKTAIL

The classic champagne cocktail can be too sweet for some. It is the brandy that gives the treat and the kick, so you could leave out the sugar!

SERVES 1

1 sugar cube
2 dashes Angostura bitters
1 measure brandy
chilled champagne

Place the sugar cube with the bitters in the bottom of a chilled flute. Pour on the brandy and top up slowly with champagne.

622 KIR ROYALE

A wicked improvement on the simple cassis and white wine drink.

SERVES 1

few drops cassis, or to taste
1/2 measure brandy
chilled champagne

Put the cassis and brandy into the bottom of a flute. Top up with champagne to taste.

621 MIMOSA

So called because it resembles the colour of a mimosa's attractive yellow bloom.

SERVES 1

flesh of 1 passion fruit
1/2 measure orange curaçao
crushed ice
chilled champagne
star fruit slice, to decorate

Scoop out the passion fruit flesh into a jug or shaker and shake with the curaçao and a little crushed ice until frosted. Pour into the bottom of a champagne flute and top up with champagne. Dress with a slice of star fruit.

623 BLACK VELVET

Don't ever say that it ruins good champagne, just enjoy a long heady draught of a timeless treasure.

SERVES 1

chilled Guinness
chilled champagne

Pour both drinks in equal quantities carefully (it may fizz up well) into a long beer or highball glass.

624
SERPENTINE

Living up to its name, this green bubbly concoction has hidden secrets. Don't forget to chill the champagne for at least 2 hours before mixing.

SERVES 1

1/2 measure green crème de menthe
cracked ice
lime peel curl or twist
champagne, chilled
1 tsp lime zest, to decorate

Pour the crème de menthe into the bottom of a flute with ice and a curl of lime peel. Top up with champagne and dress with a sprinkle of lime zest.

626
CAMPARI FIZZ

The bitter sweetness of Campari is a natural with orange juice and sparkling wine or champagne. You need very little to add the distinctive colour and flavour.

SERVES 1

1 measure Campari
1 measure orange juice
crushed ice
champagne

Shake the Campari and orange juice together over ice until frosted and pour into a flute. Top up with champagne.

625
CHICAGO

Do use a dry champagne, or even a good sparkling wine, for cocktails where you add sweet ingredients, especially if you want to sugar the rim of the glass for extra sparkle.

SERVES 1

egg white or lemon juice
icing sugar
1 measure brandy
1 dash Cointreau
1 dash Angostura bitters
ice
champagne

Frost the rim of a glass with the egg white and sugar. Shake the next three ingredients together with ice until frosted. Strain into the prepared glass and top up with champagne.

627
LONG TALL SALLY

A seriously strong champagne cocktail with the subtle perfume of herbs.

SERVES 1

1/4 measure brandy
1/4 measure dry vermouth
1/4 measure Galliano
1/4 measure mandarin liqueur
ice
champagne or sparkling wine

Stir the first four ingredients over ice and pour into a tall chilled glass. Top up with champagne.

628 DISCO DANCER

Make it nice and long and you have the perfect disco drink.

SERVES 1

1 measure crème de banane
1 measure rum
few drops Angostura bitters
ice
sparkling white wine

Shake the first three ingredients well over ice. Pour into a highball glass and top up with sparkling wine to taste. Add plenty of ice to keep you cool and lengthen your drink.

629 DAYDREAMER

You won't need more than one of these before you begin to daydream.

SERVES 1

1/3 measure brandy
1 tsp maraschino
1 tsp dark curaçao
1 tsp Angostura bitters
ice
champagne
fresh cherry, to decorate

Stir the first four ingredients over ice, strain into a cocktail glass and top up with champagne. Dress with a fresh cherry.

630 PINK SHERBET ROYALE

This is perfect for very special occasions on hot days, or after dinner watching a warm sun setting slowly.

SERVES 2

1 1/2 cups sparkling white wine, really cold
2 measures cassis
1 measure brandy
crushed ice
blackberries, to decorate

Blend half the wine in a blender with the cassis, brandy and ice until really frothy and frosted. Slowly whisk in a little more wine and pour into tall thin frosted glasses. Dress with blackberries.

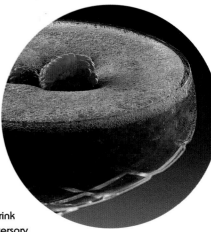

631 RASPBERRY MIST

The perfect celebration drink for a ruby wedding anniversary.

SERVES 24

6 measures Irish Mist honey liqueur
450 g/1 lb raspberries
crushed ice
4 bottles sparkling dry white wine, well chilled
24 raspberries, to decorate

Blend the liqueur and raspberries in a blender with 55 g/2 oz crushed ice. When lightly frozen, divide between chilled champagne bowls and top up with wine. Top each with a raspberry.

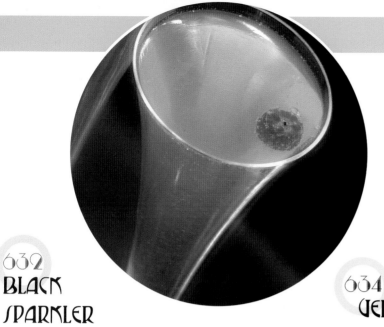

632
BLACK SPARKLER

Simply using sparkling water makes this a delicious summer party drink. If you want to make it more celebratory, use sparkling white wine instead of soda water.

SERVES 1

1³/4 measures cognac
1/4 measure crème de mure
1/4 measure lemon juice
1 tsp icing sugar
ice
soda water
frozen blackcurrants, to decorate

Shake the first four ingredients over ice until frosted. Strain into a tall chilled cocktail glass and top up with soda water. Dress with frozen blackcurrants.

633
BOMBAY SHERRY PUNCH

An unusual mix for a party, ideal to dilute as much as you like.

SERVES 16

1 bottle brandy, chilled
1 bottle sherry, chilled
1 measure maraschino
1 measure curaçao
2 bottles chilled champagne
chilled soda water
large ice cubes
  (set with fruit in them)
any combination of fruit,
  to decorate

Mix the first four ingredients in a large punch bowl. Add the champagne and soda water to taste, then add the ice cubes and fruit at the last minute.

634
VELVET COOLER

A very unusual long summer party drink, refreshing yet surprisingly strong.

SERVES 1

2–3 tbsp pineapple juice
iced lager
iced champagne

Pour the pineapple juice into the bottom of a chilled highball glass. Slowly add equal quantities of lager and champagne.

635
VELVET MULE

This mule has an interesting kick of anise and ginger – a surprisingly good mix, especially with the unique flavours supplied by the cola.

SERVES 1

1 measure cassis
1 measure black Sambuca
2 measures ginger wine
ice
cola
soda water or sparkling white
  wine

Stir the first three ingredients over ice until well frosted. Strain into a frosted flute and top up with equal quantities of cola and soda water.

636

AMARETTINE

Inexpensive sparkling white wine is the base of this pretty cocktail. Use the sweeter bubblies if you prefer a slightly sweeter drink, otherwise go for dry. And be warned, it is not just a pretty drink!

SERVES 1

1/3 measure amaretto
1/3 measure dry vermouth
sparkling white wine

Mix the amaretto and vermouth in a chilled tall cocktail glass. Top up with wine to taste.

638

JAMES BOND

Surprisingly and very definitely not shaken on this occasion, or even stirred!

SERVES 1

1 sugar cube
2 dashes Angostura bitters
1 measure chilled vodka
chilled champagne

Moisten the sugar with the bitters and place in the bottom of a chilled glass. Cover with the vodka and then top up with champagne.

637

CARIBBEAN CHAMPAGNE

Both rum and bananas are naturally associated with the Tropics, but wine does not spring so readily to mind when the Caribbean is mentioned. However, remember that France and many of the Caribbean islands, such as Martinique and Guadeloupe, share a long history.

SERVES 1

1/2 measure white rum
1/2 measure crème de banane
chilled champagne
banana slices, to decorate

Pour the rum and crème de banane into a chilled flute. Top up with champagne. Stir gently to mix and dress with slices of banana.

639

ROYAL JULEP

As with all juleps, the mint needs crushing or muddling first to help release its flavour into the sugar and water. Simply chopping it won't produce enough flavour.

SERVES 1

1 sugar lump
3 sprigs fresh mint, plus extra to decorate
1 measure Jack Daniels
chilled champagne

In a small glass, crush the sugar and mint together with a little of the whisky. When the sugar has dissolved, strain it into a chilled flute with the rest of the whisky, and top up with champagne. Dress with mint sprigs.

640
LONG JUMP

An unusual mix of creamy and bubbly. Make sure the bubbly is really cold, but the liqueur not so cold, or it might separate.

SERVES 1

1 measure Amarula liqueur
chilled champagne or sparkling
   white wine

Pour the Amarula into a chilled long glass and top up slowly with champagne. Drink immediately.

642
ALFONSO

This is a delicious way to turn a simple sparkling white wine into a sophisticated cocktail. Probably not the time to use expensive champagne.

SERVES 1

1 measure Dubonnet
1 sugar lump
2 dashes Angostura bitters
chilled champagne

Pour the Dubonnet into a chilled flute. Add the sugar lump with the bitters splashed onto it. When ready to serve, pour on chilled champagne to taste.

641
LE CRYSTAL

Poire William liqueur schnapps is a great drink on its own, but it makes a really super champagne cocktail with a very serious kick.

SERVES 1

1/2 measure Poire William
1 dash orange curaçao
ice
champagne
fresh pear slice, to decorate

Shake the first two ingredients over ice until really cold. Pour into a flute and top up with cold champagne. Dress with a slice of pear.

643
BUCK'S FIZZ

Invented at Buck's Club in London, the original was invariably made with Bollinger champagne and it is true that the better the quality of the champagne, the better the flavour.

SERVES 1

2 measures chilled fresh
   orange juice
2 measures chilled
   champagne

Half fill a chilled flute with orange juice, then gently pour in the chilled champagne.

644

DAWN (see right-hand page for picture)

Look for a good fruity sparkling wine to use in this cocktail – even a sparkling red.

SERVES 1

1 measure lime juice
1 measure medium to medium-dry sherry
chilled champagne

Stir the lime and sherry in a chilled flute. Top up with chilled champagne and stir briefly.

645

WINE TIME

A knockout version of a champagne cocktail, not to be drunk too quickly.

SERVES 1

1 measure brandy
1 measure Madeira or muscatel
3 drops curaçao
2 drops Angostura bitters
ice
chilled champagne
orange peel, to decorate

Shake the first four ingredients together over ice and strain into a chilled flute. Top up with champagne to taste and dress with orange peel.

646

MIDNIGHT COCKTAIL

Specially created to mark the beginning of the twenty-first century – and an even better way to continue it.

SERVES 1

1 measure raspberry vodka
1 measure fresh raspberry juice
1 measure orange juice
ice
chilled champagne
raspberries, to decorate

Shake the vodka, raspberry juice and orange juice vigorously over ice until well frosted. Strain into a chilled flute and top up with champagne. Stir gently to mix and dress with some raspberries.

647 CHAMPAGNE COBBLER

The Cobbler was popular in Dickens' time when it was a concoction of sherry, sugar, lemon and ice. This version has much more kick and lots more bubbles.

SERVES 1

1 glass champagne
1/2 measure curaçao
1 tsp sugar syrup
ice
fruit slices, to decorate

Mix the champagne, curaçao and syrup in a chilled mixing glass. Pour into a tall glass filled with ice and dress with slices of fruit.

649 LADY LUCK

The pear and apple flavours give a deep fruitiness to the final cocktail so you could use a sparkling white wine as the base.

SERVES 1

1 measure Calvados
1 measure pear nectar or
    1/2 measure pear liqueur
firm ripe pear slice
chilled champagne

Pour the Calvados and pear nectar into a chilled flute with a slice of pear. Top up with chilled champagne.

648 GRAPE EXPECTATIONS

Add the remaining grapes at the very last minute, then watch them liven up your drink as they jump around.

SERVES 1

5–6 red or black grapes
ice
splash of mandarin liqueur
chilled pink champagne

Save two grapes for the glass. Crush the others in a small bowl. Add ice and the liqueur, stir well and strain into a chilled champagne glass. Top up with champagne. Halve the remaining grapes and add to the glass.

650 KISMET

A romantic era produced some delightful music and this elegant drink brings that mood right up to date.

SERVES 1

1 measure gin
1 measure apricot brandy
1/2 tsp stem ginger syrup
chilled champagne
fresh mango slice, to
    decorate

Pour the gin and brandy into a chilled flute. Trickle the ginger syrup slowly down the glass and then top up with champagne. Dress with a slice of mango.

651 ORANGE SPARKLER

Serve this exotic version of a classic champagne cocktail for any occasion or simple celebration.

SERVES 1

2/3 measure brandy
1/3 measure orange liqueur
1/3 measure lemon juice
ice
iced Asti Spumante dry sparkling wine, to taste

Shake the first three ingredients well together over ice. Strain into a chilled champagne glass and top up with Asti Spumante to taste.

653 PICK-ME-UP

Champagne always gives you a lift and this cocktail, with its added ingredients, is the perfect anytime booster.

SERVES 1

ice
3 dashes Fernet Branca
3 dashes curaçao
1 measure brandy
champagne, chilled
lemon peel twist, to decorate

Place the ice in a wine glass to chill. Stir in the next three ingredients gradually and top up with champagne. Dress with a twist of lemon.

652 DEATH IN THE AFTERNOON

It is rumoured this was Ernest Hemingway's favourite drink when he lived in Paris. The anise gives it a mysterious cloudiness and it is certainly delicious!

SERVES 1

ice
1 measure Pernod
dry champagne, chilled

Put two ice cubes into a champagne glass. Pour the Pernod over them and carefully pour in the champagne. Drink quickly before the bubbles disperse!

654 JADE

You can tell good jade because it always feels cold to the touch – and that should apply to cocktails too. No cocktail bar, nor home bar, can ever have too much ice.

SERVES 1

1/4 measure Midori
1/4 measure blue curaçao
1/4 measure lime juice
dash Angostura bitters
cracked ice
chilled champagne, to taste
lime slice, to decorate

Shake the Midori, curaçao, lime juice and Angostura bitters vigorously over ice until well frosted. Strain into a chilled flute. Top up with chilled champagne to taste and dress with a slice of lime.

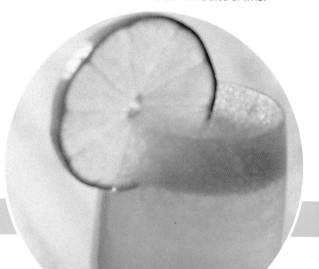

655
LONDON FRENCH 75

A variation on the classic French 75, with London gin as the main ingredient.

SERVES 1

2 measures London gin
1 measure lemon juice
1 tbsp sugar syrup
cracked ice
chilled champagne
lemon peel twist, to decorate

Shake the gin, lemon juice and sugar syrup vigorously over ice until well frosted. Strain into a chilled highball glass and top up with champagne. Dress with a twist of lemon.

657
WILD SILK

A wildly fruity cocktail topped with a riot of bubbles and really well-iced champagne.

SERVES 2

a few raspberries
1/2 measure cream
1 measure framboise or raspberry syrup
crushed ice
iced champagne

Set aside 2–3 nice raspberries. Blend the remainder with the cream, framboise and a little ice in a blender until frosted and slushy. Pour into a glass and top up with champagne. Float a raspberry or two on the top.

656
FRENCH 75

Described in a cocktail book of the early twentieth century as a drink that 'definitely hits the spot', there is some confusion about the ingredients. All recipes include champagne, but disagree about the spirits that should be included.

SERVES 1

2 measures brandy
1 measure lemon juice
1 tbsp sugar syrup
cracked ice
chilled champagne
lemon peel twist, to decorate

Shake the brandy, lemon juice and sugar syrup vigorously over ice until well frosted. Strain into a chilled highball glass and top up with champagne. Dress with a twist of lemon.

658
SAN JOAQUIN PUNCH

A fabulous bubbly punch enriched with brandy-soaked Californian dried fruit.

SERVES 4

1 tbsp raisins or chopped prunes
6 tsp brandy
1 cup sparkling white wine or champagne
1 cup white cranberry and grape juice
ice

Mix the dried fruit and brandy in a small bowl and leave to soak for 1–2 hours. In a jug, mix the sparkling wine, juice and brandy-soaked fruit. Pour into ice-filled glasses.

659
SAN REMO

Next time you cut up a citrus fruit, put any leftover slices in the freezer, as they make great flavoured ice cubes.

SERVES 1

1/2 measure grapefruit juice
1/4 measure triple sec
1/4 measure mandarin liqueur
ice
champagne
frozen citrus fruit slices,
   to decorate

Mix the first three ingredients with ice in a tall glass. Top up with champagne and dress with slices of frozen fruit.

660
THE FOOTMAN

If you are preparing several glasses, make the gin base in advance and keep it well chilled until you are ready.

SERVES 1

1/2 measure gin
1 measure orange juice
1 peach slice
1 ice cube
chilled champagne
peach slice, to decorate

Blend the first four ingredients in a blender for about 10 seconds, until smooth. Pour into a flute and top up with champagne. Dress with a slice of peach.

661
CHRISTMAS COCKTAIL

This bright and cheerful cocktail is easy to prepare for lots of guests and you certainly don't need to wait for Christmas to enjoy it.

SERVES 1

1 cube sugar
splash brandy
generous splash cranberry
   juice, chilled
champagne, chilled
few raspberries, to decorate

Place a sugar cube in the bottom of a chilled champagne glass. Add the brandy and leave to soak in, then splash on the cranberry juice. At the last moment, top up with champagne and dress with raspberries.

662
SPARKLING GOLD

For a very special occasion, such as a golden wedding anniversary, you could float tiny pieces of edible gold leaf on the top of each glass.

SERVES 1

1 measure golden rum
1/2 measure Cointreau
chilled champagne

Pour the rum and liqueur into a chilled flute and top up with champagne.

663 VALENCIA COCKTAIL

Valencia is the home of some of the best oranges. This is a forerunner of Buck's Fizz, no doubt.

SERVES 1

4 dashes orange bitters
1 tsp apricot cordial
1/3 measure orange juice
1/3 measure apricot brandy
ice
chilled champagne, to taste

Shake the first four ingredients well over ice until frosted. Strain into a tall chilled flute and top up with champagne to taste.

664 SHANGRI-LA

This an excellent mix to liven up a not-so-exciting bottle of bubbly! Also an unusual mix for several people for a party.

SERVES 1

1/2 measure gin
1/4 measure apricot brandy
1/2 measure orange juice
few drops grenadine
ice
Asti Spumante dry sparkling wine
fruit slices, to decorate

Stir the first four ingredients with ice in a chilled highball or large wine glass. Top up with sparkling wine and dress with slices of fruit.

665 SABRINA

Perfect for lovers of sweet and fruity cocktails – the base is easy to prepare in advance.

SERVES 1

1/2 measure gin
1/8 measure apricot brandy
1/2 measure fresh orange juice
1 tsp grenadine
1/4 measure Cinzano
ice
sweet sparkling wine
orange and lemon slices, to decorate

Shake the first five ingredients together over ice. Pour into a tall glass and top up with sparkling wine. Dress with slices of orange and lemon.

666 THE TRADE WINDS

Whether it blows hot or cold, champagne cocktails are a treat for any occasion and this one is as refreshing as it is colourful.

SERVES 1

1 measure gin
1/2 measure cherry brandy
1/2 measure lemon juice
2 dashes sugar syrup
crushed ice
chilled champagne
fresh cherries, to decorate

Shake the first four ingredients together over ice until frosted and strain into the bottom of a champagne glass. Top up with champagne and dress with fresh cherries.

667
THE BENTLEY

Champagne cocktails tend to get better and better the more you drink.

SERVES 1

1/2 measure cognac or brandy
1/2 measure peach liqueur, brandy or schnapps
juice of 1 passion fruit, strained
1 ice cube
champagne

Mix the first three ingredients gently together in a chilled glass. Add one ice cube and slowly pour in champagne to taste.

669
SPARKLER

The simplest and cleverest champagne cocktail. Replace the champagne with sparkling water for a non-alcoholic version.

SERVES 1

few drops Angostura bitters
ice
champagne
lime slice, to decorate

Splash the bitters into an ice-filled highball glass. Top up with champagne and dress with a slice of lime.

668
DIAMOND FIZZ

A sparkling concoction that uses champagne to liven up the gin base.

SERVES 1

2 measures gin
1/2 measure lemon juice
1 tsp sugar syrup
ice
chilled champagne

Shake the gin, lemon juice and sugar syrup over ice until well frosted. Strain into a chilled flute. Top up with chilled champagne.

670
SPARKLING JULEP

Champagne is good to enjoy at any time and this is a particularly refreshing way to drink it.

SERVES 1

1 sugar cube
2 fresh mint sprigs
chilled champagne

Place the sugar in the bottom of a chilled flute with one bruised sprig of mint. Add the champagne and the remaining sprig of mint.

671 MONTE CARLO

The motor racing world always drinks champagne, especially in Monte Carlo, so this well-laced cocktail will be very popular.

SERVES 1

1/2 measure gin
1/4 measure lemon juice
ice
champagne or sparkling white wine
1/4 measure crème de menthe
spring of fresh mint, to decorate

Stir the first two ingredients well over ice until well chilled. Strain into a chilled flute and top up with champagne. Finally drizzle the crème de menthe over the top and dress with a sprig of mint.

672 BLACKBERRY AND APPLE TIPPLE

If you ever make your own cider or blackberry gin this is the ideal drink in which to combine them.

SERVES 1

ice cubes
1 tsp blackberry purée, syrup or liqueur
1 measure apple juice
sparkling cider, to taste
blackberries, to decorate

Place one ice cube in the bottom of a tall thin glass. Spoon over the purée, then the apple juice and gently pour on the cider. Dress with a few blackberries.

673 APPLE FIZZ

Cider makes a great punch base as it can be blended with many alcoholic drinks. This mix can't be made in advance, but it's easy to prepare for several people and then add more cider at the last minute to create extra fizz.

SERVES 1

125 ml/4 fl oz sparkling cider or apple juice
1 measure Calvados
juice of 1/2 lemon
1 tbsp egg white
generous pinch sugar
ice
apple slice, to decorate

Shake the first five ingredients together over ice and pour immediately into a highball glass (it may fizz up well). Dress with a slice of apple. For more fizz top up with cider.

674 CIDER PUNCH

This may sound seriously strong but it isn't, and you can add more soda water or ice to taste once the base is made.

SERVES 10

475 ml/16 fl oz dry sparkling cider
1/2 cup cognac or brandy
1/2 cup Cointreau
ice
apple slices
2 cups soda water

Mix the first three ingredients together and chill in the refrigerator until required. Pour into a large punch bowl with ice, apple slices and soda water. Serve in small cups or glasses.

675
MINT & CUCUMBER REFRESHER

This is great to serve at a summer party – the cucumber inside the glass will be a real talking point!

SERVES 1

few mint sprigs
1 tsp icing sugar
juice 1 lime
thin cucumber slices
chilled sparkling water
ice cubes

Chop a few mint leaves and mix with the sugar. Rub a little lime juice round the rim of a glass and dip in the sugar. Leave to dry. Mix the rest of the lime juice, cucumber and mint in a jug and chill. Top up with water and ice.

676
FLIRTINI

This combination of vodka and champagne is guaranteed to bring a sparkle to the eyes and a smile to the lips – what could be more attractive?

SERVES 1

1/4 slice fresh pineapple, chopped
1/2 measure chilled Cointreau
1/2 measure chilled vodka
1 measure chilled pineapple juice
chilled champagne or sparkling white wine

Put the pineapple and Cointreau into a mixing glass or jug and muddle with a spoon to crush the pineapple. Add the vodka and pineapple juice and stir well, then strain into a glass. Top up with champagne.

677
CHAMPAGNE SIDECAR

A luxury edition of the traditional Sidecar.

SERVES 1

1 1/2 measures bourbon
1 measure Cointreau
1/4 measure lemon juice
ice
chilled champagne

Shake the bourbon, Cointreau and lemon juice over ice and strain into a chilled flute. Top up with chilled champagne.

678
PEARL COCKTAIL

No pearls or oysters here, just a pearl of a drink to enjoy before or after dinner.

SERVES 1

1/2 measure cognac
1/2 measure coffee liqueur
crushed ice
chilled champagne
fresh cherry, to decorate

Stir the first two ingredients together over ice in a chilled champagne glass. Top up with champagne and dress with a cherry.

679
BELLINI

This delicious concoction was created by Giuseppe Cipriani at Harry's Bar in Venice, around 1943.

SERVES 1

1 measure fresh peach juice, made from lightly sweetened, peeled and blended peaches
icing sugar
3 measures chilled champagne

Dip the rim of a champagne flute in some peach juice and then in some sugar to create a sugar-frosted effect. Set aside to dry. Pour the peach juice into the chilled flute. Carefully top up with champagne.

680
CHERRY KISS

A great party drink for those avoiding alcohol, this cherry drink tastes as good as it looks.

SERVES 2

8 ice cubes, crushed
2 tbsp cherry syrup
475 ml/16 fl oz sparkling water
maraschino cherries, to decorate

Divide the crushed ice between two tall glasses and pour over the cherry syrup. Fill each glass with sparkling water. Dress with maraschino cherries.

681
CHAMPAGNE PICK-ME-UP

You won't be feeling down for long with one of these in your hand.

SERVES 1

2 measures brandy
1 measure orange juice
1 measure lemon juice
dash grenadine
ice
chilled champagne

Shake the brandy, orange juice, lemon juice and grenadine vigorously over ice until well frosted. Strain into a wine glass and top up with champagne.

682
PEACEMAKER

A delightful sparkling fruit cup for summer entertaining al fresco.

SERVES 8

30 strawberries, hulled
1/2 small fresh pineapple, peeled and crushed
1–2 tbsp icing sugar
1 bottle dry champagne
1 measure maraschino
1 bottle sparkling water
ice
fresh mint leaves, to decorate

Set aside 4–5 of the largest strawberries to slice and add later. Crush the fruit and sugar with a little water in a large punch bowl. Add the remaining ingredients, mix well and serve, decorated with mint leaves and strawberries.

683
RASPBERRY LEMONADE

If you like real old-fashioned lemonade you will love this.

SERVES 4

2 lemons
115 g/4 oz icing sugar
115 g/4 oz fresh raspberries
few drops vanilla extract
crushed ice
iced sparkling water,
lemon balm sprigs,
   to decorate

Cut the ends off the lemons, scoop out and chop the flesh and place in a blender with the sugar, raspberries, vanilla extract and ice. Blend for 2–3 minutes. Strain into tall glasses and top up with ice cubes and sparkling water. Dress with sprigs of lemon balm.

685
THE NAVIGATOR

These look like surprisingly calm waters with a few white horses, but you may find it a bit of a handful!

SERVES 1

1 measure coconut liqueur
splash blue curaçao
champagne or sparkling white
   wine, to taste

Stir the liqueurs over ice in a wine glass and top up with champagne to taste.

684
UNDER THE BOARDWALK

A lovely sparkling drink that's just right for those long summer nights.

SERVES 4

crushed ice
2 measures lemon juice
1/2 tsp sugar syrup
1/2 peach, peeled, stoned
   and chopped
sparkling water
raspberries, to decorate

Blend crushed ice in a blender with the lemon juice, sugar syrup, and chopped peach until slushy. Pour into a chilled tumbler. Top up with sparkling water and stir gently. Dress with raspberries.

686
HAZELNUT COFFEE SPARKLE

A very well-chilled and refreshing glass of sparkling black coffee flavoured with a little hazelnut syrup.

SERVES 1

225 ml/8 fl oz strong black
   coffee, chilled
1 tbsp hazelnut syrup
2 tbsp brown sugar
6 ice cubes
350 ml/12 fl oz sparkling water
lemon and lime slices,
   to decorate

Blend the first four ingredients in a food processor until smooth and frothy. Pour into a tall chilled glass, top up with iced sparkling water and dress with lemon slices and lime slices.

BEST OF THE REST

From Italy to Ireland, Prague to Paris, the possibilities are endless with this international selection of wild-card cocktails. These colourful cocktails will score a direct hit. It's bombs away with the infamous B-52 or, for a more sedate slurp, try an Apple Martini. Whether you're searching for a Christmas drink or a spring nip, you'll find it here.

687 APPLE MARTINI

The Martini family just keeps on growing since the original cocktail was invented in New York in about 1900 – this is one of the newest and liveliest members.

SERVES 1

cracked ice
1 measure vodka
1 measure sour apple schnapps
1 measure apple juice

Put the cracked ice into a cocktail shaker and pour in the vodka, schnapps and apple juice. Cover and shake vigorously for 10–20 seconds, until the outside of the shaker is misted. Strain into a cocktail glass.

688 B-52

The B-52 was created in the famous Alice's restaurant in Malibu, California. The name refers to the B-52 Stratofortress long-range bomber.

SERVES 1

1 measure chilled dark crème de cacao
1 measure chilled Bailey's Irish Cream
1 measure chilled Grand Marnier

Pour the crème de cacao into a shot glass. With a steady hand, gently pour in the Bailey's to make a second layer, then gently pour in the Grand Marnier. Cover and slam.

689 ALABAMA SLAMMER

Small, but perfectly proportioned – this is a shooter with a real kick!

SERVES 1

1 measure Southern Comfort
1 measure amaretto
1/2 measure sloe gin
cracked ice
1/2 tsp lemon juice

Pour the Southern Comfort, amaretto and gin over cracked ice in a mixing glass and stir. Strain into a shot glass and add the lemon juice. Cover and slam.

690 KIR

As with the best mustard, cassis production is centred on the French city of Dijon. This cocktail is named in memory of a partisan and mayor of the city, Félix Kir.

SERVES 1

cracked ice
2 measures cassis
chilled white wine
lemon peel twist, to decorate

Put the ice cubes into a chilled wine glass. Pour the cassis over the ice. Top up with white wine and stir well. Dress with a lemon twist.

691 KIRSCH RICKEY

This cherry-themed rickey will sharpen your taste buds.

SERVES 1

2 measures kirsch
1 tbsp lime juice
crushed ice
sparkling water
fresh cherries, stoned,
   to decorate

Pour the kirsch and lime juice into a chilled tumbler half filled with crushed ice. Top up with sparkling water and stir gently. Dress with fresh cherries.

693 RAFFLES KNOCKOUT

This is as cool as its inspiration, although Raffles himself probably favoured a Singapore Sling.

SERVES 1

1 measure triple sec
1 measure kirsch
dash lemon juice
ice
lemon slices and cocktail
   cherries, to decorate

Shake the liquid ingredients vigorously over ice until well frosted. Strain into a chilled cocktail glass and dress with slices of lemon and cocktail cherries.

692 PEARDROPS

Pear is one fruit that adds an alcoholic type of flavour, whether it is in alcohol form or not. When you cook pears, they become more aromatic and in this cocktail they certainly give off a wonderfully rich and heady aroma.

SERVES 1

1 measure pear schnapps
chilled perry
cherry, to decorate

Pour the schnapps into the bottom of a chilled champagne glass and slowly add the perry. Dress with a cherry.

694 MIDNIGHT SUNSET

Punt e Mes is an unusual aperitif – as bitter as Campari but more like a sweet sherry. It is the perfect mixer in a cocktail such as this.

SERVES 1

1 measure Cinzano rosso
1/2 measure lime juice
1/2 measure Punt e Mes
ice
pineapple juice
pineapple slices, to decorate

Shake the first three ingredients well over ice. Strain into a chilled highball glass with more ice and top up with pineapple juice. Dress with pineapple slices.

695 ICE MAIDEN

If you keep frozen orange juice in the freezer, it will instantly provide the basis for many cocktails.

SERVES 1

2 tbsp frozen orange juice
2 tbsp crushed ice
1 measure dry vermouth
lemonade
2 measures Marsala
fruit slice, to decorate

Blend the orange juice, ice and vermouth to a slush in a small blender. Pour into an iced wine glass and top up with lemonade. Pour on the Marsala and dress with a slice of fruit.

697 RED DESERT

Vermouth is a fortified wine flavoured with herbs, spices and flowers, so it makes a refreshing and aromatic drink.

SERVES 1

1 measure red vermouth
1 measure dry vermouth
ice
soda water
orange slice, to decorate

Stir the two vermouths briefly with ice in a glass. Top up with soda water to taste and dress with a slice of orange.

696 MERRY WIDOW FIZZ

Dubonnet, a French vermouth-type aperitif made by adding quinine and other flavours to sweet heavy wine, makes a versatile cocktail ingredient.

SERVES 1

3 measures Dubonnet
1 measure fresh lemon juice
1 measure fresh orange juice
egg white
cracked ice
soda water

Shake the first four ingredients together over ice until well frosted. Pour into a chilled glass and top up with soda water.

698 COUNTRY CLUB

Vermouths vary from extra dry to dry or sweet, so you can vary this drink to suit your taste.

SERVES 1

2 measures dry vermouth
1 tsp grenadine
ice
soda water, to taste

Stir the vermouth and grenadine over ice in a chilled tumbler. Top up with soda water, to taste.

699
BITTER-SWEET SYMPHONY

A light, refreshing cocktail for lovers of Campari, easy anytime drinking to make as strong or as weak as you like.

SERVES 1

1 measure Campari
1 measure sweet vermouth
ice
soda water
orange peel twist,
    to decorate

Pour the Campari and vermouth into a highball glass filled with ice. Stir well and then top up with soda water. Dress with a twist of orange peel.

700
WALK TALL

Looks and smells like orange juice, but don't be deceived, there is a lot going on here!

SERVES 1

1/2 measure sweet white
    vermouth
1/4 measure gin
1/4 measure Campari
1/4 measure orange liqueur
sweet orange juice
ice
soda water
orange peel twist,
    to decorate

Mix the first five ingredients well and pour into a tall glass or large tumbler full of ice. Top up with a splash of soda water and dress with a twist of orange.

701
BLACKCURRANT COCKTAIL

If you have young children, you can make them a non-alcoholic version, using blackcurrant cordial and soda water.

SERVES 1

2 measures dry vermouth
1 measure cassis
ice
soda water
blackcurrants, to decorate

Shake the first two ingredients over ice until well frosted. Strain into a medium-sized glass and top up with soda water. Add a few blackcurrants at the last minute.

702
SPECIAL CLAM COCKTAIL

The combination of clam and tomato juice is unusual, but goes well with dry fruity sherry.

SERVES 1

1 measure schnapps
1 measure dry sherry
1/2 measure clam and tomato
    juice
3–4 dashes lemon juice
2 dashes Worcestershire sauce
ice
cayenne pepper and lemon
    zest, to decorate

Stir all the liquid ingredients together over ice and strain into an ice-filled old-fashioned glass or a tumbler. Dress with a sprinkling of cayenne pepper and lemon zest.

703

MANHATTAN DRY

(see right-hand page for picture)

This drier version of the classic Manhattan would be good even on a wet day in New York.

SERVES 1

dash Angostura bitters
2 dashes curaçao
3 measures rye whisky
1 measure dry vermouth
cracked ice
cocktail cherry, to decorate

Shake the liquids over cracked ice in a cocktail shaker and mix well. Strain into a chilled glass and dress with a cocktail cherry.

704

BROADWAY SMILE

You'll need to keep a steady hand to prevent the layers from mixing as you pour.

SERVES 1

1 measure chilled triple sec
1 measure chilled cassis
1 measure chilled Swedish
  Punsch

Pour the triple sec into a small chilled tumbler, pour the cassis on top, without mixing, then pour the Swedish Punsch on top, again without mixing.

705

EGGMANIA

No need to wait until Easter to serve this delicious mint chocolate treat. Why not serve with small chocolate eggs for added luxury?

SERVES 1

1 measure chocolate mint
  liqueur
1 measure advocaat
1/2 measure whisky
1/2 scoop vanilla ice cream
2 eggs

Blend all the ingredients except the eggs together in a small blender on a slow speed for about 10 seconds. Add the eggs and blend again for another 30 seconds, until smooth and creamy. Pour into a chilled cocktail glass.

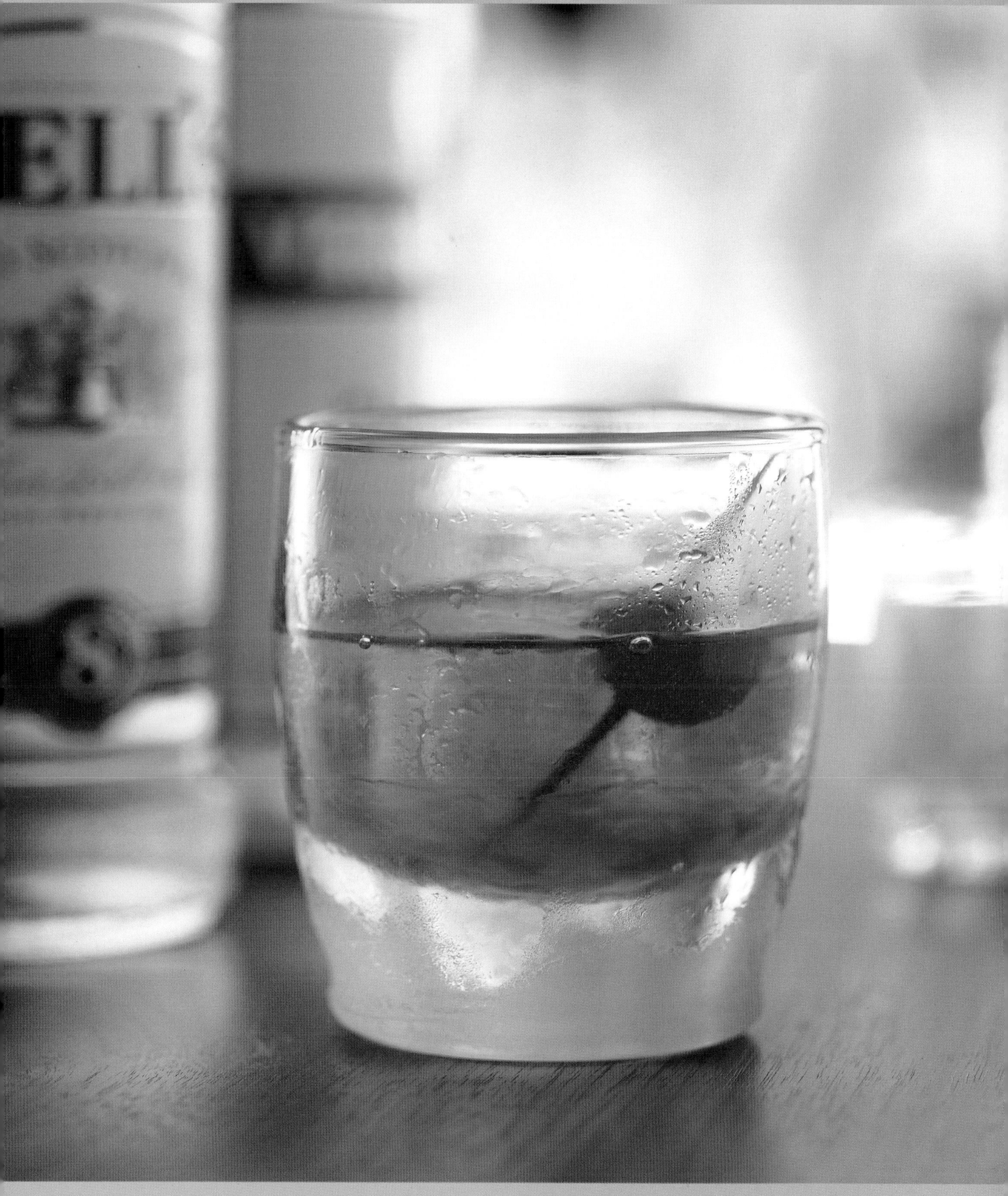

706 CACTUS CAFÉ

An exciting variation on iced coffee that will be enjoyed on any hot day and can be made in advance, ready for a crowd.

SERVES 1

1 measure coffee liqueur
1/2 measure tequila
ice
lemonade, to taste

Pour the coffee liqueur and tequila over ice in a tall glass and top up with lemonade to taste.

708 KISS-ME-QUICK

This cloudy combination is for serious anise lovers and the last few drops of bitters add a nice sharp finish.

SERVES 1

2 measures Pernod
1 tsp Cointreau
2 dashes Angostura bitters
ice
soda water, to taste

Pour the first three ingredients over the ice in a tumbler or tall glass. Top up with soda water to taste and add a few more drops of Angostura bitters.

707 MUDDY WATERS

Coffee soda with a difference – not quite non-alcoholic but it could be. Or you could add a drop more liqueur if you have added just a little too much cola!

SERVES 1

1 measure coffee liqueur
crushed ice
cola, to taste

Stir the liqueur over ice in a tall glass and top up with cola to taste.

709 SUISSESSE

This looks almost like a cool refreshing glass of milk, but don't think you will be able to fool your friends for very long!

SERVES 1

1 1/2 measures Pernod
1 measure lemon juice
1/4 measure orange flower
    water
1 egg white
ice
soda water, to taste

Shake all ingredients except the soda water over ice until well frosted. Strain into a tumbler and top up with a little soda water to taste.

710 ICEBERG

If you are an anise fan, you may want to add only a very little lemonade – it's up to you.

SERVES 1

2 measures Pernod
good squeeze of lime
cracked ice
lemonade or ginger beer, to taste
lime peel twist, to decorate

Stir the Pernod and lime over ice. Strain into a chilled highball glass with extra ice and top up with lemonade to taste. Dress with a twist of lime.

712 PACKING A PUNCH

Just sip quietly and your blues will soon drift away.

SERVES 1

1 measure coconut liqueur
1 measure blue curaçao
$1/2$ measure white rum
$1/4$ measure pineapple juice
crushed ice
toasted shredded coconut, to decorate

Blend the first five ingredients together in a blender until frothy and partly frozen. Pour into a tall iced glass, top up with more ice and dress with toasted shredded coconut.

711 MISTY MORNING

If the weather really looked like this in the morning, you'd need another one of these quickly!

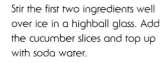

SERVES 1

$1^{1}/2$ measures Pernod or Ricard
1 measure crème de menthe
ice
cucumber slices
soda water

Stir the first two ingredients well over ice in a highball glass. Add the cucumber slices and top up with soda water.

713 LUISITA

If you are not feeling in a blue mood, remember you can buy orange curaçao and change the whole mood without changing the taste!

SERVES 1

1 measure blue curaçao
lemon barley water
few dashes lemon juice
ice
tonic water
lemon slices, to decorate

Stir the curaçao, barley water and lemon juice over ice in a chilled long tumbler. Add tonic water to taste and dress with a few slices of lemon.

714 ORANGE DEMONS

Don't despair if you think this is going to look grim. With plenty of ice and tonic water, it begins to look different!

SERVES 1

1/2 measure green crème de menthe
1 measure Dubonnet
1/3 measure orange juice
ice
soda water
orange slice, to decorate

Stir the first three ingredients with ice in a tumbler or old-fashioned glass. Top up with soda water and dress with a slice of orange.

716 WAKE-UP CALL

Very refreshing and revitalizing at any time of the day – and not just for hangovers!

SERVES 1

1/2 measure fresh orange juice
1/2 measure Fernet Branca
ice
soda water, to taste

Stir the first two ingredients over ice in a medium-sized glass and top up with soda water to taste.

715 LIME 'N' LEMON HOUR

This advocaat cocktail may look like a milkshake, but when mixed with citrus and given a kick of vodka, it certainly doesn't taste like one!

SERVES 1

1 measure advocaat
1/2 measure vodka
1/2 measure lime cordial
ice
lemonade
lime peel twist

Shake the first three ingredients well over ice until frosted. Pour into a chilled highball glass and top up with lemonade. Finish with a twist of lime peel.

717 TRICOLOUR

Despite the inclusion of Bailey's Irish Cream, the ingredients combine to make the Italian tricolour, not the Irish green, white and orange.

SERVES 1

1 measure chilled red maraschino
1 measure chilled crème de menthe
1 measure chilled Bailey's Irish Cream

Pour the maraschino into a chilled shot glass. Gently pour in the crème de menthe to make a second layer and, for the final layer, gently pour in the Bailey's Irish Cream.

718 UNION JACK

The gorgeous jewel colours of so many of the world's flags shine out from this delicious glassful.

SERVES 1

1 measure chilled maraschino
1 measure chilled grenadine
1 measure chilled blue
   curaçao

Pour the maraschino into a chilled shot glass. With a steady hand, gently pour in the grenadine to make a second layer and, finally, gently pour in the curaçao.

720 MASSIMO

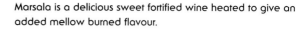

Marsala is a delicious sweet fortified wine heated to give an added mellow burned flavour.

SERVES 1

2 measures Marsala
1 measure gin
ice
fresh mint sprig
orange and lime slices
lemonade
dash Angostura bitters

Pour the Marsala and gin over ice in an old-fashioned glass. Add mint, slices of fruit and lemonade to taste, then finish with a dash of Angostura bitters.

719 FRIVOLOUS DUBONNET

A sweet and fruity favourite with the girls.

SERVES 1

1 measure Dubonnet
1 measure cherry brandy
1/2 measure lemon juice
1/2 egg white
ice
soda water
lemon slice, to decorate

Shake the Dubonnet, brandy and lemon juice over ice with the egg white until frothy. Strain into long glasses and top up with soda water. Dress with a lemon slice.

721 SNOWBALL CLASSIC

The familiar golden egg yellow of advocaat is preferred by many when it is lengthened with soda water or tonic water and given an added tang of lemon.

SERVES 1

1 measure advocaat
good dash fresh lemon juice
ice
lemonade
orange and lemon slices, to
   decorate

Stir the advocaat and lemon over ice in a mixing glass. Strain into a highball glass filled with ice and top up with lemonade. Dress with slices of orange and lemon.

722 ACE OF SPADES

This drink is long, cold and refreshing, great for warm summer evenings, but it is not as mild as it looks!

SERVES 1

1/2 measure coffee liqueur
1/2 measure Cointreau
1 measure Dubonnet
ice cubes
1/2 bottle Guinness

Mix the first three ingredients together over ice in a large glass. Slowly pour in the Guinness so it doesn't bubble over.

723 RUFFLED

This strange combination could ruffle your feathers if you have too many!

SERVES 1

1 measure Dubonnet
1/2 measure coffee liqueur
1/2 measure Calvados
ice
Guinness
apple peel twist, to decorate

Mix together the first three ingredients and pour over ice into a long glass. Top up with Guinness and dress with a twist of apple peel.

724 SPARKLING ROSE

The ever popular Dubonnet mixes with so many flavours. This combination may be new to you, so give it a try – you won't be disappointed.

SERVES 1

2 measures Dubonnet
3 measures cider
5 measures lemonade
ice
apple slice, to decorate

Stir the liquid ingredients over ice in a chilled highball glass and dress with a slice of apple.

725 BRAIN HAEMORRHAGE

This is a rare instance of a cocktail that is deliberately intended to look horrible, rather than tempting, and was probably invented to drink at Halloween.

SERVES 1

1 measure chilled peach
  schnapps
1 tsp chilled Bailey's Irish
  Cream
1/2 tsp chilled grenadine

Pour the peach schnapps into a shot glass, then carefully float the Bailey's Irish Cream on top. Finally, add the grenadine.

726 TIGER BY THE TAIL

This deceptively light cocktail may persuade you that you're as strong as a tiger!

SERVES 1

2 measures Pernod
4 measures orange juice
1/4 tsp triple sec
crushed ice
lime twist, to decorate

Blend the liquid ingredients with crushed ice until smooth. Pour into a chilled wine glass and dress with a twist of lime.

728 ADAM AND EVE

The base is sharp and astringent, while the top is sweet and frothy – no discrimination here, of course!

SERVES 1

2 measures triple sec
1 measure vodka
1 measure grapefruit juice
1 measure cranberry juice
ice
5–6 cubes of pineapple
2 tsp icing sugar
crushed ice
strawberry slice, to decorate

Shake the triple sec, vodka, grapefruit juice and cranberry juice over ice until well frosted. Strain into a chilled glass. In a blender, blend the pineapple with the sugar and 1–2 tablespoons of crushed ice to a frothy slush. Float gently on the top of the cocktail. Dress with a slice of strawberry.

727 OSBORNE

It may break all the rules about never mixing the grape with the grain, but this simple combination really works.

SERVES 1

3 measures claret
1 measure Scotch whisky

Pour the claret and whisky into a goblet and stir.

729 SANGRIA

The perfect long cold drink for a summer barbecue.

SERVES 6

juice of 1 orange
juice of 1 lemon
2 tbsp icing sugar
ice cubes
1 orange, thinly sliced
1 lemon, thinly sliced
1 bottle chilled red wine
lemonade, to taste

Shake the orange and lemon juices with the sugar and transfer to a large jug. When the sugar has dissolved, add a few ice cubes, the sliced fruit and the wine. Marinate for 1 hour, then add lemonade to taste and more ice.

730
BANANA SLIP

It takes a steady hand to float the Bailey's on top, so make these before you start drinking them.

SERVES 1
1 measure chilled crème de banane
1 measure chilled Bailey's Irish Cream

Pour the crème de banane into a shot glass. With a steady hand, gently pour in the Bailey's Irish Cream to make a second layer. Cover and slam.

731
BLONDE SANGRIA

Like its red wine-based cousin, this is an excellent party drink to prepare for a crowd at any time of year.

SERVES 10
4 measures clear acacia or almond blossom honey
2 lemons
2 oranges
8–12 cups white wine
ice
soda water

Warm the honey a little. Pour into a large jug. Cut 2–3 good slices off the fruits, then squeeze the rest of the juice into the honey and mix well. Slowly add the wine and mix. Pour over ice into tall glasses, add the fruit slices, and top up with soda water.

732
WINE WITH TEA PUNCH

This light and fruity punch is perfect for a garden party, really well iced.

SERVES 20
cracked ice
225 g/8 oz icing sugar
5 bottles Rhine wine
1.5 litres/2½ pints soda water
2 measures brandy
2 measures maraschino
2 tbsp tea, in bags, or leaves tied in muslin
fruit slices, to decorate

Surround a large punch bowl with cracked ice. Add all the ingredients, except the fruit, and leave to marinate for about 10 minutes. Remove the tea and add the slices of fruit.

733
PROST

This German cocktail is best made with one of the slightly sweeter and fruitier German Rhine wines.

SERVES 1
½ measure cherry brandy
4 measures white wine
crushed ice
soda water
2 maraschino cherries, to decorate

Shake the brandy and wine together over ice until well frosted. Pour into a tall wine goblet, top up with soda water and dress with maraschino cherries.

734
BLACK AND TAN

For a cocktail without a kick, you can use non-alcoholic ginger beer instead of the alcoholic variety.

SERVES 1
1/2 cup chilled ginger ale
1/2 cup chilled ginger beer
ice cubes
lime slices, to decorate

Pour the ginger ale and ginger beer into a tumbler over ice cubes. Do not stir. Dress with lime slices.

735
ISLAND IN THE SUN

Anise is a flavour that blends well with fruit and gives only a subtle background taste in this cocktail.

SERVES 1
1 thick-skinned orange
1 measure orange juice
1 measure ouzo or other anise spirit
3 dashes grenadine
ice
soda water
orange slice and maraschino cherry, to decorate

Cut one good orange slice and reserve. Grate 1/2 tsp zest. Stir the orange juice over ice with the orange zest, ouzo and grenadine. Mix until well frosted. Pour into a cocktail glass with more ice, top up with soda water and dress with a slice of orange and a cherry.

736
AFTER FIVE

Originally the name of a mixed cocktail finished off with lemonade, it has now been completely transformed into a layered shooter with a real kick.

SERVES 1
1/2 measure chilled peppermint schnapps
1 measure chilled Kahlúa
1 tbsp chilled Bailey's Irish Cream

Pour the peppermint schnapps into a shot glass. Carefully pour the Kahlúa over the back of a teaspoon so that it forms a separate layer. Finally, float the Bailey's Irish Cream on top.

737
POM POM

This lemony extravaganza is pretty in pink, with a frothy topping to match its frivolous name.

SERVES 1
juice of half a lemon
1 egg white
1 dash grenadine
crushed ice
lemonade
lemon slice, to decorate

Shake the lemon juice, egg white and grenadine together and strain over crushed ice in a tall glass. Top up with lemonade and dress with a slice of lemon.

738 ISLAND BABY (see right-hand page for picture)

A classic combination of peppermint and rich chocolate.

SERVES 1

2 measures peppermint
   schnapps
1 measure dark crème de
   cacao
cracked ice
soda water

Shake the peppermint schnapps and crème de cacao vigorously over ice until well frosted. Fill a small chilled tumbler with cracked ice and strain the cocktail over it. Top up with soda water.

739 SOBER SUNDAY

An interesting concoction for those not drinking and any who are driving.

SERVES 1

1 measure grenadine
1 measure fresh lemon or lime
   juice
ice
lemonade
lemon and lime slices,
   to decorate

Pour the grenadine and fruit juice into an ice-filled highball glass. Top up with lemonade and dress with slices of lemon and lime.

740 SLUSH PUPPY

Pink, pretty and refreshing – it looks serious, but you won't need to book a cab to take you home.

SERVES 1

juice of 1 lemon or
   1/2 pink grapefruit
1/2 measure grenadine
ice
few strips lemon peel
2–3 tsp raspberry syrup
soda water
maraschino cherry, to decorate

Pour the lemon juice and grenadine into a chilled tall glass with ice. Add the lemon peel, raspberry syrup and soda water to taste. Dress with a cherry.

741 RATTLESNAKE

If you can prevent your hand trembling when you make this cocktail, it really will look like a rattler's tail!

SERVES 1

1 measure chilled dark crème de cacao

1 measure chilled Bailey's Irish Cream

1 measure chilled Kahlúa

Pour the crème de cacao into a shot glass. With a steady hand, gently pour in the Bailey's Irish Cream to make a second layer, then the Kahlúa to make a third layer. Do not stir.

742 GLOOM CHASER

This bright and cheery drink is tempting enough to chase away any gloomy moods.

SERVES 1

1 measure dry vermouth

1 1/2 measures gin

1/2 tsp grenadine

2 dashes Pernod

ice

Shake the liquid ingredients together over ice and strain into a cocktail glass.

743 RED COBBLER

Although traditionally a short drink, for a cobbler to be extra refreshing, it is often drunk long over crushed ice, especially if it's very strong.

SERVES 1

orange and lemon slices or wedges

1 measure port

1 measure gin

few drops fraise

ice

Place the fruit in the shaker and crush or muddle with a wooden spoon or small pestle. Add the liquids and ice and shake well until frosted. Strain into a frosted martini glass and add the squeezed fruit.

744 CHARLESTON

This little number combines several tastes and flavours to produce a very lively drink. Don't drink it when you are thirsty, you might want too many!

SERVES 1

1/4 measure gin

1/4 measure dry vermouth

1/4 measure sweet vermouth

1/4 measure Cointreau

1/4 measure kirsch

1/4 measure maraschino

ice

lemon peel twist, to decorate

Shake all the liquids well together over ice and strain into a chilled glass. Dress with a twist of lemon.

745
WIDOW'S WISH

Nobody's sure what the widow might be wishing for – another one of these, perhaps?

SERVES 1

2 measures Benedictine
1 egg
ice cubes
single cream

Shake the Benedictine with the egg vigorously over ice until well frosted. Strain into a chilled tumbler. Top up with cream.

746
HIGH FLYER

These two unusual liqueurs combine to make a very aromatic and fruity cocktail.

SERVES 1

2/3 measure gin
1/2 measure Strega
1/2 measure Van der Hum or triple sec
ice
orange peel, to decorate

Stir the gin, Strega and Van der Hum well over ice and strain into a tumbler. Dress with some orange peel.

747
NELL GWYNN

Named after a saucy actress and mistress of King Charles II.

SERVES 1

1 measure triple sec
1 measure peach schnapps
1 measure white crème de menthe
ice
orange peel twist, to decorate

Pour the triple sec, peach schnapps and crème de menthe over ice in a mixing glass and stir well. Strain into a chilled cocktail glass and dress with an orange twist.

748
VOODOO

This enthralling mixture of flavours is guaranteed to weave a spell on your taste buds and work its magic from the first sip.

SERVES 1

1/2 measure chilled Kahlúa
1/2 measure chilled Malibu
1/2 measure chilled butterscotch schnapps
1 measure chilled milk

Pour the Kahlúa, Malibu, schnapps and milk into a glass and stir well.

749 BARTENDER

There is certainly an art to mixing and blending several different alcohols to give the best result. This classic has been much enjoyed by many generations.

SERVES 1

1/4 measure dry vermouth
1/4 measure Dubonnet
1/4 measure sherry
1/4 measure gin
dash Grand Marnier
ice
pineapple slice, to decorate

Shake the liquid ingredients together in a cocktail shaker with plenty of ice. Strain into a cocktail glass and dress with a slice of pineapple.

751 BLUE LADY

She couldn't get much bluer than this – let's hope the colour reflects her eyes, not her mood.

SERVES 1

2½ measures blue curaçao
1 measure white crème
    de cacao
1 measure single cream
ice

Shake the curaçao, crème de cacao and cream over ice until well frosted. Strain into a chilled cocktail glass.

750 PEPPERMINT PATTY

Sometimes the simple things in life are the best – one such pleasure is this delicious combination of chocolate and peppermint.

SERVES 1

cracked ice
1 measure white crème
    de cacao
1 measure white crème
    de menthe

Put the ice in a cocktail shaker and pour in the crème de cacao and crème de menthe. Shake vigorously for 10–20 seconds, until the outside of the shaker is misted. Strain into a shot glass.

752 RULE BRITANNIA

Unusually pretty and clever, this requires a few hours' forward planning to get the blue ice cubes ready in time. They melt quickly too.

SERVES 1

blue curaçao
1/4 measure Campari
1/2 measure vodka
1/4 measure pink grapefruit
    juice
ice

Make two ice cubes with 1–2 tablespoons of water and 1–2 teaspoons curaçao. Freeze well in advance. Shake the remaining liquid ingredients together over ice. Strain into a chilled cocktail glass and add an ice cube at the last minute.

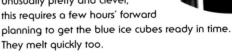

753 TITANIC

Let's hope it wasn't on the menu the night the ship went down. Perhaps it just gives you a hangover of titanic proportions?

SERVES 1

3 measures mandarin liqueur
2 measures vodka
cracked ice
sparkling water

Shake the mandarin liqueur and vodka vigorously over ice until well frosted. Half fill a chilled tumbler with cracked ice and strain the cocktail over it. Top up with sparkling water.

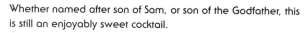

755 GODSON

Whether named after son of Sam, or son of the Godfather, this is still an enjoyably sweet cocktail.

SERVES 1

cracked ice
2 measures amaretto
orange juice

Put some cracked ice into a chilled tumbler. Pour in the amaretto and top up with orange juice. Stir well to mix

754 GODCHILD

Who wouldn't want a godchild as well-behaved and beautifully presented as this?

SERVES 1

crushed ice
1 1/2 measures amaretto
1 measure vodka
1 measure single cream

Blend some crushed ice in a blender with the amaretto, vodka and cream. Blend until smooth, then pour into a chilled champagne flute.

756 INDIAN SUMMER

The coffee liqueur is the key ingredient in this delicious long mix – it would be good with crème de noyaux or crème de cacao too.

SERVES 1

1 measure vodka
2 measures Kahlúa
1 measure gin
2 measures pineapple juice
ice
tonic water, to taste

Shake the vodka, Kahlúa, gin and pineapple juice well over ice until frosted. Strain into a medium-sized cocktail glass or wine glass and top up with tonic water to taste.

757 ISLAND BLUES

This taste of the deep blue ocean comes from those romantic rum-producing Islands.

SERVES 1

lemon juice
icing sugar
3/4 measure peach schnapps
1/2 measure blue curaçao
1 small egg white
dash fresh lemon juice
ice
lemonade

Frost the rim of a glass using the lemon juice and sugar. Set aside to dry. Place the peach schnapps, blue curaçao, egg white and lemon juice into a cocktail shaker half full of ice. Shake well and strain into a glass. Top up with lemonade.

758 ZANDER

A liquorice-flavoured liqueur, Sambuca is traditionally drunk straight, but its intense flavour is great with fruit drinks, and makes a change for a long drink.

SERVES 1

1 measure Sambuca
1 measure orange juice
dash lemon juice
ice
bitter lemon

Shake the Sambuca, orange juice and lemon juice well over ice and strain into a glass filled with ice. Top up with bitter lemon.

759 ROYALIST

Presumably this drink derives its name from its bourbon base. Louis XVI, of the Bourbon line of French kings, did not let it go to his head.

SERVES 1

1 measure bourbon
2 measures dry vermouth
1 measure Benedictine
dash peach bitters
cracked ice

Stir all the ingredients together in a mixing glass until well frosted. Strain into a glass.

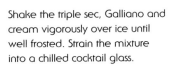

760 GOLDEN CADILLAC

A cocktail named after a car – both associated with the golden age of leisure and indolence.

SERVES 1

1 measure triple sec
1 measure Galliano
1 measure single cream
ice

Shake the triple sec, Galliano and cream vigorously over ice until well frosted. Strain the mixture into a chilled cocktail glass.

761
ROLLS-ROYCE

It's hardly surprising that several classic cocktails have been named after a famous marque. This version was created by author H. E. Bates in his popular novel *The Darling Buds of May*.

SERVES 1

cracked ice
dash orange bitters
2 measures dry vermouth
1 measure dry gin
1 measure Scotch whisky

Put the cracked ice into a mixing glass. Dash the bitters over the ice. Pour the vermouth, gin and whisky over the ice and stir to mix. Strain into a chilled cocktail glass.

762
BITTER ORANGE

This one is surprisingly cool and refreshing, sweet and lovely, with just a hint of underlying bitterness.

SERVES 1

1 measure Campari
2 measures orange juice
ice
sparkling water, to taste

Pour the Campari and orange juice over ice in a shaker. Shake vigorously until well frosted. Fill a tall glass with ice cubes and strain the cocktail over them. Top up with sparkling water to taste.

763
MELANIE HAMILTON

This gentle *Gone with the Wind* character got her man, turning Scarlett O'Hara green with envy in the process.

SERVES 1

2 measures triple sec
1 measure Midori
2 measures orange juice
ice
melon wedge, to decorate

Shake the triple sec, Midori, and orange juice vigorously over ice until well frosted. Strain the mixture into a chilled cocktail glass. Dress with a wedge of melon.

764
THE KICKER

There is certainly some kick in this cocktail, but it will be best enjoyed if you ice all the ingredients well first.

SERVES 1

2 dashes sweet vermouth
1/3 measure Calvados
2/3 measure white rum
ice

Shake the liquid ingredients well over ice and strain into a cocktail glass.

765 PORT FLIP

The sailor's favourite is a great winter warmer for anyone anytime, but be warned, it has a fair kick!

SERVES 1

1 egg
2 tsp icing sugar
grated nutmeg or
    ground ginger
300 ml/10 fl oz rum, port,
    brandy or whisky

Whisk the egg, sugar and nutmeg together. Warm the rum slightly in a saucepan over a low heat and whisk in the egg mixture. Serve (in heatproof glasses) when frothy and as warm or hot as you like (do not heat too much or the egg may curdle).

766 NINETEEN PICK-ME-UP

Nobody is sure where the name comes from – perhaps it's meant to restore you at the nineteenth hole.

SERVES 1

2 measures Pernod
1 measure gin
1/4 tsp sugar syrup
dash Angostura bitters
cracked ice
sparkling mineral water

Shake the Pernod, gin, sugar syrup and bitters vigorously over ice until well frosted. Half fill a tumbler with cracked ice and strain the cocktail over them. Top up with sparkling water.

767 VICTORY

To the victor the spoils – although there's nothing less than perfect about this drink!

SERVES 1

2 measures Pernod
1 measure grenadine
ice
sparkling mineral water

Shake the Pernod and grenadine vigorously over ice until well frosted. Strain into a chilled tumbler and top up with mineral water.

768 BLANCHE

As white as white can be – the natural result of combining clear liqueurs with cloudy pastis.

SERVES 1

1 measure Pernod
1 measure triple sec
1/2 measure clear curaçao
ice

Shake the liquid ingredients vigorously over ice until well frosted. Strain into a chilled cocktail glass.

769
WHICH WAY?

Aniseed-flavoured pastis, such as Pernod, are firm favourites in today's cocktail bars and often form the basis of almost lethally strong drinks.

SERVES 1

1 measure Pernod
1 measure anisette
1 measure brandy
cracked ice

Shake the Pernod, anisette and brandy vigorously over ice until well frosted. Strain into a chilled wine glass.

771
SAVOY SANGAREE

Truly the Savoy of sangarees – the usual red wine is replaced with rich ruby port.

SERVES 1

cracked ice
1 measure ruby port
1 tsp icing sugar
freshly grated nutmeg,
  to decorate

Put some cracked ice into a mixing glass, pour in the port and sugar and stir until dissolved. Strain into a chilled cocktail glass and sprinkle with freshly grated nutmeg.

770
MOONRISE

A warm and comforting drink – perfect for a bit of moongazing.

SERVES 1

300 ml/10 fl oz dry cider
1 tbsp brown sugar
pinch of ground cinnamon
pinch of freshly grated nutmeg
1 measure apple brandy
2 tsp single cream

Put the cider into a saucepan with the sugar, cinnamon and nutmeg. Heat gently, stirring until the sugar has dissolved. Pour into a warmed, heatproof punch glass and stir in the apple brandy. Float the cream on top by pouring it gently over the back of a teaspoon.

772
DUCHESS

Not as grand as a Grand Duchess, but pretty uplifting, all the same.

SERVES 1

cracked ice
1 measure Pernod
1 measure sweet vermouth
1 measure dry vermouth

Put some cracked ice into a mixing glass. Pour the Pernod, sweet vermouth and dry vermouth over the ice. Stir well to mix, then strain into a chilled cocktail glass.

773

DUKE (see right-hand page for picture)

A lovely fruity and frothy combination more suited to a duchess than a duke. Perhaps he designed it for her?

SERVES 1

1 measure triple sec
1/2 measure lemon juice
1/2 measure orange juice
1 egg white
dash maraschino
ice
chilled champagne

Shake the first five ingredients vigorously over ice until well frosted. Strain into a chilled wine glass. Top up with chilled champagne.

774

PISCO SOUR

Pisco is the national tipple of Chile and Peru – this is a very cooling drink, ideal for the heat of South American summers, but deceptively strong.

SERVES 1

2 measures pisco
1 measure lemon juice
1 tsp icing sugar
dash orange bitters (optional)
egg white (optional)
cracked ice

Shake the first five ingredients well over ice until frosted and strain into a glass. The egg white is optional, but it does help to bind the flavours together and also improves the drink's appearance.

775

GREENBRIAR

The origin of this potion is obscure. It may be named from the Greenbrier district of West Virginia, one of the homes of the Mint Julep.

SERVES 1

2 measures dry sherry
1 measure dry vermouth
dash peach bitters
cracked ice
mint sprig, to decorate

Stir the liquid ingredients together over ice in a wine glass until well chilled. Dress with mint.

776 GRANDMA'S SURPRISE

We all know Grandma loves sherry, especially on the quiet, so this one hidden in fresh orange juice will really please her!

SERVES 1

1/2 measure cream sherry
1/2 measure medium-dry
   vermouth
dash Angostura bitters
fresh orange juice
orange peel strip,
   to decorate

Stir the sherry and vermouth together with ice in a small tumbler. Add a dash Angostura bitters. Top up with orange juice and dress with a strip of orange peel.

777 SANTA VITTORIA

Dedicate this to any victorious match you have recently watched and enjoy the success all over again.

SERVES 1

1 measure Cinzano rosso
1 measure gin
1 measure fresh orange juice
1/4 measure Cointreau
ice
rose petals, to decorate

Shake the first four ingredients well over ice and strain into a chilled cocktail glass. Dress with rose petals.

778 RAFFLES

A popular cocktail from the old colonial days, before tonic stole the show.

SERVES 1

1 measure white vermouth
1/4 measure gin
1/4 measure Campari
ice
orange slice

Stir the first three ingredients over ice in a chilled medium-sized tumbler. Squeeze in a slice of orange and place it in the glass.

779 ADONIS

The sherry you choose makes all the difference to this drink, be it dry, sweet or the slightly nutty medium-sweet amontillado.

SERVES 1

1 measure sherry
1/2 measure red vermouth
dash orange bitters
ice
orange peel strip,
   to decorate

Stir the liquid ingredients over ice in a chilled medium-sized tumbler. Dress with a strip of orange peel.

780
THE CAPITOL

This is a surprisingly dry drink until the sugar from the rim kicks in, but you may prefer it without.

SERVES 1

few drops cherry brandy
1 tbsp icing sugar
2 dashes Angostura bitters
2 dashes sugar syrup
1 measure dry vermouth
1/2 measure brandy
ice
maraschino cherry, to decorate

Brush the rim of a shallow cocktail glass with the cherry brandy and dip in sugar. Leave to dry. Shake the liquid ingredients well together, strain into the cocktail glass, add a large ice cube and dress with a maraschino cherry.

782
PORT WINE COBBLER

Port is not usually thought of as a cocktail ingredient – this is like a chilled version of the winter warmer, hot port.

SERVES 1

1 tsp icing sugar
2 measures sparkling water
cracked ice
3 measures ruby port
orange slice and cocktail
   cherry, to decorate

Put the sugar into a chilled wine glass and add the water. Stir until the sugar has dissolved. Fill the glass with ice and pour in the ruby port. Dress with a slice of orange and a cocktail cherry.

783
SHERRY COBBLER

A long drink made with syrup and fresh fruit garnishes, Sherry Cobbler is the original, but there are now numerous and often more potent variations.

SERVES 1

crushed ice
1/4 tsp sugar syrup
1/4 tsp clear curaçao
4 measures amontillado sherry
pineapple wedges and lemon
   peel twist, to decorate

Fill a wine glass with crushed ice. Add the sugar syrup and curaçao and stir until frosted. Pour in the sherry and stir well. Dress with pineapple wedges and a twist of lemon peel.

781
BULLFROG

Fresh lemon is so important in cocktails, especially when it is one of the key ingredients, so look for really fresh unwaxed lemons and keep them in a warm place to encourage easier juicing.

SERVES 1

1 measure dry vermouth
1 measure triple sec
1 measure lemon juice
ice
green cherry and lime slices,
   to decorate

Shake the liquid ingredients well over ice until frosted. Strain into a chilled cocktail glass and dress with a green cherry and some slices of lime.

784 BOMBSHELL

Tequila will give any cocktail a good kick, but this concoction is really not as strong as its name implies!

SERVES 1

2 measures dry Marsala
1 measure tequila
splash Campari
splash cherry brandy
ice
lemon slice, to decorate

Mix the liquid ingredients straight into a small tumbler or cocktail glass with ice. Dress with a slice of lemon.

785 BANSHEE

A surprising number of cocktails are named after ghouls, ghosts and things that go bump in the night. It seems unlikely that this one will get you wailing (except with delight), but it might make your hair stand on end.

SERVES 1

2 measures crème de banane
1 measure crème de cacao
1 measure single cream
cracked ice

Shake the crème de banane, crème de cacao and cream vigorously over ice until a frost forms. Strain into a chilled wine glass.

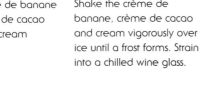

786 CANDY FLOSS

Banana freezes well, so it is great to use as a stirrer or finish to banana cocktails. Cut the fruit into long thin strips or diagonal slices and freeze briefly.

SERVES 1

1 measure peach schnapps
1 measure banana liqueur
1 measure apricot brandy
1–2 measures orange juice
ice
fresh or frozen banana pieces,
   to decorate

Mix the first three ingredients well with orange juice to taste. Pour into a tumbler full of ice and dress with banana pieces.

787 CUPID

A sweet and wholesome concoction – probably the original food of love!

SERVES 1

2 measures dry sherry
1 tsp sugar syrup
1 egg
dash Tabasco sauce
ice

Shake the sherry, sugar syrup, egg and Tabasco sauce vigorously over ice until well frosted. Strain into a chilled cocktail glass.

788 FROZEN APPLES

Like vodka, schnapps can be kept in the freezer as it never completely freezes and is ready iced for use.

SERVES 1

1 measure iced apple schnapps
1 measure white cranberry and apple juice
ice

Stir the liquid ingredients well over ice and strain into a chilled cocktail glass.

790 HAZY LADY

The bright pink grenadine soon trickles through these rich nutty-flavoured liqueurs to give a pretty base layer.

SERVES 1

1/2 measure crème de noyaux
1/2 measure coffee liqueur
1/2 measure brandy
1/2 measure orange juice
dash egg white
ice
dash grenadine
grated nutmeg, for sprinkling

Shake the first five ingredients together over ice until frosted. Strain into an iced cocktail glass and add a dash grenadine and a sprinkling of nutmeg.

789 ORANGE BITTER-SWEET

Izarra is a French floral liqueur based on Armagnac and eau de vie. The green is stronger than the yellow, whose sweetness is balanced here by the citrus and the Campari.

SERVES 1

1 measure yellow Izarra
1 measure Campari
juice of 1 orange
ice
orange slice, to decorate

Shake the liquid ingredients over ice until well frosted. Strain into a chilled cocktail glass and dress with a slice of orange.

791 PARADISO

As with most short cocktails, the best results come from using iced drinks. The very high-sugar liqueurs and spirits can be kept in the freezer without freezing.

SERVES 1

1 measure Parfait Amour
1 measure Cointreau or triple sec
ice cubes
orange peel twist, to decorate

Pour the liqueurs into a small chilled liqueur glass with ice. Dress with a twist of orange peel.

792 MUDSLIDE

Despite its ominous-sounding name, this is a richly flavoured creamy concoction that is delicious whatever the weather.

SERVES 1

1½ measures Kahlúa
1½ measures Bailey's Irish Cream
1½ measures vodka
ice
cracked ice

Shake the Kahlúa, Bailey's Irish Cream and vodka vigorously over ice until well frosted. Strain into a chilled glass.

794 TROPICAL MINT

Amarula is a very rich and exotic liqueur that is best served and drunk really cold – but not on ice, as that would dilute its real character.

SERVES 1

¾ measure chilled crème de menthe
¾ measure chilled Amarula

Pour the crème de menthe into the base of a slim cocktail glass or shot glass. Pour the Amarula slowly over the back of a spoon to create a layer over the mint.

793 LAST TANGO

Use the mango slices here as added ice cubes. They look and taste great and do a good job.

SERVES 1

1½ measures Mandarine Napoleon
½ measure kirsch
crushed ice
2–3 thin slices ripe mango, part-frozen, to decorate

Shake the liqueurs well over ice until frosted. Pour into a chilled cocktail glass and dress with the slices of mango.

795 MINT IMPERIAL

This is a strong combination with a long-lasting effect, so enjoy with caution or add lots of ice to cool it down.

SERVES 1

dash Pernod
icing sugar
1 measure green crème de menthe
½ measure Drambuie
2 dashes sugar syrup
ice

Rub a little Pernod around the rim of a chilled cocktail glass and then dip in sugar. Shake the next three ingredients together well over ice. Strain into the frosted glass and add one ice cube.

796
FOGGY TOWN

The anisette will turn cloudy only when you start stirring over ice – if you use white crème de menthe you could have a simple white fog.

SERVES 1

1/2 measure anisette
1/2 measure crème de menthe
few drops Angostura bitters
crushed ice

Stir the liquid ingredients over ice and pour into an ice-filled cocktail glass.

797
GALLANT GALLIANO

You can use green crème de menthe if you prefer, but this one is prettier and tastes just as good.

SERVES 1

1 measure Galliano
1/2 measure white crème de menthe
1/2 measure brandy
ice

Shake the first three ingredients well over ice. Strain into a chilled liqueur glass.

798
PINK SQUIRREL

Crème de noyaux has a wonderful, slightly bitter, nutty flavour, but is, in fact, made from peach and apricot kernels. It is usually served as a liqueur, but combines well with some other ingredients in cocktails.

SERVES 1

2 measures dark crème de cacao
1 measure crème de noyaux
1 measure single cream
cracked ice

Shake the crème de cacao, crème de noyaux and single cream vigorously over ice until well frosted. Strain into a chilled glass.

799
FIRELIGHTER

If you are looking for a cocktail to give you a real kick, this is it. The infamous absinthe is a seriously strong spirit and not to be treated lightly!

SERVES 1

1 measure iced absinthe
1 measure iced lime juice cordial
ice

Ice a glass. Shake the absinthe and lime over ice and, when well frosted, strain into the glass.

800
BLACK HOLE

Get yourself out of a hole when you need something really unusual. Black Sambuca is certainly different and will intrigue your friends.

SERVES 1

2 measures iced black
  Sambuca
2 measures iced dry vermouth
cracked ice
soda water, to taste

Stir the first two ingredients over ice until frosted. Strain into an old-fashioned glass and top up with soda water to taste.

801
FIREWIRE

This delicate and refreshing-looking drink will set you alight, ready for an eventful evening or some serious foot stomping.

SERVES 1

1 measure Pernod
1 measure Cointreau
1/2 measure fresh lemon juice
crushed ice
lemon peel twist,
  to decorate

Shake the first three ingredients well with crushed ice until frosted. Strain into a chilled cocktail glass and dress with a twist of lemon.

802
TRIPLE
CHAMPION

Pink or ruby grapefruit juices are sweeter and gentler flavours than classic white grapefruit juice, so are very good mixers in cocktails.

SERVES 1

1 measure Cinzano bianco
1 measure triple sec
1–2 measures pink or ruby
  grapefruit juice
1/2 measure ruby port
ice

Mix the liquid ingredients in a tall tumbler with ice.

803
WILLIAM TELL

Any schnapps would do, but pear is the best flavour combination here.

SERVES 1

2 measures pear schnapps
1 measure maraschino
ice
2 measures apple juice
soda water, to taste

Stir the first two ingredients with ice in a tumbler or highball glass. Add the apple juice and top up with soda water to taste.

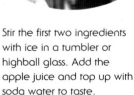

804
WHAT A PEACH

Vermouth is a popular light spirit and, mixed with fruit and sparkling water, makes an interesting long and refreshing drink.

SERVES 1

1 measure dry vermouth
1/2 measure amaretto
2 measures peach nectar
ice
peach-flavoured sparkling water
flowers, to decorate

Shake the first three ingredients together over ice until frosted. Strain into a chilled tall glass and top up with water to taste. Dress with flowers.

805
CHRISTMAS PUNCH

In the bleak midwinter, a glass of this piping hot punch will really hit the spot.

SERVES 8

4 cups red wine
4 tbsp sugar
1 cinnamon stick
350 ml/12 fl oz boiling water
90 ml/3 fl oz brandy
90 ml/3 fl oz sherry
90 ml/3 fl oz orange liqueur, such as Cointreau
2 seedless oranges, cut into wedges
2 apples, cored and cut into wedges

Put the wine, sugar and cinnamon into a large saucepan and stir. Warm over a low heat, stirring, until simmering. Do not boil. Remove from the heat and strain. Discard the cinnamon stick. Return the wine to the pan and stir in remaining liquids. Add the fruit wedges and warm gently over a very low heat, but do not boil. Remove from the heat and pour into a heatproof punch bowl.

806
ONE ENCHANTED EVENING

A long refreshing drink for any occasion when you need cheering up a little.

SERVES 1

2 measures pineapple juice
1 measure crème de banane
1 measure Mount Gay rum
ice
few drops grenadine

Shake the first three ingredients well over ice and pour into an ice-filled highball glass. Top with a few drops of grenadine.

807
JUICY LUCY

Harvey Wallbanger without the vodka – very nice, very simple, and it could be a long drink too.

SERVES 1

2 measures Galliano
4 measures fresh orange juice
ice

Mix the Galliano and orange juice straight into an ice-filled tumbler.

808
AMARETTO STINGER

(see right-hand page for picture)

The vital ingredient in a stinger is crème de menthe. Here it's white, therefore hidden, and capable of providing a real sting.

SERVES 6

2 measures amaretto
1 measure white crème de menthe
ice

Pour the amaretto and crème de menthe over ice. Shake vigorously until well frosted and strain into a chilled cocktail glass.

809
CARIBBEAN CHILL

A long and refreshing party punch that you could prepare well in advance ready to mix in the glass at the last minute.

SERVES 6

5 measures Malibu
3 measures crème de banane
10 measures fresh orange or pineapple juice
ice
soda water

Mix the first three ingredients well together and chill. When required, pour over ice in highball glasses and top up with soda water.

810
BANANA COCKTAIL

This can be sweet and rich, so enough ice and the right touch of soda water are important.

SERVES 1

1 measure advocaat
1 measure crème de banane
1 ripe banana
1/2 cup crushed ice
soda water, to taste

Blend all the ingredients except the soda water in a blender until smooth and well frosted. Pour into a chilled highball glass and top up with soda water to taste.

811
PINEAPPLE JULEP

In place of the traditional mint, this julep has pineapple, which needs to be finely chopped or mashed in the glass with the ice.

SERVES 6–8

juice of 2 oranges
2 measures raspberry vinegar
3 measures maraschino
3 measures gin
1 bottle sparkling white wine
1 small ripe pineapple, cut into small pieces
crushed ice

Muddle or mash the orange, vinegar, maraschino, gin, wine and pineapple well together. Pour into iced tumblers filled with crushed ice and drink through straws before the ice begins to melt.

812
MELON & GINGER CRUSH

A refreshing summer drink, this melon crush is quick and simple to make. If you can't buy kaffir limes, ordinary limes are fine.

SERVES 4

1 melon, peeled, deseeded and coarsely chopped
6 tbsp ginger wine
3 tbsp kaffir lime juice
crushed ice
1 lime, thinly sliced, to decorate

Place the melon flesh in a blender with the ginger wine and lime juice and blend on high speed until smooth. Place crushed ice in four medium-sized straight-sided glasses and pour over the melon and ginger crush. Dress with slices of lime.

813
PROHIBITION PUNCH

Prohibition era cocktails were designed to look non-alcoholic – this one, however, actually is as innocent as iced tea.

SERVES 6–8

125 ml/4 fl oz apple juice
350 ml/12 fl oz lemon juice
125 ml/4 fl oz sugar syrup
cracked ice
2.2 litres/3¾ pints ginger ale
orange slices, to decorate

Pour the apple juice, lemon juice and sugar syrup into a large jug. Add ice and the ginger ale. Stir gently to mix. Serve in chilled tumblers, dressed with slices of orange.

814
FRUIT RAPTURE

A silky smooth mix for fruit drink sophisticates. Perfect for any time of the day, unless, of course, you do not want to share...

SERVES 2

125 ml/4 fl oz milk
125 ml/4 fl oz peach yogurt
90 ml/3 fl oz orange juice
225 g/8 oz canned peach slices, drained
6 ice cubes
fresh orange peel strips, to decorate

Pour the milk, yogurt and orange juice into a food processor and process gently until combined. Add the peach slices and ice cubes and process until smooth. Pour the mixture into glasses and dress with strips of fresh orange peel.

815
WHITE CHARGER

Definitely a summertime drink. You could try it with other freezes, such as lemon sorbet, for instance, and it is especially good for a fun barbecue cocktail.

SERVES 1

1/2 scoop vanilla ice cream
1 measure gin
2 measures chilled white wine or soda water, to taste

Shake together the ice cream and gin until well mixed. Pour into a medium-sized chilled glass and stir in wine to taste.

817
ESPRESSO GALLIANO

One of the many variations on the original Irish Coffee, but this one is best without the cream.

SERVES 1

2 1/2 measures strong hot coffee
1 1/2 measures Galliano
orange juice, to taste
sugar, to taste
orange peel twist, to decorate

Pour the coffee and Galliano into an Irish coffee glass and add orange juice and sugar to taste. Dress with an orange peel twist.

816
APPLE TODDY

A toddy is traditionally served warm, but in fact this one is just as good served cold during not-so-cold weather.

SERVES 1

1 measure whisky, rum or brandy
3 measures cider or apple juice
lemon slice, to decorate

Warm the whisky and cider gently together and pour into a medium-sized tumbler. Dress with a slice of lemon.

818
MEXICAN COFFEE

Another heady mix of coffee and liqueur – probably best drunk in the cool of a Northern winter, though.

SERVES 1

2 1/2 measures strong hot coffee
1 1/2 measures Kahlúa
1 tbsp whipped cream
1 tbsp grated chocolate

Pour the coffee and Kahlúa into an Irish coffee glass. Top with some whipped cream and grated chocolate.

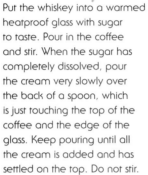

819
IRISH COFFEE

This is thought to have been created by Joe Sheridan in the 1940s when he was head chef at Shannon Airport, Ireland.

SERVES 1

2 measures Irish whiskey
sugar, to taste
freshly made strong black
    coffee
2 measures double cream

Put the whiskey into a warmed heatproof glass with sugar to taste. Pour in the coffee and stir. When the sugar has completely dissolved, pour the cream very slowly over the back of a spoon, which is just touching the top of the coffee and the edge of the glass. Keep pouring until all the cream is added and has settled on the top. Do not stir.

820
JAGGER TAE

Take this in a thermos when walking in the mountains and you will never be alone.

SERVES 1

hot fresh tea without milk
sugar, to taste
2–3 measures schnapps or
    brandy
lemon slice, to decorate

Pour the hot tea into a warmed heatproof glass or mug, add sugar to taste and stir until it is dissolved. Add the schnapps and dress with a slice of lemon. Serve hot.

821
TORNADO

If these liqueurs are really well iced, you will certainly create a tornado in your glass when you pour one into the other – just sit and watch them swirling for a moment!

SERVES 1

1 measure peach or other
    favourite schnapps, frozen
1 measure black Sambuca,
    frozen

Pour the schnapps into an iced shot glass. Then gently pour on the Sambuca over the back of a spoon. Leave to stand for a few minutes to settle and separate before you down it.

822
BROWN COW

Not very brown, but with all that milk, it certainly has a pronounced bovine quality.

SERVES 1

1 measure Kahlúa
3 measures chilled milk
cracked ice

Shake the Kahlúa and milk vigorously over ice until well frosted. Half fill a small chilled tumbler with ice and strain the cocktail over.

823
WATERMELON MAN

Watermelon is such a colourful and tasty fruit that it makes a great mixer. Don't be tempted to add more though, unless you want to dilute the strength of your cocktail.

SERVES 1
4 measures dry white wine
1 dash grenadine
4 cubes or chunks of watermelon, plus extra to decorate
crushed ice

Blend all the ingredients together in a blender for 10 seconds, until well frosted. Pour into a tall glass and dress with melon.

825
CHOCOLATE STINGER

A combination of two mellow liqueurs – hard to imagine where the sting comes from!

SERVES 1
1 measure dark crème de cacao
1 measure white crème de menthe
ice

Pour the crème de cacao and crème de menthe over ice. Shake vigorously until well frosted. Strain into a chilled cocktail glass.

824
IRISH STINGER

Bailey's Irish Cream is more potent than its sweet smooth taste suggests – take it easy with these if you don't want to fall over when you stand up.

SERVES 1
1 measure Bailey's Irish Cream
1 measure white crème de menthe
ice

Pour the Bailey's Irish Cream and crème de menthe over ice. Shake vigorously until well frosted and strain into a chilled shot glass.

826
BALTIMORE EGGNOG

Most nogs are hot or warmed through. This one is cold, but it is still extremely good.

SERVES 1
1 egg
1 tsp sugar
3 measures Madeira
1/2 measure brandy
1/2 measure dark rum
milk
ice
grated nutmeg, to decorate

Shake the first five ingredients together over ice with a little milk. Strain into a large tumbler and top with grated nutmeg.

827
ALBERTINE

Although originally an after-dinner cocktail, this drink is good any time and it certainly has a soothing and calming effect.

SERVES 1

1/3 measure kirsch
1/3 measure Cointreau
1/3 measure Chartreuse
few drops maraschino
ice
maraschino cherry, to decorate

Shake all the liquid ingredients together well over ice and strain into a small chilled cocktail glass. Dress with a maraschino cherry.

828
NUCLEAR FALLOUT

This is similar to a pousse-café, where the liqueurs are layered, but, in this case, the heaviest liqueur is coldest and added last, to create the slow dropping effect.

SERVES 1

1 tsp raspberry syrup
1/4 measure maraschino liqueur
1/4 measure yellow Chartreuse
1/4 measure Cointreau
1/2 measure well-iced blue
    curaçao

Chill all the liqueurs but put the curaçao in the coldest part of the freezer. Chill a shot glass. Carefully pour the raspberry syrup and all the liqueurs except the curaçao in layers over the back of a spoon. Finally, pour in the curaçao.

829
STARS AND
SWIRLS

You will need a steady hand for this one – preferably two steady hands.

SERVES 1

1 measure Malibu
large ice cube
1/2 measure strawberry or
    raspberry liqueur
1 tsp blue curaçao

Chill a small shot glass. Pour in the Malibu and add the ice cube. Carefully pour in the strawberry liqueur and curaçao from opposite sides of the glass very slowly so they fall down the sides and swirl around.

830
CAPUCINE

Well-iced liqueurs are often served over finely crushed ice as a frappé. This version is tiered for twice the effect.

SERVES 1

crushed ice
1 measure iced blue
    curaçao
1 measure iced Parfait
    Amour

Pack a small cocktail or shot glass with finely crushed ice. Pour in the curaçao slowly and then carefully add the Parfait Amour.

831
TRAFFIC LIGHTS

Best to keep out of the driver's seat after even one of these colourful cocktails.

SERVES 1

¹/₂–1 measure blue curaçao
¹/₂–1 measure orange brandy
¹/₂–1 measure cherry brandy
crushed ice

Pour the ingredients carefully, one at a time, into a straight-sided cocktail glass filled with crushed ice.

833
WHITE DIAMOND FRAPPÉ

This combination works well once you've added the lemon. Extra ice at the last minute brings out the separate flavours.

SERVES 1

¹/₄ measure peppermint schnapps
¹/₄ measure white crème de cacao
¹/₄ measure anise
¹/₄ measure lemon juice
crushed ice

Shake all the liquid ingredients over ice until frosted. Strain into a chilled shot glass and add a small spoonful of crushed ice.

832
MINT FRAPPÉ

This is the classic original frappé. Simply pour your favourite liqueur – in this case crème de menthe – over finely crushed ice to dilute it slightly, and enjoy.

SERVES 1

2 measures crème de menthe
crushed ice

Fill a small cocktail glass with crushed ice and pour in the crème de menthe.

834
GRASSHOPPER

Experts disagree on the original recipe and there seem to be at least three versions with the same name – as well as numerous variations. The recipe given here is also known as a Grasshopper Surprise.

SERVES 1

2 measures green crème de menthe
2 measures white crème de cacao
2 measures single cream
cracked ice

Shake the crème de menthe, crème de cacao and cream over ice until a frost forms. Strain into a chilled goblet.

835
ANGEL'S DELIGHT

This is a modern version of the classic pousse-café, an unmixed mixed drink, in that the ingredients form separate layers in the glass – providing you have a steady hand. You can drink it as a slammer or sip it.

SERVES 1

1/2 measure chilled grenadine
1/2 measure chilled triple sec
1/2 measure chilled sloe gin
1/2 measure chilled single cream

Pour the grenadine into a chilled shot glass or pousse-café glass, then, with a steady hand, pour in the triple sec to make a second layer. Add the sloe gin to make a third layer and, finally, add the cream to float on top.

837
SPRINGBOK COFFEE

A fruity but rather rich coffee to serve hot or iced.

SERVES 1

1 cup strong black coffee
1 measure apricot brandy
1 measure Amarula
whipped cream and toasted flaked almonds, to decorate

Pour the coffee into a tall heatproof glass or cup. Pour in the brandy and then carefully pour in the Amarula. Dress with a swirl of whipped cream and a few flaked almonds.

836
CHOCOLATE-COVERED CHERRY

The 'cherry' is supposedly the striking red grenadine sitting at the bottom of the glass.

SERVES 1

1 measure grenadine
1 measure crème de cacao
1 measure Bailey's Irish Cream

Pour the grenadine into a shot glass. Carefully pour in the crème de cacao over the back of a spoon, so that it floats on the grenadine. Gently pour in the Bailey's over the spoon.

838
CAFÉ BRULOT

Serve this when you have time to linger and enjoy. For a really dramatic display, flambé it at the table using the peel of a whole orange.

SERVES 2

1/2 stick cinnamon
several cloves
peel of 1 orange, in one strip or thick pieces
3 sugar cubes
150 ml/5 fl oz brandy
1–2 tbsp curaçao, warmed
2 cups hot fresh coffee

Warm the spices, orange peel, sugar and brandy in a saucepan until the sugar has dissolved. Remove the orange peel with tongs. Flambé the curaçao and pour it over the orange peel into the pan. Gradually add the coffee and stir until the flames die down. Serve in a heatproof glass.

839
JEALOUSY

This really is an after-dinner cocktail – if you want a change, you could flavour the cream with a different liqueur.

SERVES 1

1 tsp crème de menthe
1–2 tbsp double cream
2 measures coffee or
   chocolate liqueur

Gently beat the mint liqueur into the cream until thick. Pour the coffee liqueur into a very small iced glass and carefully spoon on the whipped flavoured cream.

841
PASSION

Almonds, cocoa and the fruity Amarula make a great combination and, although it is creamy, it is not too rich.

SERVES 1

1 measure amaretto
1 measure crème de cacao
1 measure Amarula
1 measure single cream
ice

Shake the first four ingredients well over ice and strain into a small chilled cocktail glass.

840
AMARETTO COFFEE

This is a lovely variation of Irish coffee. Amaretto is a deliciously sweet, almond-flavoured liqueur made from apricot kernels. It is delicious drunk on its own, but it also forms the basis of a number of cocktails.

SERVES 1

2 tbsp amaretto
1 cup hot black coffee
1–2 tbsp double cream

Stir the amaretto into the hot coffee. Carefully pour the cream on top over the back of a spoon to form a layer.

842
CAFÉ CRÈME WITH ATTITUDE

A delicious way to end a light meal, as it is very rich.

SERVES 1

2 measures Tia Maria
2 measures Kahlúa
ice
1 measure Bailey's Irish Cream
1/2 measure cream
chocolate-covered coffee
   beans, to decorate

Mix the Tia Maria and Kahlúa with ice in a mixing glass. Strain into a small cocktail glass. Carefully pour on the Bailey's over the back of a spoon, then do the same with the cream. Dress with the coffee beans.

843

SNOWBOAT (see right-hand page for picture)

This is such a good combination, it is perfect for special occasions, such as Christmas, and could easily be made into an ice cream or creamy dessert.

SERVES 2

1 measure chocolate mint
  liqueur, iced
1 measure milk, iced
1/2 measure Malibu, iced
small scoop coconut ice cream
crushed ice
chocolate flakes, to decorate

Blend the first five ingredients together in a blender until frothy and well-chilled. Pour or spoon into iced cocktail glasses and dress with chocolate flakes.

844

THE BABYSITTER

Perhaps the babysitter should just have the ice cream sundae part, and add the liqueurs for those with fewer responsibilities.

SERVES 1

2 measures coconut liqueur
1 measure crème de cacao
1/2 scoop vanilla ice cream
cola
chocolate flakes, to decorate

Blend the first three ingredients in a blender for about 5 seconds, until thick and frothy. Pour into a large chilled glass and top up with cola to taste. Dress with chocolate flakes.

845

DEPTH CHARGE

Anise is a particularly unusual drink in that it turns cloudy when mixed with water but not when mixed with other alcoholic drinks, until the ice starts melting. So drink it slowly, with care, and watch it change.

SERVES 1

1 measure gin
1 measure Lillet
2 dashes Pernod
ice

Shake the ingredients over ice until well frosted. Strain into a chilled glass.

846
YANKEE DOODLE

Serve this delicious concoction after dinner on a warm evening.

SERVES 1
1 measure crème de banane
1 measure cognac
1 measure Royal Mint
  Chocolate
ice

Shake the liquid ingredients together over ice until well frosted and strain into a small cocktail glass.

848
SMART ALEC

If the glasses and the liqueurs are really well iced, they will stay in layers, but you can't tell until you drink it as they are almost all the same colour!

SERVES 1
³/4 measure chilled crème
  de cacao
¹/2 measure orange curaçao
¹/2 measure chilled cream
cocoa powder, to decorate

Pour the crème de cacao slowly into the bottom of an iced elgin glass or liqueur glass, then add the curaçao. Finally, carefully pour the cream in a layer over the top. Dress with a sprinkle of cocoa powder.

847
TOFFEE SPLIT

You should not need a dessert as well, but you could always pour it over some ice cream.

SERVES 1
crushed ice
2 measures Drambuie
1 measure iced toffee liqueur

Fill a small cocktail glass or shot glass with crushed ice. Pour on the Drambuie and pour in the toffee liqueur carefully from the side of the glass so it layers on top.

849
FIFTH AVENUE

After-dinner cocktails often include cream and this one also has the delicate flavours of apricot and cocoa.

SERVES 1
1 measure dark crème de
  cacao, iced
1 measure apricot brandy,
  iced
1 measure cream

Pour the ingredients, one at a time, into a chilled glass. Pour the layers slowly over the back of a spoon resting against the edge of the glass. Each layer should float on top of the previous one.

850
TOASTED ALMONDS

You can't beat this for a wonderfully rich after-dinner treat. Serve with sugared almonds for a good effect.

SERVES 1

2 ice cubes
2 measures amaretto
1 measure brandy
1–2 measures double cream
toasted flaked almonds, to
    decorate

Place two ice cubes in a chilled cocktail glass. Stir in the amaretto and brandy to mix well and chill. With the help of a spoon, pour the cream in a layer over the top and dress with a few toasted flaked almonds.

852
AVALANCHE

Amaretto is a rich almond-flavoured liqueur, so this would be delicious after dinner, instead of a dessert.

SERVES 1

1 measure amaretto
1/2 measure apricot brandy
1 measure apricot juice or
    mango juice
1 scoop vanilla ice cream

Blend all the ingredients in a blender until well frosted and frothy. Pour into an iced cocktail glass.

851
FIVE FIFTEEN

Don't be fooled by the cream, this is a serious concoction.

SERVES 1

1/3 measure curaçao
1/3 measure dry vermouth
1/3 measure sweet cream
ice

Shake all the ingredients together well over ice and strain into a small glass.

853
MELON FREEZE

A very refreshing and cooling cocktail for warm summer days, but don't try to make too many at once, as it needs to be kept well frozen.

SERVES 1

2 measures iced Midori, plus
    extra for spooning over
1 measure fresh lemon juice
1 small scoop vanilla ice cream
a little crushed ice
green melon slice,
    to decorate

Blend the first three ingredients with ice in a blender, then pour into a well-chilled cocktail glass. Spoon over a few drops of Midori and dress with melon.

854
MEXICAN DAWN

Creamy and richly flavoured with a hint of daring,
just like Mexico.

SERVES 1

1 measure coconut liqueur
1 measure tequila
1 scoop strawberry ice cream
dash strawberry liqueur
dash tamarind syrup
fresh coconut flake, to
    decorate

Blend all the liquid ingredients
slowly in a blender for about
10 seconds. Pour into a chilled
cocktail glass and dress with a
sliver of fresh coconut.

856
VINTAGE
CADILLAC

Luxury and style all rolled into one sophisticated drink.

SERVES 1

1 measure Galliano
1 measure crème de cacao
1 measure cream
ice

Shake all the ingredients together
with ice and strain into a small
chilled glass.

855
DOWN UNDER

Here is a fruit salad mix of liqueur flavours that produces
a great-tasting cocktail.

SERVES 1

1 measure crème de banane
1 measure strawberry liqueur
1 measure orange curaçao
1 measure orange juice
small scoop ice cream
fresh strawberry, to decorate

Blend the first five ingredients
in a blender for about
10 seconds, until smooth
and almost frozen. Pour into
a chilled cocktail glass and
dress with a strawberry.

857
SNOWY
RIDGE

Cream-topped liqueurs are
delicious after-dinner drinks.
Any favourite can be used but it
works best with a well-chilled liqueur.

SERVES 1

1 measure crème de cacao,
    chilled
1/2 measure double cream

Pour the crème de cacao
into a small cocktail glass.
Carefully pour the cream
over the back of a spoon
on top of the liqueur so that
it floats. Sip slowly through
the cream.

858
LOUISA

Blue cocktails look such fun, so enhance the effect with a few coloured ice cubes.

SERVES 1

³/4 measure blue curaçao
¹/2 measure vodka
¹/4 measure barley water
squeeze lemon juice
ice
soda water, to taste
blue ice cubes

Mix the first four ingredients in a long glass full of ice. Top up with soda water to taste. Finish with blue ice cubes.

860
MINTED DIAMONDS

Make these stunning ice cubes well in advance and take them out of the freezer only at the very last second.

SERVES 1

1 tsp green crème de menthe
1 tbsp iced water
1 measure white crème de menthe
2 measures apple schnapps or pear schnapps
ice

Mix the green crème de menthe with the iced water and freeze into 1 or 2 small ice cubes. Stir the other liqueurs over ice until well frosted. Strain into a chilled cocktail glass and float the mint ice cubes on top.

859
COLD COMFORT

Ice-cold drinks are very soothing during really hot weather, especially when mixed with herbal liqueurs, such as kümmel.

SERVES 1

1 measure cream, chilled
¹/2 measure kümmel
¹/2 measure kirsch
few drops orange flower water
1–2 measures pineapple juice
ice
fruit or cherry slices, to decorate

Shake all the liquid ingredients together over ice until well frosted. Strain into a large cocktail glass or wine glass and dress with fruit.

861
GREEN DAZE

Looks like it should smell of newly mown grass in early summer, but at least you can dream all through the winter.

SERVES 1

1 measure chilled Midori
1 measure chilled green Chartreuse
¹/2 measure chilled cream
¹/2 measure lime juice
cracked ice
star fruit slice, to decorate

Stir all the liquid ingredients together over ice until well frosted. Strain into a chilled cocktail glass and dress with a slice of star fruit.

862
MINTY CAPPUCCINO

You could add a good sifting of cocoa powder on top.

SERVES 1
1 measure white crème de menthe
1 measure chocolate cream liqueur
1 measure coffee liqueur
1 tbsp single cream
crushed ice
soda water, to taste

Stir the first four ingredients well over the crushed ice and pour into a chilled cocktail glass.

863
AROUND THE WORLD

Flavours from all around the world go into this glorious mix, so serve it on a cosmopolitan occasion.

SERVES 1
1 measure Mandarine Napoleon
1 measure Polish vodka
1/2 measure Campari
1/2 measure crème de banane
1/2 measure coconut liqueur
ice
lemonade
mandarin halves, to decorate

Shake the first five ingredients over ice until frosted. Strain into an ice-filled glass, top up with lemonade and dress with mandarin halves.

864
ANGEL'S WINGS

Drink slowly through a straw to appreciate the minty flavours and the subtle frothy vanilla topping.

SERVES 3
1 egg white
4 measures advocaat
1 measure Cointreau
ice
1 measure green crème de menthe

Shake the egg white, advocaat and Cointreau over ice until frothy and frosted. Place an ice cube in each chilled glass and slowly pour on the crème de menthe and the frothy egg mixture. The colours will separate.

865
JOHN WOOD

Vermouth is an immensely useful cocktail flavouring because it contains more than 50 herbs and spices and combines well with many spirits. It had fallen in popularity as a base for cocktails but is now enjoying a revival.

SERVES 1
2 measures sweet vermouth
1/2 measure kümmel
1/2 measure Irish whiskey
1 measure lemon juice
cracked ice
dash Angostura bitters

Shake the vermouth, kümmel, whiskey and lemon juice vigorously over ice with a dash Angostura bitters until well frosted. Strain into a chilled wine glass.

866
MULLED MARSALA

Perfect for serving as a stirrup cup if you are not riding, or on a bitterly cold Sunday morning before lunch.

SERVES 8
1 bottle Marsala
575 ml/18 fl oz water
6 cloves
4 measures amaretto
sugar

Heat all the ingredients except the sugar together slowly and bring almost to the boil. Remove from the heat, add the sugar and stir to dissolve before serving in very small heatproof glasses.

867
DR. JOHNSON'S MULL

This is definitely a medicinal mulled wine, much stronger than most of us are used to, so drink in small quantities.

SERVES 16
1 litre/1³/4 pints claret
1 sliced orange
12 cubes sugar
6 cloves
2¹/4 cups water
wine glass of brandy
nutmeg

Pour the claret into a medium saucepan with the orange slices, sugar, and cloves. Bring almost to a boil. Boil the water and pour into the pan. Add the brandy and nutmeg, then pour into warmed heatproof cups or glasses.

868
PORT & LEMON MULL

The clove-studded lemon is a very successful old-fashioned way of adding a subtle amount of flavour to a pot of wine or port.

SERVES 10
1 bottle port
pinch allspice
55 g/2 oz sugar cubes
2 lemons, 1 studded with
   cloves and warmed

Pour the port into a saucepan and bring to scalding. Boil a pint of water and add the allspice. Rub sugar cubes over the non-studded lemon and squeeze out half the juice. Add everything to the pan of port and heat to dissolve the sugar. Serve in heatproof glasses.

869
GLÜHWEIN

The skier's favourite 'Après' warmer can be enjoyed on most cold winter nights, with no need for the snowy excuse.

SERVES 8
3 bottles red wine
a few pieces of lemon zest
good pinch each ground
   ginger, cinnamon and cloves
55 g/2 oz sugar
cinnamon sticks, to serve

Heat the wine in a saucepan with the zest, spices and sugar. When the sugar has dissolved and the wine is hot, steep for 5–10 minutes. Dilute with water to taste. Serve in heatproof glasses with cinnamon sticks.

870
THE ARCHBISHOP

If you are feeling brave, you can flambé this just before serving, then cool it slightly.

SERVES 4

few cloves
1 small orange
575 ml/18 fl oz port
2 tbsp soft brown sugar

Push the cloves into the orange and place in a small saucepan with the port and brown sugar. Heat through gently. Serve when well mulled, in warmed heatproof glasses.

872
NEGUS

Named after Colonel Francis Negus, who invented it in the eighteenth century, when sherry or wine was more readily available than most other drinks.

SERVES 18

1 bottle cream sherry
1 lemon, sliced and halved
1.2 litres/2 pints boiling water
nutmeg
sugar, to taste
1–2 measures brandy

Warm the sherry slowly in a medium-sized saucepan. Add the lemon and boiling water, grated nutmeg, sugar to taste and brandy. Warm through well and serve in small heatproof glasses.

871
CIDER-BERRY PUNCH

This bright and cheery punch can be well spiced and you may need to add sugar, preferably brown, to taste, or use a sweet cider. Perfect for a cold Christmas Eve.

SERVES 10

1.2 litres/2 pints cider
1 cinnamon stick
pinch grated nutmeg
115 g/4 oz cranberries
475 ml/16 fl oz red wine
sugar, to taste
sugar swizzle sticks, to serve

Heat the cider, spices and cranberries until the fruit bursts. Add the wine and bring almost to the boil. Add sugar to taste and then strain into a serving jug. Serve with swizzle sticks.

873
TWELFTH NIGHT

The longer you allow this mixture to marinate the better the final result will be. You may want to add sugar to taste, but try it first.

SERVES 8

1 apple, studded with cloves
1 bottle red wine, heated
hot water

Place the clove-studded apple in a large bowl or saucepan with the heated red wine and boiled water to taste. Leave to mull for 5–15 minutes. Serve in small heatproof glasses.

874
STIRRUP CUP

This should really stir up the winter gathering on a cold morning, as it is strong when well warmed. Small cups are ideal.

SERVES 24

1 bottle red wine
7–8 measures dark rum
3 dashes Angostura bitters
1 tsp ground cinnamon
few cloves
8 measures fresh orange juice
100 g/3½ oz sugar
1 bottle cider

Gently heat all the ingredients except the cider together in a large saucepan until really warmed through and mulled, but do not allow to boil. Add the cider just before serving in small heatproof glasses.

876
SANTA'S SIP

Unusually, this is unsweetened, so if you find it too dry when warmed through, add a cube of brown sugar to each glass.

SERVES 20

4 bottles red wine
1 litre/1³/4 pints water
¼ bottle dark rum
1 lemon, studded with cloves
½ tsp cinnamon
nutmeg

Heat the wine, water and rum together in a saucepan. Add the lemon and cinnamon. Heat through until almost boiling, reduce the heat and leave to mull for 5–10 minutes. Sprinkle with nutmeg and serve in heatproof glasses.

875
MISTLETOE MULL

There are numerous ways to make a mulled wine, but this one is by far the simplest and easiest. You can always add more wine if you prefer a stronger brew!

SERVES 8

475 ml/16 fl oz water
sugar, to taste
1 stick cinnamon
4 cloves
2 lemons, sliced
1 bottle red Burgundy

Boil the water with the sugar, cinnamon and cloves for 3–5 minutes. Add the lemon slices and leave to stand for about 10 minutes. Add the wine and heat through slowly without boiling. Serve piping hot.

877
HET PINT

An old-fashioned mix originating in Scotland to keep the cold out and help ward off winter colds.

SERVES 6

4 egg yolks
4 tbsp brown sugar
grated nutmeg, plus extra to decorate
2 egg whites, beaten
1 litre/1³/4 pints pale ale, heated

Beat the egg yolks with the sugar and nutmeg and gently whisk in the egg whites. Slowly pour on the ale, whisking constantly. Using two jugs, pour from one to another until you have a frothy mix. Sprinkle with nutmeg.

878

TAMAGOZAKE (see right-hand page for picture)

This is a brave drink for some rare tasting occasions, but be careful not to burn away all the sake. You might want to blow it out before all the flavour and spirit has been burned up.

SERVES 1

1 egg
1 tsp sugar
6 measures sake

Lightly beat the egg and sugar together. Boil the sake and ignite it. Remove from the heat and stir in the egg and sugar mixture. Serve in a heatproof glass.

879

MANHATTAN COOLER

Nothing like the classic Manhattan cocktail, more like a red wine punch.

SERVES 1

2 measures claret or good red wine
3 dashes dark rum
juice 1/2 lemon
2 tsp icing sugar
ice
lemon slice, to decorate

Stir the first four ingredients together well with ice until the sugar has dissolved. Strain into a chilled wine goblet and dress with a slice of lemon.

880

AVOCADO CHILL

Because avocados are packed with vitamins, this can be considered as a healthy cocktail and included in your diet – no pretending any more!

SERVES 1

1/4 ripe avocado
juice of 1/2 lime
1 tsp icing sugar
1/2 measure dry vermouth
1 measure gin (optional)
ice
tonic water
ice cube with frozen lime slice

Blend the avocado, lime and sugar together until smooth. Then shake well with the vermouth and gin, if using, over ice. Strain into a chilled long cocktail glass and top up with tonic water. Float a lime ice cube on the top.

NON-ALCOHOLIC

Non-alcoholic cocktails are a great alternative for those who are driving or a treat for health-conscious fruit lovers – they can also be enjoyed by children. Accompany those sunny spring days with a fresh and fruity Peachy Melba, or why not try the innocent, but seductively sweet Shirley Temple for some real family fun?

881 MELON & PINEAPPLE CRUSH

When you are feeling jaded, this will give you a boost.

SERVES 2

125 ml/4 fl oz pineapple juice
4 tbsp orange juice
125 g/4 1/2 oz galia melon, cut into chunks
225 ml/8 fl oz frozen pineapple chunks
crushed ice
melon slices, to decorate

Pour the pineapple juice and orange juice into a food processor and process gently until combined. Add the melon, pineapple and crushed ice and process to a slushy consistency. Pour the mixture into glasses and dress with slices of melon.

883 RED PEPPER REACTOR

Not for the faint-hearted, this fiery mix will certainly wake you up if you're having a mid-morning snooze.

SERVES 2

225 ml/8 fl oz carrot juice
225 ml/8 fl oz tomato juice
2 large red peppers, deseeded and coarsely chopped
1 tbsp lemon juice
pepper
shredded carrot strips, to decorate

Pour the carrot juice and tomato juice into a food processor with some pepper and process until smooth. Add the red peppers and lemon juice. Pour the mixture into glasses and dress with strips of shredded carrot.

882 PEAR & RASPBERRY DELIGHT

Pink, light and fruity, this refreshing smoothie is simply delicious. If you don't like the seeds, you can use a strainer to make it silken smooth.

SERVES 2

2 large ripe Anjou pears, peeled, cored and chopped
140 g/5 oz frozen raspberries
175 ml/6 fl oz ice-cold water
honey, to taste
fresh raspberries, to decorate

Put the pears and raspberries into a food processor with the raspberries and water and process until smooth. Taste and sweeten with honey to taste. Pour into glasses and dress with fresh raspberries.

884 WATERMELON REFRESHER

A great favourite in Greece, where roadside stalls sell enormous watermelons.

SERVES 2

watermelon wedge, weighing about 350 g/12 oz, derinded
ice cubes
watermelon slices, to decorate

Chop the watermelon into chunks, discarding any seeds. Put the chunks into a food processor and process until smooth. Place ice cubes in the glasses. Pour the watermelon mixture over the ice and dress with slices of melon.

885
PERKY PINEAPPLE

This is a great energy booster and is packed full of nutrients. The tangy taste is extremely refreshing as well.

SERVES 4
cracked ice
2 bananas
225 ml/8 fl oz pineapple juice, chilled
125 ml/4 fl oz lime juice
pineapple slices, to decorate

Put the cracked ice into the blender. Peel the bananas and slice directly into the blender. Add the pineapple and lime juice and process until smooth. Pour into chilled glasses and dress with slices of pineapple.

887
WATERMELON SUNSET

Watermelon seeds can be roasted and eaten, and the rind is used in pickles and relishes, making every part edible.

SERVES 2
1 watermelon, halved and seeded
6 tbsp ruby grapefruit juice
6 tbsp orange juice
dash lime juice
watermelon slice, to decorate

Scoop the melon flesh into a blender and add the grapefruit juice, orange juice and lime juice. Process until smooth, pour into chilled glasses and dress with a slice of watermelon.

886
STRAWBERRY COLADA

Strawberries are a delicious way to get your daily requirement of iron, potassium and vitamins A and C.

SERVES 2
450 g/1 lb strawberries
125 ml/4 fl oz coconut cream
600 ml/1 pint chilled pineapple juice

Reserve four strawberries to decorate. Halve the remainder and place in the blender. Add the coconut cream and pineapple juice and process until smooth, then pour into chilled glasses and dress with the reserved strawberries.

888
APPLE COOLER

The distinctive flavour of fragrant, ripe apples combines with fresh strawberries and freshly squeezed orange juice to give you a really zingy smoothie.

SERVES 2
2 ripe apples, peeled and roughly chopped
115 g/4 oz strawberries, hulled
juice of 4 oranges
sugar, to taste
apple slices, to decorate

Put the apples, strawberries and orange juice into a food processor and process until smooth. Taste and sweeten with sugar if necessary. Dress with slices of apple.

889

MAIDENLY MIMOSA

This non-alcoholic 'cocktail' is a delicious alternative for non-drinkers and drivers at a brunch or lunch party.

SERVES 2

175 ml/6 fl oz freshly squeezed orange juice
175 ml/6 fl oz sparkling white grape juice

Divide the orange juice between two chilled wine glasses or champagne flutes. Top up with grape juice.

890

RASPBERRY & APPLE QUENCHER

Quick and easy to make, this is a simple and elegant drink.

SERVES 2

8 ice cubes, crushed
2 tbsp raspberry syrup
475 ml/ 16 fl oz chilled apple juice
whole raspberries and pieces of apple, to decorate

Divide the crushed ice between two glasses and pour over the raspberry syrup. Fill each glass with apple juice and stir well. Dress with raspberries and pieces of apple.

891

BLACK GRAPE FIZZ

Use large dark grapes for this foamy, refreshing cooler.

SERVES 2

140 g/5 oz black grapes, deseeded or seedless
175 ml/6 fl oz sparkling mineral water
2 large scoops of lemon sorbet
lime slices, to decorate

Put the grapes, mineral water and lemon sorbet in a food processor and process until smooth. Pour into glasses and dress with slices of lime.

892

ST. CLEMENTS

Anyone familiar with the nursery rhyme will know immediately what the ingredients of this refreshing drink are.

SERVES 2

cracked ice
2 measures orange juice
2 measures bitter lemon
orange and lemon slices, to decorate

Put the ice cubes into a chilled tumbler. Pour in the orange juice and bitter lemon. Stir gently and dress with slices of orange and lemon.

893
LONG BOAT

A long and pleasant cocktail, with a gentle hint of ginger.

SERVES 1
ice
1 measure lime cordial
ginger beer
wedge lime and mint sprig,
   to decorate

Fill a chilled highball or tall glass two-thirds full with ice and pour in the lime cordial. Top up with ginger beer and stir gently. Dress with a wedge of fresh lime and a sprig of mint.

895
GINGER FIZZ

This is a cool, refreshing cocktail for a hot day, easiest made in a blender.

SERVES 1
ginger ale
fresh mint sprigs
cracked ice
raspberries and a sprig of mint,
   to decorate

Put the ginger ale and several mint leaves into a blender and blend together. Strain into a chilled highball glass two-thirds filled with ice. Dress with a few raspberries and a sprig of fresh mint.

894
LEMON GINGER BITTER

For occasions when you are drinking the real thing, drivers and the younger members of the family can also join in.

SERVES 6
600 ml/1 pint chilled
   lemonade
475 ml/16 fl oz chilled cola
475 ml/16 fl oz chilled dry
   ginger
juice of 1 orange
juice of 1 lemon
few drops Angostura bitters
fruit slices and mint sprigs, to
   decorate
ice

Mix the first six ingredients together in a large jug or punch bowl. Float in the fruit and mint, keep in a cold place and add the ice cubes at the last minute.

896
THE GUNNER

A good alternative to a glass of beer in a bar; no one will know what it is but they will all want to try it.

SERVES 1
few ice cubes
1 measure lime juice
2–3 dashes Angostura bitters
   or to taste
175 ml/6 fl oz ginger beer
175 ml/6 fl oz lemonade

In a long glass, mix all the ingredients, adding equal quantities of ginger beer and the lemonade. Taste and add more Angostura bitters if you want.

897

HEAVENLY DAYS (see right-hand page for picture)

The blend of hazelnut and lemon may not appear to be a match made in heaven, but they work very well together.

SERVES 1

2 measures hazelnut syrup
2 measures lemon juice
1 tsp grenadine
cracked ice
sparkling water
star fruit slice, to decorate

Shake the first three ingredients vigorously over ice until well frosted. Half fill a tumbler with cracked ice and strain the cocktail over them. Top up with sparkling water. Stir gently and dress with a slice of star fruit.

898

ITALIAN SODA

Italian syrup comes in a wide variety of flavours, including a range of fruit and nuts, and is available from most Italian delicatessens and supermarkets. French syrups are similar. You can substitute your favourite and vary the quantity to taste.

SERVES 1

cracked ice
1 1/2 measures hazelnut syrup
sparkling water
lime slice, to decorate

Fill a chilled Collins glass with cracked ice. Pour the hazelnut syrup over and top up with sparkling water. Stir gently and dress with a slice of lime.

899

SHIRLEY TEMPLE

The Shirley Temple is one of the most famous non-alcoholic drinks – it's named after the very popular 1930s child movie star.

SERVES 1

2 measures lemon juice
1/2 measure grenadine
1/2 measure sugar syrup
cracked ice
ginger ale
orange slice and cocktail cherry, to decorate

Shake the lemon juice, grenadine and sugar syrup vigorously over ice until well frosted. Strain into a small, chilled glass half filled with cracked ice. Top up with ginger ale and dress with an orange slice and a cocktail cherry.

900 NEW ENGLAND PARTY

The party won't get too boisterous if this is the cocktail on offer.

SERVES 2

crushed ice
dash Tabasco sauce
dash Worcestershire sauce
dash lemon juice,
1 carrot, chopped
2 celery sticks, chopped
225 ml/8 fl oz tomato juice
125 ml/4 fl oz clam juice
salt and pepper
celery stick, to decorate

Put the ingredients in a blender and blend until smooth. Transfer to a jug, cover with clingfilm and chill for about 1 hour. Pour into two chilled tumblers, season with salt and pepper and dress with a stick of celery.

901 VIRGIN MARY

This is simply a Bloody Mary without the vodka, but it is still a great pick-me-up.

SERVES 1

3 measures tomato juice
1 measure lemon juice
2 dashes Worcestershire sauce
1 dash Tabasco sauce
cracked ice
pinch celery salt
pepper
lemon wedge and celery stick,
   to decorate

Shake the first four ingredients vigorously over ice and season with celery salt and pepper. Strain into an iced old-fashioned glass. Dress with a lemon wedge and a celery stick.

902 CLAM DIGGER

A good cocktail for a Sunday brunch, when alcoholic drinks can be too soporific and you end up wasting the rest of the day, but you still want something to set the tastebuds tingling.

SERVES 1

cracked ice
Tabasco sauce
Worcestershire sauce
4 measures tomato juice
4 measures clam juice
1/4 tsp horseradish sauce
ice
celery salt
pepper
lime wedge, to decorate

Put the first six ingredients in a cocktail shaker. Shake vigorously until well frosted. Fill a chilled Collins glass with cracked ice and strain in the cocktail. Season to taste with celery salt and pepper and dress with a lime wedge.

903 FERDINAND THE BULL

Most cocktails are suitable for vegetarians, but this, with a healthy dose of beef stock, is for carnivores only.

SERVES 1

4 measures tomato juice,
4 measures chilled beef stock
1 measure lime juice
dash Worcestershire sauce
dash Tabasco sauce
cracked ice
salt and pepper
slice of lime, to decorate

Shake the first five ingredients over ice until well frosted. Half fill a tall chilled tumbler with ice and strain the cocktail over. Season to taste with salt and pepper and dress with a slice of lime.

904
RANCH GIRL

Surprisingly spicy, but then it does come from Texas.

SERVES 1
1 measure lime juice
1 measure barbecue sauce
dash Worcestershire sauce
dash Tabasco sauce
ice
tomato juice
lime slices, to decorate

Shake the first four ingredients over ice until well frosted. Pour into a chilled tumbler, top up with tomato juice and stir. Dress with slices of lime.

906
COCOBELLE

If you have a steady hand, this drink can be served with pretty swirls of colour up the sides.

SERVES 1
3 measures cold milk
1 measure coconut cream
2 scoops vanilla ice cream
3–4 ice cubes
dash grenadine
desiccated coconut, toasted, for sprinkling

Blend the first four ingredients in a blender until slushy. Chill a tall glass and gently dribble a few splashes of grenadine down the insides. Pour in the slush slowly and top with the toasted coconut.

907
COCONUT ISLANDER

This can be very rich, so enjoy in small quantities or dilute a little with soda water.

SERVES 1
1 pineapple
4 measures pineapple juice
4 tbsp creamed coconut
4 measures milk
2 tbsp crushed pineapple
3 tbsp shredded coconut
crushed ice
fresh cherry, to decorate

Cut the top off the pineapple and remove the flesh. Blend all the ingredients except the cherry in a blender with a little ice for 30–40 seconds. When smooth and frothy, pour into the shell and dress with a fresh cherry.

905
SANGRIA SECA

The literal translation of this is 'dried blood'. Perhaps it sounds better in Spanish.

SERVES 4
475 ml/16 fl oz tomato juice
225 ml/8 fl oz orange juice
3 measures lime juice
1/2 measure Tabasco sauce
2 tsp Worcestershire sauce
1 jalapeño chilli, deseeded and finely chopped
celery salt
freshly ground white pepper
cracked ice

Pour the first five ingredients into a jug. Add the chilli. Season to taste with celery salt and pepper and stir well. Cover with clingfilm and chill in the refrigerator for at least 1 hour. To serve, half fill chilled tumblers with cracked ice and strain the cocktail over them.

908
MOCHA SLUSH

Definitely for people with a sweet tooth, this is a chocoholic's dream and is popular with adults, as well as children.

SERVES 1

crushed ice
2 measures coffee syrup
1 measure chocolate syrup
4 measures milk
grated chocolate, to decorate

Blend the crushed ice in a small blender with the coffee syrup, chocolate syrup and milk until slushy. Pour into a chilled goblet and sprinkle with grated chocolate.

910
CITRUS FIZZ

This is a clever and refreshing variation on the classic Buck's Fizz, which is perfect for all ages in the family.

SERVES 1

2 measures fresh orange juice, chilled
icing sugar
few drops Angostura bitters
squeeze lime juice
2–3 measures sparkling water, chilled

Rub the rim of a flute with orange or lime juice and dip into icing sugar. Stir the rest of the juices together with the bitters and then pour into the glass. Add sparkling water to taste.

909
LASSI

Originally, lassi was simply a flavoured yogurt drink, slightly sour, often savoury or spiced.

SERVES 2

125 ml/4 fl oz plain yogurt
225 ml/8 fl oz milk
1 tbsp rose water
3 tbsp honey
1 ripe mango, peeled and diced
6 ice cubes
rose petals, to decorate

Pour the yogurt and milk into a food processor and process until combined. Add the rose water and honey and process until blended, then add the mango and ice cubes and blend until smooth. Pour into chilled glasses. Dress with rose petals.

911
SOFT SANGRIA

This is a version of the well-known Spanish wine cup that has caught out many an unwary tourist. A Soft Sangria poses no such danger of unexpected inebriation, but is just as refreshing and full of flavour. Chill everything thoroughly first.

SERVES 4

1.2 litres/2 pints red grape juice
225 ml/8 fl oz orange juice
3 measures cranberry juice
2 measures lemon juice
2 measures lime juice
4 measures sugar syrup
ice
lime slices, to decorate

Pour all the juices and the sugar syrup into a chilled punch bowl and stir well. Add the ice and the lime slices and serve in chilled glasses.

912 SUNRISE SMOOTHIE

The secret of smoothie success – non-alcoholic and alcoholic – is to blend on medium speed until just smooth.

SERVES 1

1 banana, peeled and thinly sliced
200 g/7 oz strawberries
85 g/3 oz stoned dates
4 1/2 tsp clear honey
1 cup orange juice
crushed ice

Put the banana, strawberries, dates and honey in a blender and blend until smooth. Add the orange juice and crushed ice and blend again until smooth. Pour into a chilled glass.

914 SUMMER FRUIT SLUSH

This medley of summer berries makes an inspired drink.

SERVES 2

4 tbsp orange juice
1 tbsp lime juice
125 ml/4 fl oz sparkling water
250 g/9 oz frozen summer berries, such as strawberries, raspberries and blueberries
4 ice cubes

Pour the orange juice, lime juice and sparkling water into a food processor and process gently until combined. Add the summer fruits and ice cubes and process until a slushy consistency has been reached. Pour into glasses.

913 HONEYDEW

The natural texture of the honeydew melon lends itself to this delicate smoothie. For best results, make sure the melon is truly ripe.

SERVES 2

250 g/9 oz/ honeydew melon
300 ml/10 fl oz sparkling mineral water
2 tbsp clear honey

Cut the rind off the melon. Chop the melon into chunks, discarding any seeds. Put into a food processor with the water and honey and process until smooth. Pour into glasses.

915 SUMMER BERRIES SMOOTHIE

The rich flavours and colours of summer fruits in a great smoothie.

SERVES 2

350 ml/5 fl oz orange juice
1 banana, sliced and frozen
280 g/10 oz frozen summer berries, such as strawberries, raspberries and blueberries
slices of fresh orange, to decorate

Pour the orange juice into a food processor. Add the banana and half the berries and process until smooth. Add the remaining berries and process until smooth. Pour the mixture into tall glasses and dress with orange slices.

916 CRANBERRY ENERGIZER

Sweet and sour combine to make a deliciously energizing juice packed full of goodness.

SERVES 2

300 ml/10 fl oz cranberry juice
125 ml/4 fl oz orange juice
55 g/2 oz fresh raspberries
1 tbsp lemon juice
fresh orange slices, to decorate

Pour the cranberry juice and orange juice into a food processor and process gently until combined. Add the raspberries and lemon juice and process until smooth. Pour the mixture into glasses and dress with slices of orange.

917 BANANA & APPLE BOOSTER

Ginger and cinnamon spice up these everyday fruits to make a great energizer for a cold winter morning.

SERVES 2

225 ml/8 fl oz apple juice
1/2 tsp ground cinnamon
2 tsp grated fresh ginger
2 bananas, sliced and frozen
fresh apple chunks, to decorate

Pour the apple juice into a food processor. Add the cinnamon and ginger and process gently until combined. Add the bananas and process until smooth. Pour the mixture into tall glasses and dress with apple chunks.

918 KIWI COOLER

Use a strawberry ice cream to contrast with the glorious green colour of this smoothie, or a lime sorbet to tone in with it. Whichever you choose, the combination will be delightful.

SERVES 2

4 ripe kiwi fruit, peeled and cut into quarters
175 ml/6 fl oz traditional lemonade
2 large scoops of ice cream or sorbet

Put the kiwi fruit and lemonade into a food processor and process until smooth. Pour into glasses and top with ice cream.

919 PINEAPPLE TANGO

This long, cool thirst-quencher will revitalize you when you are feeling tired or stressed.

SERVES 2

125 ml/4 fl oz pineapple juice
juice of 1 lemon
125 ml/4 fl oz water
3 tbsp soft light brown sugar
175 ml/6 fl oz plain yogurt
1 peach, cut into chunks and frozen
140 g/5 oz frozen pineapple chunks
fresh pineapple wedges, to decorate

Pour the pineapple juice, lemon juice and water into a food processor. Add the sugar and yogurt and process until blended. Add the peach and pineapple chunks and process until smooth. Pour the mixture into glasses and dress with wedges of fresh pineapple.

920
MOCHA CREAM

The heavenly pairing of coffee and chocolate can be improved only by the addition of whipped cream.

SERVES 2

175 ml/6 fl oz milk
60 ml/2 fl oz single cream
1 tbsp brown sugar
2 tbsp cocoa powder
1 tbsp coffee syrup
6 ice cubes
whipped cream and grated chocolate, to decorate

Put the milk, cream and sugar into a food processor and process gently to combine. Add the cocoa and coffee syrup and process, then add the ice and process until smooth. Pour into glasses. Top with whipped cream and scatter with grated chocolate.

921
CITRUS COOLER

A pretty cocktail, reputed to have been created during the Prohibition era.

SERVES 1

cracked ice
juice 1/2 orange
juice 1/2 lemon
juice 1/2 lime
1/2 egg yolk
dash grenadine
orange slice and fresh mint sprig, to decorate

Shake the first six ingredients vigorously over ice and strain into a chilled highball glass. Dress with a slice of orange and a sprig of fresh mint.

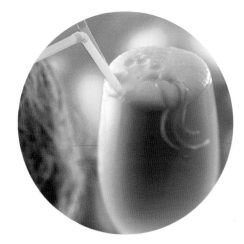

922
TROPICANA

Coconut milk and coconut cream are very similar but both need mixing up and shaking before they can be used easily.

SERVES 1

1 measure banana cream
4 measures grapefruit juice
2 measures coconut milk
ice
soda water or lemonade
lemon peel twists, to decorate

Shake the first three ingredients well over ice. Strain into a chilled tall glass. Add more ice and soda water to fill. Dress with fine twists of lemon peel and serve with straws.

923
TONGA

This is fruity, fun and a great drink to offer drivers instead of the ubiquitous orange juice or cola!

SERVES 1

juice of 1/2 lemon
2 measures pineapple juice
1–2 measures grapefruit juice
dash grenadine
1 egg white
ice
lemonade
slice of kiwi fruit, to decorate

Shake the first five ingredients vigorously over ice. Strain into a tall glass with some ice cubes and top up with lemonade. Dress with a slice of kiwi fruit.

924
PINKY PINK

This is also delicious made with raspberries and framboise.

SERVES 1

1 measure lemon juice
1 measure orange juice
2–3 strawberries, mashed
1 measure fraise
1/2 egg yolk
dash grenadine
ice
strawberry slice, to decorate

Shake all the ingredients except the slice of strawberry really well together. Pour into a cocktail glass and dress with a slice of strawberry.

925
FAUX KIR ROYALE

Looks just like the real thing, but won't get you into a right royal state.

SERVES 1

cracked ice
1 1/2 measures raspberry syrup
sparkling apple juice

Put some cracked ice into a mixing glass. Pour the raspberry syrup over the ice. Stir well to mix, then strain into a wine glass. Top up with apple juice and stir.

926
KNICKS VICTORY COOLER

The perfect drink for lovers of tangy fruit flavours.

SERVES 1

cracked ice
2 measures apricot juice
raspberry lemonade
orange peel twist and fresh raspberries, to decorate

Half fill a tall chilled tumbler with cracked ice. Pour over the apricot juice, top up with raspberry lemonade, and stir gently. Dress with a twist of orange peel and some fresh raspberries.

927
FAUX KIR

A non-alcoholic version of a classic wine cocktail, this drink is just as colourful and tasty. French and Italian fruit syrups are often the best quality and have the most flavour.

SERVES 1

1 measure chilled raspberry syrup
chilled white grape juice

Pour the raspberry syrup into a chilled wine glass. Top up with grape juice. Stir well to mix.

928
BERRY CREAM

Pure fruit blended to a perfectly smooth cream but with no wicked cream added!

SERVES 2

350 ml/12 fl oz orange juice
1 banana, sliced and frozen
280 g/10 oz frozen summer
  berries, such as strawberries,
  raspberries and blueberries
fresh strawberry slices, to
  decorate

Pour the orange juice into a food processor. Add the banana and half the berries and process until smooth. Add the remaining berries and process until smooth. Pour the mixture into tall glasses and dress the rims with slices of a fresh strawberry.

929
ORCHARD PICKINGS

Long, cool and refreshing for any hot summer day. Make plenty as it will soon go, especially if you make your own elderflower cordial.

SERVES 1

1 measure elderflower cordial
2 measures apple juice
1/2 measure blackberry syrup
  or cordial
ice
apple-flavoured sparkling
  water
apple slices, to decorate

Shake the first three ingredients over ice until frosted. Strain into a chilled highball glass and top up with sparkling water. Dress with slices of apple.

930
MEMORY LANE

We all have many happy summer memories of freshly crushed blackberry or elderberry drinks. This version needs just a few berries from the store and some fresh citrus.

SERVES 1

a few blackberries
1 tbsp icing sugar
crushed ice
juice of 1/2 lemon
juice of 1/2 lime
lemonade

Reserve a few berries. Place the remaining fruit in a chilled tumbler with the sugar and crush until well mashed. Add ice and the fruit juices and top up with lemonade. Top with the reserved whole berries.

931
CHERRY ORCHARD

Any orchard fruit could be used in this fruity mix. Experiment with your own favourite flavours or fresh juices in season.

SERVES 1

1 measure apple juice
1 measure pear juice
2 measures cranberry juice
ice
pink lemonade or cherryade
fresh or glacé cherries and a
  pineapple wedge, to
  decorate

Mix the fruit juices together over ice in a chilled glass. Top up with lemonade to taste and dress with cherries and pineapple.

932

COCOBERRY (see right-hand page for picture)

An unusual but successful mixture of raspberries and coconut.

SERVES 1

85 g/3 oz raspberries
crushed ice
1 measure coconut cream
150 ml/5 fl oz pineapple juice
pineapple wedge and fresh
   raspberries, to decorate

Press the raspberries through a strainer with the back of a spoon and transfer the purée to a blender. Add ice, the coconut cream and the pineapple juice. Blend until smooth, then pour the mixture, without straining, into a chilled tumbler. Dress with pineapple and fresh raspberries.

933

PARSON'S PARTICULAR

You can get more juice out of oranges and lemons if you soak them in hot water for a few minutes before squeezing them. Then let grenadine perform its pastel magic on the juice!

SERVES 1

2 measures fresh orange juice
1 measure fresh lemon juice
1 egg yolk
4 dashes grenadine
cracked ice
cocktail cherry, to decorate

Shake the first four ingredients together over ice until well frosted and strain into a long glass. Dress with a cocktail cherry.

934

BERRY BERRY RED

This combination is delicious with fresh or frozen raspberries, so you can make it all year round. Cut down on the meringue if you find it too sweet a finish.

SERVES 1

55 g/2 oz raspberries
4 measures cranberry and
   raspberry juice
crushed ice
1 small meringue, crumbled
blackberry-flavoured
   sparkling water

Set aside a couple of nice berries. In a blender, blend the rest of the fruit with the juice and crushed ice. Put half the meringue in the bottom of a chilled tall glass, pour on the fruit slush, and top up with water. Dress with the reserved raspberries and the remaining crumbled meringue.

935
EYE OF THE HURRICANE

A vast range of fruit juices and syrups is now widely available, perfect for non-alcoholic mixed drinks, once dependent on the old favourites – orange, lemon and lime juices.

SERVES 1

2 measures passion fruit syrup
1 measure lime juice
cracked ice
bitter lemon
lemon slice, to decorate

Pour the syrup and lime juice over cracked ice in a mixing glass. Stir well to mix and strain into a chilled tumbler. Top up with bitter lemon and dress with a slice of lemon.

936
BRIGHT GREEN COOLER

More light than bright, but definitely cool!

SERVES 1

3 measures pineapple juice
2 measures lime juice
1 measure green peppermint
   syrup
cracked ice
ginger ale
cucumber and lime slices,
   to decorate

Shake the first three ingredients vigorously over ice until well frosted. Half fill a tall chilled tumbler with cracked ice and strain the cocktail over them. Top up with ginger ale and dress with slices of cucumber and lime.

937
GRAPEFRUIT COOLER

This wonderfully refreshing drink is ideal for serving at a family barbecue. Start making it at least four hours before serving to allow plenty of time for the mint to steep in the syrup.

SERVES 6

55 g/2 oz fresh mint
2 measures sugar syrup
475 ml/16 fl oz grapefruit juice
4 measures lemon juice
cracked ice
sparkling mineral water
fresh mint sprigs, to decorate

Muddle fresh mint leaves in a small bowl with the sugar syrup. Set aside for at least 2 hours to steep, mashing again from time to time. Strain into a jug and add the grapefruit juice and lemon juice. Cover with clingfilm and chill for at least 2 hours, until required. To serve, fill 6 chilled Collins glasses with cracked ice. Divide the cocktail between the glasses and top up with sparkling water. Dress with fresh mint.

938
BABY BELLINI

Sparkling, just like its alcoholic namesake, but as innocent as a baby.

SERVES 6

2 measures peach juice
1 measure lemon juice
sparkling apple juice

Pour the peach juice and lemon juice into a chilled champagne flute and stir well. Top up with sparkling apple juice and stir.

939
SALTY PUPPY

The salt and sugar on the rim of the glass make this lip-lickin' good!

SERVES 6

sugar
coarse salt
lime wedge
cracked ice
1/2 measure lime juice
grapefruit juice

Mix equal quantities of sugar and salt in a saucer. Rub the rim of a small, chilled tumbler with the lime and dip in the sugar and salt mixture to frost. Fill the glass with ice and pour the lime juice over. Top up with grapefruit juice.

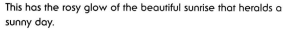

941
SUNRISE

This has the rosy glow of the beautiful sunrise that heralds a sunny day.

SERVES 1

cracked ice
2 measures orange juice
1 measure lemon juice
1 measure grenadine
sparkling mineral water

Put cracked ice into a chilled tumbler. Pour the orange juice, lemon juice and grenadine over the ice. Stir well and top up with sparkling mineral water.

940
COOL COLLINS

Minty cool and refreshingly light, this can be as long or as short as you like.

SERVES 6

6 fresh mint leaves
1 tsp icing sugar
2 measures lemon juice
cracked ice
sparkling water
fresh mint sprig and lemon wedge, to decorate

Put the mint leaves into a tall chilled tumbler and add the sugar and lemon juice. Crush the leaves with a spoon until the sugar has dissolved. Fill the glass with cracked ice and top up with sparkling water. Stir gently and dress with a fresh sprig of mint and a wedge of lemon.

942
JUICY JULEP

Taken from the Arabic word meaning a 'rose syrup', it seems likely that a julep was always intended to be non-alcoholic.

SERVES 1

1 measure orange juice
1 measure pineapple juice
1 measure lime juice
1/2 measure raspberry syrup
4 crushed fresh mint leaves
cracked ice
ginger ale
fresh mint sprig, to decorate

Shake the first five ingredients vigorously over ice until well frosted. Strain into a chilled Collins glass, top up with ginger ale and stir gently. Dress with mint.

943
APPLE FRAZZLE

You will feel the opposite of frazzled when you've had a few sips of this.

SERVES 1

4 measures apple juice
1 tsp sugar syrup
1/2 tsp lemon juice
ice
sparkling mineral water
apple slice, to decorate

Shake the apple juice, sugar syrup and lemon juice vigorously over ice until well frosted. Strain into a chilled tumbler and top up with sparkling mineral water. Dress with a slice of apple.

944
BITE OF THE APPLE

The apple sauce makes this so substantial that you might be forgiven for eating rather than drinking it.

SERVES 1

crushed iced cubes
5 measures apple juice
1 measure lime juice
1/2 tsp orgeat
1 tbsp apple sauce or apple
   purée

Blend crushed ice in a blender with the apple juice, lime juice, orgeat and apple sauce until smooth. Pour into a chilled tumbler.

945
RED APPLE SUNSET

Grenadine is a red pomegranate-flavoured syrup that is used a lot in non-alcoholic cocktails. It gives this drink its lovely sunset glow.

SERVES 1

2 measures apple juice
2 measures grapefruit juice
dash grenadine
ice

Shake the liquid ingredients over ice until well frosted. Strain into a chilled cocktail glass.

946
LEMON FIZZ

A refreshing summer fizz to enjoy with no effort – keep some in the refrigerator ready to fizz up at the last minute.

SERVES 1

2 fresh lemons
crushed ice
peel of 1/2 lemon
1 tbsp sugar
iced lemonade

Squeeze the lemons and pour the juice into a chilled highball glass filled with crushed ice. Add the piece of peel and sugar to taste and stir briefly. Top up with lemonade to taste.

947
LITTLE PRINCE

Sparkling apple juice is a great mixer, adding flavour and colour, as well as fizz. Use it as a substitute for champagne in non-alcoholic versions of cocktails such as Buck's Fizz.

SERVES 1

cracked ice
1 measure apricot juice
1 measure lemon juice
2 measures sparkling apple juice
lemon peel twist, to decorate

Put the cracked ice into a mixing glass. Pour the apricot juice, lemon juice and apple juice over the ice and stir well. Strain into a chilled highball glass and dress with a lemon twist.

949
PEACHY MELBA

The only thing missing from this dessert-like cocktail is the meringue.

SERVES 1

3 measures peach juice
1 measure lemon juice
1 measure lime juice
1 measure grenadine
ice
peach slice, to decorate

Shake the peach juice, lemon juice, lime juice and grenadine over ice until well frosted. Strain into a small chilled tumbler and dress with a slice of peach.

948
PEACHY CREAM

Nothing more, and nothing less, than pure and simple peaches and cream.

SERVES 1

2 measures chilled peach juice
2 measures single cream
cracked ice

Shake the peach juice and cream vigorously over ice until well frosted. Half fill a small chilled tumbler with cracked ice and strain the cocktail over it.

950
RASPBERRY COOLER

You can't beat this glass of apple and raspberry, really well iced, on a hot summer day. It is great with other fruit syrups too, such as passion fruit and apricot.

SERVES 2

8 ice cubes, crushed
2 tsp raspberry syrup
475 ml/16 fl oz chilled apple juice
fresh raspberries and apple pieces

Put the ice in the glasses and pour over the raspberry syrup. Top up each glass with apple juice and stir well. Dress with the raspberries and pieces of apple.

951
SPARKLING PEACH MELBA

This simple but perfect partnership of peaches and raspberries, originates in the dessert invented by the Savoy Hotel chef Georges-Auguste Escoffier in honour of Australian opera singer Dame Nellie Melba.

SERVES 1

55 g/2 oz raspberries, puréed
4 measures peach juice
crushed ice
sparkling water

Shake the raspberry purée and peach juice vigorously over crushed ice until well frosted. Strain into a tall chilled tumbler, top up with sparkling water, and stir gently.

952
TROPICAL COOLER

Cool, fruity and reviving, this cooler is a taste of the Tropics with a hint of summer.

SERVES 1

2 measures passion fruit juice
2 measures guava juice
2 measures orange juice
1 measure coconut milk
1–2 tsp ginger syrup
ice
star fruit slice, to decorate

Shake the first five ingredients vigorously over ice until well frosted. Strain into a chilled highball glass or tall wine glass and dress the rim with a thin slice of star fruit.

953
LEMON SODA

This can be bottled and kept in the refrigerator for a few days.

SERVES 6

8 large lemons
25 g/1 oz icing sugar
175 ml/6 fl oz boiling water
ice
soda water

Finely grate the peel and squeeze the juice of 7 lemons into a large heatproof bowl. Thinly slice the remaining lemon and reserve. Stir sugar and boiling water into the lemon juice and chill. Strain into a jug with ice and dilute with soda water to taste. Serve in chilled glasses, dressed with lemon slices.

954
STRAWBERRY CRUSH

This is almost a bowl of strawberries, so add cream to it as well if you like...

SERVES 1

1 egg white
icing sugar
55 g/2 oz ripe strawberries
juice of 1/2 lemon
150 ml/5 fl oz lemonade, chilled
crushed ice
sugar, to taste
mint sprig, to decorate

Lightly whisk the egg white, dip the rim of the glass into it and then into the sugar and leave to dry. Set aside 1 strawberry, hull the rest, and blend with the lemon juice, the lemonade, crushed ice and sugar for 2–3 minutes, until smooth but frothy. Pour into a frosted glass and dress with mint.

955
CARROT CREAM

Carrots have a strong hint of sweetness that makes them and their juice an excellent and delicious base for mixed drinks.

SERVES 1

2 measures carrot juice
cracked ice
2 1/2 measures single cream
1 measure orange juice
1 egg yolk
orange slice, to decorate

Pour the carrot juice, cream and orange juice over ice in a shaker and add the egg yolk. Shake vigorously until well mixed. Strain into a chilled glass and dress with a slice of orange.

957
BABYLOVE

Avocado is so luxuriously smooth when blended that this cocktail risks needing a spoon.

SERVES 2

300 ml/10 fl oz cold milk
12–14 strawberries, hulled
1/2 ripe avocado
1 measure lemon juice

Place all the ingredients except 2 strawberries in a blender and blend for 15–20 seconds, until smooth. Pour into iced glasses and dress each with a strawberry.

956
CINDERS

Yes, it's non-alcoholic but no one needs to know if you dress it up well.

SERVES 1

juice of 1/2 orange
juice of 1 lime
150 ml/5 fl oz pineapple juice
several drops Angostura bitters
ice
soda water or dry ginger ale,
   to taste
fruit slices, to decorate

Shake the first four ingredients well together with ice. Strain into a chilled glass and top up with soda water to taste. Finish with a few more drops of bitters and dress with slices of fruit.

958
APPLE SOUR

There is a hint of sharpness to this cocktail, but it is soon masked by the sweet honey and apple flavours.

SERVES 1

4 measures pure apple juice
juice of 1 lemon
juice of 1 lime
1 measure clear honey
1 small egg white
crushed ice
4–5 raspberries
long apple peel strip, to
   decorate

Blend all the ingredients except the raspberries in a blender until frothy and partly frozen. Put the raspberries in the bottom of an iced tall glass, crush with a wooden spoon and pour in the fruit slush. Dress with a strip of apple peel.

959
ANGELINA

Use canned pineapple in this recipe and you are bound to be tempted to make some of this delicious concoction for all the family too.

SERVES 1

2 measures orange juice
10 pineapple cubes
ice
splash of raspberry or strawberry cordial or syrup

Blend the first three ingredients in a blender for about 10 seconds until frothy and well mixed. Put a good splash of cordial in the bottom of a chilled long glass and slowly pour in the cocktail. Splash with a little more cordial.

961
SWEET DREAMER

Wonderfully creamy and thick with fruit and goodness, the perfect wake-up package or early evening settler.

SERVES 2

1 measure orange juice
2 measures passion fruit nectar or juice
1 small banana
1/4 ripe mango or pawpaw
few drops vanilla extract
crushed ice

Blend all the ingredients together in a blender or processor until smooth yet slushy. Pour into large cocktail glasses or goblets.

960
SUMMER CITRUS SLUSH

Great for a group of friends spending an afternoon in the garden with the kids.

SERVES 2

4 tbsp orange juice
1 tbsp lime juice
125 ml/4 fl oz sparkling water
280 g/10 oz frozen summer berries, such as strawberries, raspberries and blueberries
4 ice cubes
selection of fresh berries, to decorate

Pour the orange juice, lime juice and sparkling water into a food processor and process gently until combined. Add the berries and ice cubes and process until slushy. Pour the mixture into chilled glasses and dress with berries.

962
ISLAND COOLER

Nothing could be more refreshing than this colourful combination.

SERVES 1

2 measures orange juice
1 measure lemon juice
1 measure pineapple juice
1 measure pawpaw juice
1/2 tsp grenadine
cracked ice
sparkling water
pineapple wedges and maraschino cherries, to decorate

Shake the fruit juices and grenadine vigorously over ice until well frosted. Half fill a chilled Collins glass with cracked ice and pour the cocktail over. Top up with sparkling water and stir gently. Dress with pineapple wedges and maraschino cherries.

963
MUDDY PUDDLE

Reminiscent of the mess children make when mixing drinks! Well, in fact that's just how this murky-looking but surprisingly refreshing drink was created.

SERVES 1

juice of 1/2 lemon
juice of 1/2 orange
crushed ice
iced cola
orange slice, to decorate

Pour the fruit juice over ice in a chilled long glass and top up with cola. Dress with a slice of orange.

964
CRANBERRY & ORANGE CRUSH

Long and refreshing but it can be sharp, so taste first, then sweeten if necessary.

SERVES 1

juice of 2 blood oranges
150 ml/5 fl oz cranberry juice
2 tbsp raspberry or other fruit syrup
sugar, to taste
crushed ice
raspberries, to decorate

Shake the first four ingredients well together until really frothy. Pour straight into a tall ice-filled glass. Dress with raspberries.

965
CRANBERRY PUNCH

A sophisticated, non-alcoholic punch, this can also be served hot for a winter party as well as chilled in the summer.

SERVES 10

600 ml/1 pint cranberry juice
600 ml/1 pint orange juice
150 ml/5 fl oz water
1/2 tsp ground ginger
1/4 tsp cinnamon
1/4 tsp freshly grated nutmeg
cracked ice, frozen cranberries and their leaves (optional), to serve

Put all the ingredients into a saucepan and bring to the boil. Reduce the heat and simmer for 5 minutes. Remove from the heat and pour into heatproof glasses. If serving cold, chill and add cracked ice and dress with frozen cranberries and their leaves.

966
MELON MEDLEY

Choose a very ripe, sweet-fleshed melon, such as a cantaloupe, for this lovely fresh-tasting cocktail, perfect for sipping on a hot summer's evening.

SERVES 1

crushed ice
55 g/2 oz diced melon flesh
4 measures orange juice
1/2 measure lemon juice

Blend crushed ice in a blender with the diced melon, orange juice and lemon juice until slushy. Pour into a chilled glass.

967

BANANA COFFEE BREAK

(see right-hand page for picture)

Thanks to the coffee, this a very adult-tasting smoothie-style cocktail. In warm weather, it makes an excellent pick-me-up.

SERVES 2

300 ml/10 fl oz milk
4 tbsp instant coffee powder
1 small scoop vanilla ice cream
2 bananas, sliced and frozen
soft light brown sugar, to taste
pineapple wedges, to
    decorate

Pour the milk into a food processor, add the coffee powder, and process gently until combined. Add half of the ice cream and process gently, then add the remaining ice cream and process until well combined. When the mixture is blended, add the bananas and sugar and process until smooth. Pour into glasses and dress with pineapple wedges.

968

RASPBERRY CRUSHER

This might be one way of persuading children to take an extra portion of fruit or milk without a big battle.

SERVES 1

4 measures cold milk
1 measure grenadine
12 raspberries
1 ripe banana
3–4 ice cubes
1 tsp raspberry syrup or cordial

Blend all the ingredients except the syrup slowly in a blender for 5–10 seconds. Pour into a chilled tall glass and splash with syrup.

969

JUNIOR DANCER

Smooth, sweet and healthy too, full of energy for dancing the night away.

SERVES 1

1/2 banana
2 large strawberries
2 tbsp cream or natural
    yogurt
1 tbsp sugar syrup
dash grenadine
crushed ice
tonic water or lemonade

Blend the first five ingredients with the ice in a blender until almost frozen. Pour into a tall glass and top up with tonic water.

970
STRONG, BLACK & SWEET

This is an early morning espresso with a bit of extra zing – perfect for waking up to.

SERVES 1

1 measure orange syrup
1/2 measure chocolate syrup
espresso coffee
sugar swizzle stick

Pour the first two ingredients into a small coffee cup. Add the espresso and stir with the swizzle stick.

972
PINEAPPLE SODA

This looks great when served in pineapple shells and will certainly put you in the holiday mood.

SERVES 2

175 ml/6 fl oz pineapple juice
90 ml/3 fl oz coconut milk
small scoop vanilla ice cream
55 g/2 oz frozen pineapple chunks
175 ml/6 fl oz sparkling water

Blend the pineapple juice and coconut milk with the ice cream and pineapple chunks until smooth. Pour the mixture into tall glasses, until two-thirds full. Top up with sparkling water.

971
APPLE PIE CREAM

It's so good you will come back for more!

SERVES 1

4 measures apple juice
1 small scoop vanilla ice cream
crushed ice
soda water
cinnamon sugar and apple slice, to decorate

Blend the first two ingredients with ice in a blender for 10–15 seconds, until frothy and frosted. Pour into a chilled long glass and top up with soda water. Dress with cinnamon sugar and a slice of apple.

973
CINNAMON TEA

If you like herbal or fruit teas, you will enjoy this spicy, citrusy blend. It's also good cold.

SERVES 2

350 ml/12 fl oz water
4 cloves
1 small cinnamon stick
2 tea bags
3–4 tbsp lemon juice
1–2 tbsp soft light brown sugar
fresh lemon slices, to decorate

Bring the water, cloves and cinnamon to the boil. Remove from the heat and add the tea bags. Steep for 5 minutes, then remove. Stir in the lemon juice, sugar and some hot water to taste. Heat through gently and strain into glasses. Dress each with a lemon slice.

974
ORANGE & LIME ICED TEA

Even if you are not a keen tea drinker, this version is especially fresh and fruity. Keep some in the refrigerator if you don't use it all.

SERVES 2

125 ml/4 fl oz orange juice
4 tbsp lime juice
1–2 tbsp sugar, to taste
325 ml/11 fl oz fresh tea, chilled
lime wedges
8 ice cubes
orange slices, to decorate

Add the orange juice, lime juice and sugar to the tea. Take two glasses and rub the rims with a lime wedge, then dip them in sugar to frost. Fill the glasses with ice and pour on the tea. Dress with slices of orange.

975
CITRUS SLUSH

Youngsters often don't like bits of greenery in their drinks, so you could use a little extract instead of the mint or strain it before serving.

SERVES 1

1 grapefruit or 1 orange and 1 lemon, peeled
4 measures cold milk
1 scoop vanilla ice cream
1 scoop crushed ice
6 mint leaves, plus extra to decorate

Place the fruit in a blender with the rest of the ingredients and blend for 15–20 seconds, until slushy. Pour into a chilled sundae glass and dress with mint.

976
ALMONDINE

A smooth and velvety cocktail with loads of goodness in it. Enjoy immediately and add more fruit juice to taste.

SERVES 1

2 measures peach juice
4 measures cold milk
few drops almond extract
1–2 tbsp clover honey
1 small egg
ice cubes
toasted almonds, to decorate

Shake the first six ingredients well together until frosted. Pour into a large cocktail glass or wine glass and sprinkle the almonds on top.

977
ROSE SUNSET

You won't need much of this as it is wonderfully flavoured and also delightfully scented with the rose water.

SERVES 2

125 ml/4 fl oz natural yogurt
475 ml/16 fl oz milk
1 tbsp rose water
3 tbsp honey
1 ripe mango, peeled, stoned and diced
6 ice cubes
edible rose petals, to decorate

Process the yogurt and milk in a food processor gently until combined. Add the rose water and honey, process until thoroughly blended, then add the mango and ice cubes and process until smooth. Pour into glasses and dress with rose petals.

978
MINI COLADA

Children love the flavour of coconut and milk, so this junior cocktail should be very popular.

SERVES 2

6 measures cold milk
4 measures pineapple nectar
3 measures coconut cream
1/2 scoop crushed ice
pineapple cubes and cherry,
    to decorate

Shake the first four ingredients together until well chilled. Pour into long glasses with more ice cubes, and dress with pieces of pineapple and a cherry on a cocktail stick.

980
FUZZYPEG

A child's delight both in taste and its incredibly strange colour! It could be made with other drinks too.

SERVES 1

2 scoops vanilla ice cream
1 measure lime cordial
cola
ice

Blend the ice cream and lime cordial together for 5–10 seconds with a little cola. Pour into a tall glass filled with ice and top up with cola.

979
KIWI DREAM

This is a luscious ice cream-based smoothie with the refreshing tang of kiwi fruit and lime. Enjoy it as soon as it's ready.

SERVES 2

150 ml/5 fl oz milk
juice of 2 limes
2 kiwi fruit, peeled and
    chopped
1 tbsp sugar
115 g/4 oz vanilla ice cream
kiwi fruit slices and lime peel
    strips, to decorate

Process the milk and lime juice in a food processor gently until combined. Add the kiwi fruit, sugar and ice cream and process until smooth. Pour into iced glasses and dress with slices of kiwi fruit and strips of lime peel.

981
PEPPERMINT
ICE

This luxury smoothie can vary in colour – if you use mint chocolate chip ice cream it may be almost white. You could add a few drops of colouring to make it brighter.

SERVES 1

150 ml/5 fl oz milk
2 tbsp peppermint syrup
115 g/4 oz peppermint or
    mint choc ice cream
fresh mint sprigs, to decorate

Pour the milk and peppermint syrup into a food processor and process gently until combined. Add the ice cream and process until smooth. Pour the mixture into an iced glass and dress with mint.

982 SPICED HOT CHOCOLATE

This is a seriously good version of hot chocolate, not for everyday but perhaps as a treat after building a snowman.

SERVES 4

900 ml/1½ pints milk
200 g/7 oz plain chocolate, broken into small pieces
2 tsp sugar
1 tsp allspice
4 cinnamon sticks
2 tbsp whipped cream

Put the milk, chocolate, sugar and allspice into a saucepan over a medium heat. Whisk, stirring, until the chocolate has melted and the mixture is simmering but not boiling. Remove from the heat, pour into heatproof glasses with cinnamon sticks and top with cream.

984 BANANA COCKTAIL

Here's how to pack all your day's nutrition into one delicious glass, but serve it cool or chilled for the nicest result.

SERVES 1

1 small banana
60 ml/2 fl oz thick natural yogurt
1 egg
1–2 tbsp soft light brown sugar
ice
mint sprig, to decorate

Blend the banana, yogurt, egg and sugar in a blender with one or two ice cubes for about 2 minutes. Pour into a tall glass and dress with mint.

983 SUGAR & SPICE

Mexican chocolate is well worth using – the flavour and texture are different.

SERVES 6

750 ml/1¼ pints water
25 g/1 oz tortilla flour
5-cm/2-inch piece cinnamon stick
750 ml/1¼ pints milk
85 g/3 oz plain chocolate, grated
sugar, to taste
grated chocolate, to decorate

Pour the water into a large saucepan, stir in the flour, and add the cinnamon. Stir over a low heat for 5–10 minutes, until thickened and smooth. Gradually stir in the milk and beat in the grated chocolate, until melted and fully incorporated. Remove from the heat, discard the cinnamon and add the sugar. Ladle into heatproof glasses and dress with grated chocolate.

985 TROPICAL DELIGHT

A velvety-smooth, delicately scented drink without alcohol. This can be served at any time of day – and it's delicious for breakfast.

SERVES 4

2 large ripe mangoes, peeled, stoned and coarsely chopped
1 tbsp icing sugar
350 ml/12 fl oz coconut milk
5 ice cubes

Place the mango flesh in a blender with the sugar and blend until smooth. Add the coconut milk and ice and blend until frothy. Pour into 4 tall glasses.

986 PINOMINT SPLASH

Green food colouring gives the effect without the alcohol.

SERVES 1
4 measures cold milk,
1/4 measure peppermint cordial
1 measure coconut cream
2 measures pineapple juice
ice
dash green food colouring

Shake the first four ingredients together over ice until well frosted. Dribble or paint the tiniest drops of food colouring down the inside of a chilled tall thin glass. Slowly pour in the cocktail and add some more green food colouring.

987 MELON COCKTAIL

If you cannot find all three melons at any one time, don't be put off – two types will do well, as long as you have watermelon and one of the other two.

SERVES 2
225 ml/8 fl oz natural yogurt
100 g/3 1/2 oz each galia melon, canteloupe melon and watermelon, cut into chunks
6 ice cubes
fresh cherries, to decorate

Put the yogurt and the galia and canteloupe melon chunks in a food processor and process until smooth. Add the watermelon chunks with the ice cubes and process until smooth. Pour into glasses and dress with cherries.

988 PINEAPPLE SMOOTHIE

This is a popular combination for a smoothie – one smooth sweet fruit and one tangy and textured fruit. You might like to try your own variation.

SERVES 2
125 ml/4 fl oz pineapple juice
juice of 1 lemon
90 ml/3 fl oz water
3 tbsp soft light brown sugar
175 ml/6 fl oz natural yogurt
1 peach, chopped and frozen
100 g/3 1/2 oz frozen pineapple chunks
pineapple wedges, to decorate

Blend all the ingredients in a food processor until smooth. Pour into glasses and dress with wedges of pineapple.

989 THE BIG APPLE

This is a fun cocktail to make with the children. Prepare several together for convenience.

SERVES 1
1 crisp apple
juice of 1/2 lemon
juice of 1 orange
1/2 measure grenadine
crushed ice

Scoop out the centre of the apple to form a cup, leaving the base intact. Rub the inside with lemon juice. Discard the core and place the flesh in a blender with the juices, grenadine and ice. Blend to an icy pulp and spoon back into the shell.

990
LIME & LEMON COOLER

If you're looking for something stronger, add a shot of gin or vodka to each glass.

SERVES 4

beaten egg white
3–4 tbsp icing sugar
2 limes, cut into eighths
1 small lemon grass stick, chopped
4 ice cubes
125 ml/4 fl oz water
4 lime slices
soda water

Rim the glasses with egg white and a little sugar. Place the lime pieces and lemon grass in a blender with the rest of the sugar and the ice cubes. Add the water and process for a few seconds. Strain the mixture into the frosted glasses, add a lime slice to each glass and top up with soda water.

991
FRUIT COOLER

A great breakfast energizer and healthy start to the day, once you have done your work-out!

SERVES 2

225 ml/8 fl oz orange juice
125 ml/4 fl oz natural yogurt
2 eggs
2 bananas, sliced and frozen
slices of banana, to decorate

Pour the orange juice and yogurt into a food processor and process gently until combined. Add the eggs and frozen bananas and process until smooth. Pour the mixture into glasses and dress the rims with slices of banana.

992
SPICY BANANA SHAKE

Banana blends well even when partly frozen and it creates a luxuriously thick finished drink.

SERVES 1

300 ml/10 fl oz milk
1/2 tsp allspice
small scoop banana ice cream
2 bananas, sliced and frozen

Blend the milk in a food processor with the allspice, ice cream and half the frozen bananas. Add the remaining bananas gradually and process until well blended. Pour into a tall iced glass.

993
CARROT CHILL

Carrot is really very sweet, especially when raw and very young. It combines well with the peppery watercress.

SERVES 2

475 ml/16 fl oz carrot juice
25 g/1 oz watercress
1 tbsp lemon juice
fresh watercress sprigs, to decorate

Pour the carrot juice into a blender. Add the watercress and lemon juice and process until smooth. Transfer to a jug, cover with clingfilm and chill in the refrigerator for at least 1 hour. Pour into glasses and dress with watercress.

994 GINGER CRUSH

A fiery mix for ginger lovers, so be prepared!

SERVES 2

225 ml/8 fl oz carrot juice
4 tomatoes, peeled,
    deseeded and roughly
    chopped
1 tbsp lemon juice
25 g/1 oz fresh parsley
1 tbsp grated fresh ginger
6 ice cubes
125 ml/4 fl oz water
chopped parsley, to decorate

Put the carrot juice, tomatoes and lemon juice into a food processor and process gently until combined. Add the parsley, ginger and ice cubes. Process until well combined, pour in the water and process until smooth. Pour the mixture into tall glasses and dress with the chopped parsley.

995 FIG 'N' HAZELNUT SMOOTHIE

An unusual combination for very special occasions when you find figs in season.

SERVES 2

350 ml/12 fl oz hazelnut yogurt
2 tbsp freshly squeezed orange
    juice
4 tbsp maple syrup
8 large fresh ripe figs, chopped
6 ice cubes
toasted chopped hazelnuts, to
    decorate

Pour the yogurt, orange juice and maple syrup into a food processor and blend gently until thoroughly combined. Add the figs and ice cubes and process again until smooth. Pour into glasses and scatter toasted chopped hazelnuts on top.

996 SUNSET SMOOTHIE

Orange and carrot are a classic combination. Because carrot is sweet, the orange simply brings out the full flavour.

SERVES 2

175 ml/6 fl oz carrot juice
175 ml/6 fl oz orange juice
small scoop vanilla ice cream
6 ice cubes
orange slices and orange peel
    strips, to decorate

Pour the carrot and orange juices into a food processor and process. Add the ice cream and process until thoroughly blended, then add the ice cubes and process until smooth. Pour into chilled glasses and dress with orange slices and peel.

997 CARROT COCKTAIL

Pineapple and carrot combine to produce a refreshing drink full of vitamins.

SERVES 1

85 g/3 oz raw carrots,
    peeled and roughly
    chopped
1 slice pineapple, roughly
    chopped
1 tsp lemon juice
1 tbsp clear honey
ice
parsley or mint sprig, to
    decorate

Place the carrot, pineapple, lemon juice and honey in a blender and blend for 1–2 minutes until smooth. Serve over ice and dress with a sprig of parsley.

998
ORCHARD FRUIT SMOOTHIE

The brief cooking of the fruit mellows the flavours and allows the colours from the plums to seep into the apples and pears.

SERVES 2

1 pear, peeled and chopped
1 apple, peeled and chopped
2 large red plums, halved and stoned
4 ripe dark plums, halved and stoned
175 ml/6 fl oz water
fruit slices, to decorate

Put the fruit and water into a small saucepan. Cover tightly, then bring slowly to the boil. Take off the heat and leave to cool. Chill. Put the fruit and water into a food processor and process until smooth. Pour into glasses and dress with fruit slices.

1000
NECTARINE MELT

This smoothie is packed with fruit, flavour and vitamins, so you don't need to feel too guilty!

SERVES 1

225 ml/8 fl oz milk
2 scoops lemon sorbet
1 ripe mango, peeled, stoned and diced
2 ripe nectarines, peeled, stoned and diced

Gently blend the milk with half the sorbet until combined. Add the remaining sorbet and process until smooth. When the mixture is well blended, add the fruit and process until smooth. Pour into a chilled glass.

999
THAI FRUIT COCKTAIL

When choosing your favourite combination of juices, try using some of the delicate Asian flavours.

SERVES 1

1 measure pineapple juice
1 measure orange juice
1/2 measure lime juice
1 measure passion fruit juice
2 measures guava juice
crushed ice
flower, to decorate

Shake all the juices together with the crushed ice. Pour into a chilled long glass and dress with a flower.

1001
PRAIRIE OYSTER

For times when you really can't lift your head off the pillow, it's the only thing to try.

SERVES 1

Worcestershire sauce
vinegar
ketchup
1 egg yolk
cayenne pepper

Mix equal quantities of the first three ingredients and pour into a chilled glass. Add the egg yolk carefully without breaking. Do not stir, sprinkle with cayenne pepper, and down in one!

Index